£15.99

KU-062-849

European Union Foreign and Security Policy

The end of the Cold War presented a major challenge to Western Europe and to the European Union. It led not only to a whole new set of countries seeking to join the EU but also to a strong demand for a more intensive EU engagement in the broader regional context. This book assesses whether the EU has successfully faced up to this challenge and has adapted its policies towards its immediate neighbourhood in a coherent and strategic manner.

This volume examines EU policy from all its major regional dimensions including assessments of:

- The enlargement process in East-Central Europe
- The increasing engagement of the EU in conflict resolution, most notably in the Balkans but also towards the Arab–Israeli conflict
- Policies towards the countries and regions of the former Soviet Union, such as Russia, Ukraine and the Caucasus
- The complexities of EU policy towards Turkey and the rest of the Middle East
- The transatlantic dimensions of the EU's neighbourhood policies

The European Union's engagement with its 'near abroad' represents one of the most dynamic and important areas of its foreign and security policy. As such, it has direct and immediate implications for the future evolution of the EU, its external identity, and its capacity to be a powerful and strategic actor in international affairs.

This book will interest students and researchers of international relations, the EU and European politics.

Roland Dannreuther is Senior Lecturer in International Relations at the University of Edinburgh.

LIVERPOOL JOHN MOORES UNIVERSIT
Aldham Robarts L.R.C.
TEL. 0151 231 3701/3634

LIVERPOOL JMU LIBRARY

3 1111 01229 9879

European Union Foreign and Security Policy

Towards a neighbourhood strategy

Edited by Roland Dannreuther

LIVERPOOL JOHN MOORES UNIVERSITY
Aldham Robarts L.R.C.
TEL. 0151 231 3701/3634

 Routledge
Taylor & Francis Group

LONDON AND NEW YORK

First published 2004
by Routledge
2 Park Square, Milton Park, Abingdon, Oxon, OX14 4RN

Simultaneously published in the USA and Canada
by Routledge
270 Madison Avenue, New York, NY 10016

Reprinted 2005

Routledge is an imprint of the Taylor & Francis Group

© 2004 editorial matter and selection, Roland Dannreuther;
individual chapters, the contributors

Typeset in Times by Wearset Ltd, Boldon, Tyne and Wear
Printed and bound in Great Britain by The Cromwell Press,
Trowbridge, Wiltshire

All rights reserved. No part of this book may be reprinted or
reproduced or utilized in any form or by any electronic, mechanical,
or other means, now known or hereafter invented, including
photocopying and recording, or in any information storage or
retrieval system, without permission in writing from the publishers.

British Library Cataloguing in Publication Data
A catalogue record for this book is available from the British Library

Library of Congress Cataloging in Publication Data
European Union foreign and security policy : towards a
neighbourhood strategy / edited by Roland Dannreuther.
        p. cm.
Includes bibliographical references and index.
 1. European Union. 2. Europe—Foreign relations—1989–
I. Dannreuther, Roland.

  JZ1570.E9335 2004
  327.4—dc22

                                      2003015519

ISBN 0–415–32297–9 (hbk)
ISBN 0–415–32298–7 (pbk)

For Antoine Tardy

Contents

Contributors

Roland Dannreuther is Senior Lecturer in International Relations at the School of Social and Political Studies, Edinburgh University.

Gilles Dorronsoro is Professor of Political Science, Institut d'Études Politiques, Rennes, and is also affiliated to the Institut français d'études anatoliennes (IFEA), Istanbul.

Pál Dunay is Faculty Member and Director of the International Training Course of the Geneva Centre for Security Policy.

John Gault is an independent energy consultant and associate member of the Geneva Centre for Security Policy.

Ettore Greco is Deputy Director of the Istituto Affari Internazionali, Rome.

Hiski Haukkala is a Researcher at the Finnish Institute of International Affairs, Helsinki.

S. Neil MacFarlane is Lester B. Pearson Professor of International Relations, St Anne's College, Oxford University and Faculty Member of the Geneva Centre for Security Policy.

Antonio Missiroli is Research Fellow, European Union Institute for Security Studies, Paris.

Fred Tanner is Deputy Director of the Geneva Centre for Security Policy.

William C. Wohlforth is Associate Professor of Government at Dartmouth College, Hanover, New Hampshire.

Andrei Zagorski is Deputy Director of the Institute for Applied International Research, Moscow.

Acknowledgements

The editor is grateful for the generous financial support provided by the Geneva Centre for Security Policy (GCSP), which made possible the initial seminar bringing together the contributors in May 2002 and for the interim conclusions presented at the International Security Forum in Zürich in October 2002. Particular thanks are extended to Ulrich Lehner, former Director of the GCSP, and Fred Tanner, Deputy Director, for their enthusiastic support for the project; and to Nicole Pinter-Krainer and Joanna Schemm for their friendly and efficient assistance in conference management and editorial support. More generally, the editor wishes to thank all those at the GCSP who made his two-year secondment to the centre so enjoyable and memorable.

Abbreviations

AC	Arctic Council
ACP	African, Caribbean and Pacific countries
AKP	Justice and Development Party (Turkey)
BEAC	Barents Euro-Arctic Council
bcm/yr	billion cubic metres per year
BTC	Baku–Tbilisi–Ceyhan pipeline
CAP	Common Agricultural Policy
CARDS	Community Assistance for Reconstruction, Development and Stabilization (Community assistance programme for the Western Balkans)
CBSS	Council of the Baltic Sea States
CEEA	(EU–Russia) Common European Economic Area
CEFTA	Central European Free Trade Agreement
CERM	Coordinated Emergency Response Measures
CFSP	Common Foreign and Security Policy (of the European Union)
CIS	Commonwealth of Independent States
CIVCOM	Committee of the Civilian Aspects of Crisis Management
CMEA	Council for Mutual Economic Assistance
CMS	Common Mediterranean Strategy
CPC	Caspian Pipeline Consortium
CSCE	Conference for Security and Cooperation in Europe
DEP	Democracy Party (Turkey)
EA	Europe Agreement
EBRD	European Bank for Reconstruction and Development
EC	European Community
ECE	East-Central Europe; East-Central European
ECHO	European Community Humanitarian Office
ECSC	European Coal and Steel Community
EEC	European Economic Community
EIB	European Investment Bank
EMP	Euro-Mediterranean Partnership

LIVERPOOL JOHN MOORES UNIVERSITY
Aldham Robarts L.R.C.
TEL. 0151 231 3701/3634

EPC	European Political Cooperation
ESDP	European Security and Defence Policy (of the European Union)
EU	European Union
EUROMARFOR	European Maritime Force
FDI	foreign direct investment
FRY	Former Republic of Yugoslavia
FSU	former Soviet Union
GATT	General Agreement on Tariffs and Trade
GCC	Gulf Cooperation Council
GDP	gross domestic product
GNI	gross national income
HCNM	(OSCE) High Commissioner for National Minorities
ICBM	intercontinental ballistic missile
ICTFY	International Criminal Tribunal for the Former Yugoslavia
IEA	International Energy Agency
IMF	International Monetary Fund
IMU	Islamic Movement of Uzbekistan
INOGATE	Interstate Oil and Gas Transport to Europe
Interreg	Community assistance programme aiming to stimulate inter-regional cooperation within the EU
IPTF	(United Nations) International Police Task Force
KFOR	NATO Kosovo Force
LNG	liquefied natural gas
MEDA	Community Assistance Programme for the Mediterranean Countries
MEPP	Middle East peace process
MFN	most-favoured-nation (status)
MGK	National Security Council (Turkey)
MHP	National Action Party (Turkey)
mmbd	million barrels per day
mmtpy	million tonnes per year
NATO	North Atlantic Treaty Organization
ND	EU Northern Dimension Policy
NDEP	Northern Dimension Environmental Partnership
NEI	(US) Northern European Initiative
NGO	non-governmental organization
NIS	Newly Independent States (Armenia, Azerbaijan, Belarus, Georgia, Turkmenistan, Kazakhstan, Kyrgyzstan, Moldova, Tajikistan, Ukraine, Uzebekistan)
ODA	Official Development Assistance
ODIHR	(OSCE) Office for Democratic Institutions and Human Rights
OEEC	Organization for European Economic Co-operation

OHR	Office of the High Representative (Bosnia-Herzegovina)
OPEC	Organization of Petroleum Exporting Countries
OSCE	Organization for Security and Cooperation in Europe
PCA	Partnership and Cooperation Agreement
PfP	Partnership for Peace
PHARE	Pologne-Hongrie – Assistance à la restructuration des économies (Community assistance programme for the Central European candidate countries)
PIC	Peace Implementation Council (Bosnia-Herzegovina)
PKK	Kurdish Workers' Party
PLO	Palestine Liberation Organization
PPP	purchasing power parity
REDWG	Regional Economic Development Working Group
RMA	revolution in military affairs
SAA	Stabilization and Association Agreement
SAP	Stabilization and Association Process
SPSEE	Stability Pact for South-Eastern Europe
TACIS	Technical Assistance to the Commonwealth of Independent States
TEPSA	Trans-European Policy Studies Association
TRACECA	Transport Corridor Europe-Caucasus-Asia
TREVI	Terrorism, Radicalism, Extremism and International Violence (EU Internal Security Group)
TRNC	Turkish Republic of North Cyprus
UN	United Nations
UNHCR	United Nations High Commission for Refugees
UNMIK	United Nations Interim Administration in Kosovo
WMD	weapons of mass destruction
WTO	World Trade Organization

1 Introduction

Setting the framework

Roland Dannreuther

The main objective of this volume is to examine the extent to which Western Europe, meaning the European Union (EU) and its member states, has been able to respond as a coherent and strategic actor towards the countries in its immediate neighbourhood or periphery since the end of the Cold War. From a broader perspective, this is clearly a partial and incomplete picture of the full scope of the EU's foreign and security policy. As most accounts of EU foreign policy highlight, the EU is most clearly a coherent international actor when dealing with economic and trade issues; the EU is also an influential actor in many more distant parts of the world, such as Asia and Latin America; and the EU is a significant development body and aid donor, with a particularly involved relationship with the former colonial countries of Africa and the Caribbean.[1]

Nevertheless, the EU's engagement with its immediate neighbourhood over the past decade can justifiably be considered a highly distinctive and dynamic feature of Europe's foreign and security policy, the engagement which also most clearly differentiates EU foreign and security policy from the Cold War period. The end of the Cold War and the collapse of Soviet hegemony after 1989 quickly created the demand, not only from the newly liberated countries but from Western capitals including Washington, for Europe to assume the responsibilities of engaging decisively in the economic and political stabilization of the region.[2] As a consequence, this dimension of Europe's foreign and security policy has gained a new centrality and significance since the end of the Cold War, partially overshadowing the other dimensions. The strategic challenge was for Europe to fill the vacuum which had emerged with the withdrawal of Soviet power and the widespread expectation of US reorientation of its interests away from Europe.

The challenge represented, though, something more than a traditional geopolitical opportunity. It also had a more fundamental and even existential quality to it, reaching into the very heart of the European project. From its origins, the ideal or 'vocation' of Europe has been to ensure peace between former warring European nation-states and to provide the conditions for geopolitical stability built on the foundations of a commitment to liberal democracy. Such an ideal, despite or in spite of European traditions of *realpolitik*, has become a critical constituent element of European foreign policymaking. As Helen and William Wallace argue, there is an embedded European commitment to forms of liberal democracy, 'not as a monopoly of west Europeans but as [a] strongly to be preferred system to be defended against competing models in the immediate neighbourhood'.[3] Accordingly, the internal logic of European integration dictates that the acquired gains should not be limited to the western part of the Eurasian landmass but should be extended beyond those borders. Inevitably, there has been and continues to be strong resistance to such an extension, since it raises the costs for existing member states and increases fears among Western publics of the dangers of an opening up to the East and South. However, the future of European integration is very much linked to the success and failure of the strategic engagement of the EU with the countries and regions in its immediate neighbourhood.

The assumption of this volume is, therefore, that the EU's engagement with its immediate periphery represents a highly important, and possibly the most important, post-Cold War geopolitical challenge for its foreign and security policy. The nature of this challenge can be considered to have three major dimensions to it. First, there has been the challenge of the enlargement of the European Union, to take on new members and to define the new borders of the Union. To some degree, this has been a joint project loosely coordinated with the North Atlantic Treaty Organization (NATO) which culminated in the NATO summit in Prague and the EU summit in Copenhagen in late 2002 broadly welcoming the same group of candidates from East-Central Europe.[4] However, these summits took place at a time when NATO has appeared increasingly marginalized and when Europe's role in providing for the broader security of the region has correspondingly grown. The impact of EU enlargement is also not limited to the accession of new members but involves the definition of new borders and the creation of new neighbours with their particular demands and interests.[5] The Copenhagen summit has thus opened up new questions of Europe's policies towards these countries and regions, which represent a broad geographical arc from Russia and the other former Soviet states, to Turkey, the Middle East and North Africa.

The second dimension of this challenge has been the impact of the EU's ambition to provide a political union to complement its economic union. The Common Foreign and Security Policy (CFSP) and the European Security and Defence Policy (ESDP) represent the most visible aspects of this political ambition. There are numerous studies highlighting the weaknesses and failures of the CFSP, and the lack of progress on ESDP, and expectations of what these policies are likely to produce has become increasingly more realistic, if not pessimistic.[6] As part of this greater realism, there is a recognition that it is likely to be in the EU's immediate neighbourhood, rather than on the broader international stage, that the EU will have the greatest opportunity to utilize the full range of its instruments, not just economic but also political and military. Thus, the EU's 'near abroad' represents a testing ground for its broader political and foreign policy ambitions and its capacity to emerge as a more coherent and strategic actor.

The third dimension is driven by the security challenges emanating from Europe's periphery and the demands for an effective crisis management capability. Clearly, it was the Balkan conflicts which first exposed this need for such a capacity and demonstrated the complete lack of preparedness of the EU. As Ettore Greco in this volume demonstrates, European capacities have improved, leading to a much more substantial EU role in stabilizing the Balkans. However, ethnic and religious conflict is not limited to the Balkans but extends to the post-Soviet borderlands and the Middle East. In addition, the European periphery is viewed by EU member states as the primary source of many of the non-traditional security threats, such as terrorism, migration and transnational organized crime, which in turn compels a European engagement with the countries of these regions. The EU's internal security agenda, arguably the most dynamic area of European integration, particularly since the terrorist attacks of 11 September 2001, is therefore a highly significant dimension of Europe's strategic engagement with its neighbourhood.[7]

The underlying assumption of this book is, therefore, that the geostrategic consequences of the end of the Cold War have required the EU to prioritize and sharpen the focus of its foreign and security policy towards the countries and regions in its immediate neighbourhood. Concentrating on this dynamic area of EU foreign and security policy should contribute to the ongoing debate about the EU as an international actor and Europe's prospects for translating its economic might into political and strategic influence. In addition, the fact that the EU's strategic engagement with its immediate neighbourhood is inextricably entwined with the evolving self-definition of Europe's borders, identity and purpose should contribute to the broader debate over Europe – whether, as set out by Jan Zielonka, it is developing into a classical Westphalian state, which rigidly demarcates between internal and external, citizen and alien, or into an alternative post-modern entity in which these divisions are collapsed or sublimated.[8]

These debates have become even more intense in the aftermath of the al-Qaida terrorist attacks of 11 September 2001 and the subsequent international crisis over Iraq, which culminated in military action spearheaded by the United States and the United Kingdom in March 2003. To put it mildly, this period has not been the most auspicious for the EU's foreign and security policy. The Iraq crisis has again demonstrated the internal divisions between the EU member states, the continuing primacy of national foreign policies, and the conflicting national interests and threat assessments which undermine the potential for a coherent European foreign and security policy. The majority of commentators have assumed a gloomy perspective, judging the latest crisis as confirming the EU's impotence in foreign policy, its internal structural deficiencies, and its paralysis of action.[9] Others, most notably Jacques Chirac, argue that it is precisely when responding to its failures that Europe is invigorated and radical advances are made in the process of European integration.[10] Only time will tell whether the EU is entering a period of 'Euro-paralysis' or a renewed period of expansion and growth in the aftermath of its intense disunity during the Iraqi crisis and war.

It should, though, be stated that the most notable feature of European policy towards Iraq is the absence of such a policy, at least since the intense European divisions, most notably between France and the United Kingdom, emerged in the mid-1990s. Europe failed over Iraq not because it failed to implement a previously agreed policy but because it never succeeded in formulating such a policy. Hence, Iraq and the broader Gulf region, with the partial exception of Iran, does represent the clear limits of a common European foreign policy, and it is this absence of a policy which has been the main reason why Europe's policies towards Iraq and the Gulf have not been covered in this volume. But the failure to develop common policies towards Iraq should not obscure the existence of common European policies to the other countries and regions in the EU's immediate neighbourhood, however partial and limited these might be. In focusing on the divisions brought out by the Iraq crisis, the success symbolized by the Copenhagen summit of November 2002 should also not be completely forgotten. More generally, addressing the question of what the various policies and strategies adopted by the EU towards its neighbourhood add up to, and whether they constitute something reasonably coherent and strategic, remains a legitimate research question as well as focus of this volume.

Chapter breakdown

The key research question that all the contributors were asked to address was the extent to which, in their particular area of concern, Europe can be considered to have become a more coherent and strategic actor. The more specific and derivative questions related to this broad overarching research question included:

- How has the policy of the EU and its member states developed since the end of the Cold War?
- To what extent can the EU be viewed as having increased its strategic presence and influence?
- What have been the main strengths and weaknesses of EU policy?
- To what extent is the EU acting as an autonomous actor and to what extent is it driven by the policies of key member states?

- To what extent do other actors – such as the United States, NATO, the UN and sub-regional organizations – impinge on and influence the activities of the EU?
- To what extent has the EU moved from being a developmental and economic actor (civilian power) to being a politico-security and strategic actor?

The majority of the chapters of the book focus on the principal regions neighbouring the EU. These chapters seek to provide a detailed and comprehensive survey of Europe's engagement with its immediate neighbourhood. The first chapter, by Antonio Missiroli, provides a broad survey of the policies adopted by the EU to its neighbourhood since the end of the Cold War and argues that a twin-track approach has been adopted: stabilization and integration. Pál Dunay then examines the evolution and, as he argues, the success of the EU's strategic engagement with the candidate countries of East-Central Europe. Gilles Dorronsoro provides a more qualified assessment of the EU's policies towards Turkey, an applicant country but with a special status, but nevertheless argues that the EU has stimulated a radical reform programme within the country. Ettore Greco sets out the factors behind the EU's current expansive role in the Balkans, which has increasingly taken over and subsumed the functions and roles played by other international and regional institutions in the region, such as the UN, the Organization for Security and Cooperation in Europe (OSCE) and NATO.

The following set of chapters cover what might be called the northern (Russia and the other former Soviet states) and southern dimensions (the Middle East) of the EU's foreign relations. Hiski Haukkala sets out the evolution and development of the originally Finnish initiative for a Northern Dimension to EU policy which sought to build bridges between the northern EU members and their neighbours, Russia and the Baltic states. Haukkala raises the question of the future purpose of this initiative once the Baltic states become full members of the EU. Andrei Zagorski analyses and compares EU policy towards the East European former Soviet states Russia, Ukraine, Belarus and Moldova, noting the inconsistencies and limitations of the EU's strategic engagement. Neil MacFarlane reaches a more unqualified conclusion that the EU's policies adopted towards the Caucasus and Central Asia effectively constitute a 'non-strategy'. Moving on to the 'southern dimension', Fred Tanner assesses the impact of the Euro-Mediterranean Programme on the countries of North Africa, and highlights the weaknesses and contradictions in the policies and instruments used to implement this programme. Roland Dannreuther reaches a cautiously more optimistic assessment of the EU's engagement in the Middle East peace process and how, particularly from the mid-1990s, the EU has secured a more significant role in the negotiation process.

The chapter by John Gault deviates from the pattern of regional analyses and offers an in-depth assessment of Europe's energy security in relation to its periphery. There are two reasons why this contribution has been included in this volume. First, as Gault himself states, energy is the 'umbilical cord' which connects Western Europe to its eastern and southern periphery, most notably to Russia, Central Asia, the Middle East and North Africa (p. 182). It is the key economic resource that the EU needs for its economic vitality and for which it will become increasingly dependent on its immediate neighbourhood. Second, the chapter highlights the critical but sometimes ignored role that private business must play in the development of Europe's neighbourhood and the policies that the EU and national governments can promote to facilitate the private investment desperately needed by these countries.

The final substantive chapter by William Wohlforth also breaks the pattern of regional studies by providing a transatlantic perspective to the issue of the EU's emerging regional role and questioning whether this represents a fundamental challenge to US hegemony. Using structural realism as his theoretical framework, Wohlforth argues that the EU has filled some of the regional vacuum created by the end of the bipolar East–West confrontation but that the EU remains constrained in promoting its interests and preferences over the United States even within its immediate neighbourhood. This challenging analysis provides the starting point for Roland Dannreuther to draw together the broader conclusions of the contributions in the volume and to assess the extent to which a clearer picture has emerged of the EU as a strategic actor in its immediate neighbourhood and the significance of this for international order.

Framework of analysis

This volume seeks principally to make a contribution to an empirical and policy-relevant assessment of the EU's foreign and security policy rather than to provide a new theoretical or conceptual construct for understanding this policy. However, any such empirically grounded and policy-related study is bound to build upon existing theoretical and conceptual foundations and potentially to offer new insights.

In terms of existing conceptualization of European foreign and security policy, this volume adopts the increasingly accepted view that such a policy must be considered to be broader than the CFSP as a policy and the EU as an institution. In this conceptualization, European foreign policy emerges from three distinct but interdependent systems of decision-making:[11] first, the coordination of national foreign policies;[12] second, the policies, principally focused on the economic and trade sphere, promoted by the European Community and the European Commission or from the first pillar; and third, EU policies centred on the CFSP or second pillar. These three different systems are deeply interpenetrated, and considerable overlap and cooperation exist, as well as lack of coordination and conflict. This is particularly the case for the EU's policies towards its immediate neighbourhood since all three arenas of decision-making have asserted a strong interest and set of preferences in their respective policies of engagement. One should also note that these three centres of foreign policy are not constitutive of all that can be considered to be European foreign policy. As Susan Strange has consistently argued, and John Gault highlights in this volume, large European business firms and corporations are increasingly significant foreign policy actors, whose interests and policies must be taken into account.[13]

This broader conception of the EU's foreign and security policy has two particular advantages. First, it qualifies the simple equation that a failure of the CFSP necessarily represents a failure for 'Europe'. Failure in developing CFSP and ESDP is certainly a negative development for Europe in terms of seeking to project itself as an international actor, but Europe's powers and influence are more expansive and pervasive than is captured by these policies. Second, the complexity of European decision-making, and the multiple actors involved, underlines that the EU is not a classical nation-state actor and that its foreign policy should not be judged in these terms. In fact, it is an inherently difficult task to identify what precisely constitutes an EU foreign policy or even whether it is correct even to say that there is such a policy. What can properly be said is that the EU has a number of dimensions of a foreign policy and that the task of an analyst of EU foreign policy is to identify and assess these different dimensions. Only once this has been done is it possible to judge whether the parts make a coherent whole in terms of a meaningful foreign and security policy.

It is this essentially inductive and bottom-up approach that this study adopts. In terms of the study of foreign policy, the focus is more on the outcomes of the foreign policy process than on an analysis of the foreign policy itself.[14] The principal concern of the contributors is to offer an evaluation of the impact of the policies that the EU and its member states have adopted towards the various parts of the immediate neighbourhood and focus less on the procedural and institutional mechanisms of how these policies emerged.[15] Although the classical concerns of foreign policy analysis are considered in this volume, it is generally in the context of how the internal processes of policymaking facilitated or hindered the effective implementation of policy.

The fact that the volume breaks down into the study of the EU's impact on differing regions and sets of countries is itself a reflection and recognition of the fact that there has been no common template for the EU's engagement but that policies have been adopted and adapted on a frequently ad hoc and often disconnected fashion. Most obviously in this regard, some countries and regions have enjoyed a much more intensive set of relations than others. Consequently, the picture of the EU's engagement with its immediate neighbourhood represents a complex mosaic in which it is particularly difficult to gain an overall impression or image that is greater than the sum of its parts. Nevertheless, the objective of this volume is to provide, through a focus on the EU's immediate neighbourhood, a more holistic and coherent conceptualization of European foreign policy than more wide-ranging and comprehensive accounts have traditionally offered. Although even the policies adopted to the EU's neighbouring regions tend to be fragmented and often disconnected from one another, there are nevertheless often subtle indirect linkages.

For example, there has been a certain complementarity between the southern dimension of the EU's policies, most notably the Euro-Mediterranean policy, and the process of eastward enlargement. These two processes have frquently developed in parallel. Likewise, the development of the Northern Dimension was created to foster an EU engagement with the North which would complement its existing southern and eastern policies. The process of enlargement also creates new demands from the new potential neighbours and indirectly enforces an EU involvement which had earlier been resisted. In addition, the complementarity between the EU and NATO has led to pressures for the EU to assume responsibilities in the Balkans and to prepare itself for a more sustained and expansive military-security role.

The issue of how to describe the complex and multi-dimensional entity which is nevertheless producing something that can be called a European foreign and security policy necessarily confronts all the contributors to this volume. In general, the practice has been to follow the conceptualization of the EU as a 'presence' or as an 'actor' with the qualification that the implied referent is not a classical nation-state but a *sui generis* multi-dimensional entity.[16] The variant of this volume is to bring a *strategic* perspective: to ask whether Europe can be considered to be acting strategically in its policies towards its immediate neighbourhood.

The term 'strategy' in this context refers to the means that policymakers choose to attain desired ends. The utility of this ends–means analysis is that it emphasizes that a coherent strategic actor has to have not only adequate means, such as the necessary instruments and policies, but also clearly defined ends and objectives. It also involves recognition that good strategy is about adapting the limited resources at one's disposal to the pursuit of realistic and attainable goals. Failure to do this is a failure of strategy. But, as some of the contributors to this volume argue, the absence of a strategy is not necessarily a failure of strategy; rather, it can be considered a realistic response to the absence of clearly defined interests and goals and the limitations of available means. Europe's coherence as a strategic actor might be as much in limiting its strategic engagement as in expanding that engagement without the necessary means or without clearly defined objectives.

Finally, the picture that emerges of the nature and extent of the EU's strategic engagement with its immediate neighbourhood contributes to some of the broader debates about the EU as an international actor. For example, it raises the question of whether one can discern a normative value to the EU's engagement which provides a distinctive, if not unique, feature to European foreign policy.[17] Is the EU's soft power projection a strength or weakness in its outward engagement?[18] What should be the respective roles played by the United States and Europe, particularly in ensuring the stability and prosperity of the western part of the Eurasian continent?[19] This study seeks to provide insights into these vital questions through a particular focus on the EU's engagement with its immediate neighbourhood. This is, as noted above, only a partial dimension of the totality of the EU's foreign and security policy. However, it is a critical one, since the ultimate strategic purpose or vision of the European project is to provide for the geopolitical stabilization of Europe and the spread of a unique form of economic and political governance based on democratic ideals. The extent to which this ideal can be gradually spread from its historical base in Western Europe will be a significant indicator of the success or failure of the EU as a strategic international actor.

Notes

1 For some recent more general overviews of EU foreign policy, see C. Bretherton and J. Vogler, *The European Union as a Global Actor*, London: Routledge, 1999; R. H. Ginsberg, *The European Union in International Politics: Baptism by Fire*, Oxford: Rowman and Littlefield, 2001; R. Whitman, *From Civilian Power to Superpower?*, Basingstoke, UK: Macmillan, 1998; and C. Piening, *Global Europe: The European Union in World Affairs*, Boulder, Colo.: Lynne Rienner, 1997.
2 For a historical coverage of this early post-Cold War period, see S. J. Nutall, *European Foreign Policy*, Oxford: Oxford University Press, 2000.
3 H. Wallace and W. Wallace, 'Introduction', in H. Wallace and W. Wallace (eds), *Policymaking in the European Union*, Oxford: Oxford University Press, 2000, p. 50.
4 The overlap is not perfect, as Romania and Bulgaria were invited to join NATO while their application to join the EU was postponed. For an assessment of the dual enlargement process, see S. Croft, J. Redmond, G. Wyn Rees and M. Webber, *The Enlargement of Europe*, Manchester: Manchester University Press, 1999; and R. Dannreuther, *Eastward Enlargement: NATO and the EU*, Oslo: Institutt for Forvarstudier, 1997.
5 G. Amato and J. Batt, *The Long-Term Implications of EU Enlargement: The Nature of the New Border*, Florence: European University Institute, 1999.
6 For example, J. Peterson and H. Sjursen (eds), *A Common Foreign Policy for Europe? Competing Visions of the CFSP*, London: Routledge, 1998; D. Allen, *The Common Foreign and Security Policy of the European Union*, New York: Addison-Wesley, 2000; and F. Cameron, *The Foreign and Security Policy of the European Union*, Sheffield: Sheffield University Press. For the best-known diagnosis of the problems of CFSP, see C. Hill, 'Closing the Capability–Expectations Gap?', in Peterson and Sjursen (eds), *A Common Foreign Policy for Europe*, pp. 18–38.

7 For a good overview of the development of the EU's internal security agenda, see M. Den Boer and W. Wallace, 'Justice and Home Affairs: Integration through Incrementalism?', in Wallace and Wallace, *Policymaking in the European Union*, pp. 439–519. For a more detailed analysis, see J. Monar, *Enlargement-Related Diversity in EU Justice and Home Affairs: Challenges, Dimensions and Management Instruments*, The Hague: Scientific Council for Government Policy, 2000. For an assessment of the implications of the terrorist attacks of 11 September, see M. Den Boer and J. Monar, 'Keynote Article: 11 September and the Challenge of Global Terrorism to the EU as a Security Actor', *Journal of Common Market Studies*, 2002, vol. 40: 11–28.

8 J. Zielonka, 'How New Enlarged Borders Will Reshape the European Union', *Journal of Common Market Studies*, 2001, vol. 39: 507–36. See also O. Waever, 'Imperial Metaphors: Emerging European Analogies to Pre-nation-state Imperial Systems', in O. Tunander, P. Baev and V. I. Einagel (eds), *Geopolitics in Post-Wall Europe*, London: Sage, 1997, pp. 59–93; and J. A. Caporaso, 'The European Union and Forms of State: Westphalian, Regulatory or Post-modern', *Journal of Common Market Studies*, 1996, vol. 34, no. 1: 29–52.

9 For academic analyses reaching similar conclusions, see P. H. Gordon, 'Europe's Uncommon Foreign Policy', *International Security*, 1997/8, vol. 11, no. 3: 27–74; and J. Zielonka, *Explaining Euro-paralysis: Why Europe Is Unable to Act in International Politics*, Basingstoke, UK: Macmillan, 1998.

10 French Embassy London: *Statements*, SAC/03/87. For an analysis which suggests that Europe has made such advances in reaction to the terrorist attacks of 11 September, see J. Peterson, 'Europe, America and 11 September', *Irish Studies in International Affairs*, 2002, vol. 13: 23–42.

11 This follows B. White, *Understanding European Foreign Policy*, Basingstoke, UK: Palgrave, 2001, pp. 40–1.

12 C. Hill (ed.), *The Actors in Europe's Foreign Policy*, London: Routledge, 1996; and I. Manners and R. Whitman (eds), *The Foreign Policies of EU Member States*, Manchester: Manchester University Press, 2001.

13 J. Stopford, S. Strange and J. S. Henley, *Rival States and Firms*, Cambridge: Cambridge University Press, 1991.

14 In this way, the volume follows most closely the approach taken in Ginsberg, *The European Union in International Politics*. For a more theoretical contribution, see J. Jupille, 'The European Union and International Outcomes', *International Organization*, 1999, vol. 23, no. 2: 410–25.

15 This is more fully covered in White, *Understanding European Foreign Policy*; Peterson and Sjursen (eds), *A Common Foreign Policy for Europe?*; and K. Smith, *The Making of EU Foreign Policy: The Case of Eastern Europe*, Basingstoke, UK: Macmillan, 1999.

16 For the notion of 'presence', see D. Allen and M. Smith, 'The European Union's Security Presence: Barrier, Facilitator, or Manager', in C. Rhodes (ed.), *The European Union in the World Community*, Boulder, Colo.: Lynne Rienner, 1998, pp. 41–59. For assessments of the EU as an international actor, see Paul Taylor, 'The European Communities as an Actor in International Society', *Journal of European Integration*, 1982, vol. 6: 205–28; J. Caporaso and J. Jupille, 'States, Agency and Rules: The EU in Global Environmental Politics', in Rhodes, *The European Union in the World Community*; and Bretherton and Vogler, *The European Union as a Global Actor*.

17 I. Manners, 'Normative Power Europe: A Contradiction in Terms', *Journal of Common Market Studies*, 2002, vol. 40, no. 2: 235–58.

18 J. Nye, 'Europe Is Too Powerful to Be Ignored', *Financial Times*, 11 March 2003. The 'civilian power' debate goes back to François Duchene, 'Europe's

Role in the International System', in W. Hager and M. Kornstamm, *A Nation Writ Large*, London: Macmillan, 1973; and H. Bull, 'Civilian Power Europe: A Contradiction in Terms?', *Journal of Common Market Studies*, 1982, vol. 21, no. 1: 149–70.

19 'Special Report: America and Europe: Who Needs Whom?', *The Economist*, 9–15 March 2002.

2 The EU and its changing neighbourhood

Stabilization, integration and partnership

Antonio Missiroli

Over the past decade, the European Union has pursued at least two distinct approaches (and policies) towards its immediate neighbourhood:

- an approach aiming, first and foremost, at *stabilization*, mainly based on fostering regional cooperation and broad partnerships ('regionality'); and
- an approach (in addition to, or instead of, the above), aiming at *integration* proper, i.e. at bringing neighbouring countries directly into the EU through a bilateral process based on strict 'conditionality'.

The stabilization approach

The first policy approach – stabilization as a goal, regionality as a means – is typical of the security policy of any regional power. It was first tentatively adopted vis-à-vis the crumbling Yugoslav Federation in the early 1990s, but with very little success.[1] It was then applied to the Central European countries and the Baltic States – the Balladur Pact of 1993–5 (the first Stability Pact proper) – and, in both cases, with a significant degree of success. In South-Eastern Europe, however, the same approach bore little or no fruit until it was blended with the second approach, which envisages integration as a goal (however distant) and conditionality as a means (however strict). Furthermore, between 1994 and 1995 the EU signed so-called Partnership and Cooperation Agreements (PCAs) with Russia, Ukraine, Moldova and Belarus. With the exception of Belarus (owing to objections on the EU side to President Lukashenka's policies), the agreements have been ratified by all the countries concerned and have taken effect: they combine a Western interest in bilateral political cooperation and dialogue on democratic foundations with an Eastern interest in economic cooperation, managed through the Union's TACIS (Technical Assistance to the Commonwealth of Independent States) programme. Strictly speaking, however, these agreements cannot be considered as aimed at *stabilizing* the countries concerned. The PCAs with Ukraine and Russia were then supplemented by a 'Common Strategy' for each, approved in June and December 1999 respectively, in the context of the Union's Common Foreign and Security Policy (CFSP). Neither, however, adds much to the existing policies, or envisages eventual EU membership.[2] More recently, Moldova has been included in the Stability Pact for South-Eastern Europe as a recipient country, although it does not entirely belong to the region geographically or politically: in fact, the dividing line between the Russian and the Ottoman Empires ran though its current territory – and still does, in a way, with Transdniestria now cut off from the the rest of what could now qualify as a small 'Balkan' country.

The Euro-Mediterranean Conference initiated in 1995 – now more commonly referred to as the Barcelona Process or Euromed – can be considered a by-product of this approach in that it was not, and still is not, meant to lead to full integration into the EU. Arguably, it was rather meant to prevent just such an eventuality, at least for the foreseeable future, by setting up an alternative form of partnership based on economic and trade cooperation and a rather unspecified political 'basket'. Yet the lack of solid incentives (the 'carrots', as opposed to the sticks) on the Union's side, coupled with the heterogeneity of the Mediterranean partners involved in the Euromed framework (let alone the different priorities of the EU member states), has made it less and less effective: the relevant 'Common Strategy' adopted in June 2000 says next to nothing as to the way ahead in the process.[3]

Finally, over the years the EU has set up a wide array of multilateral and bi-regional arrangements – the so-called 'group-to-group' diplomacy – with areas far away from the European continent: Central and Latin America, Asia with the Asia-Europe Meeting (ASEM) and Africa, not to mention the peculiar world of the former European colonies that are tied to the EU through preferential trade arrangements, the so-called African, Caribbean and Pacific (ACP) countries.[4] None of the latter properly fits in the neighbourhood policy of the Union, although they shape a wider web of relations based on historical and economic ties.

The 'Balladur' pact

The first Stability Pact was launched by the then French Prime Minister, Edouard Balladur, in the spring of 1993 as an instrument of preventive diplomacy in post-Communist Europe: its main objective was to set out in detail and implement some basic principles with regard to borders and minorities in the area and to organize and coordinate the action of the institutions involved, especially the EU, the Conference/Organization for Security and Cooperation in Europe (CSCE/OSCE) and the Council of Europe. It also built upon the existing web of multilateral sub-regional relations established through the Central European Free Trade Agreement (CEFTA), launched in late 1992 by the Visegrad group and later extended to fellow applicants, and other partnerships in the area, all partly supported also by the EU's Interreg-CBC programme. In December 1993 the EU Council approved a CFSP 'joint action' to support this initiative, and in May 1994 a conference was held in Paris with the participation of the nine European countries that had then signed the Europe Agreements (Slovenia would follow suit in 1996–7). Regional round tables were organized in the following months, and a concluding conference took place in Paris, once again, in March 1995. The resulting Stability Pact consisted of a political declaration and about 100 bilateral agreements, the most tangible one being a treaty between Slovakia and Hungary regarding the Magyar minority in Slovakia. It included also a series of projects on regional cross-border economic, cultural and environmental cooperation to be funded by the PHARE programme (*Pologne–Hongrie – Assistance à la restructuration des économies*: the acronym borrows the French word for 'lighthouse'). The Pact's follow-up was handled by the OSCE and has left a mixed record. On the one hand, of the approximately 50 bilateral agreements or arrangements concluded between the EU member states and the East-Central European associates/candidates, only half have been registered with the OSCE. On the other hand, the OSCE – and notably its Commissioner for national minorities – played an important (if hardly visible) role in advising the Baltic States on how to solve the thorny issue of Russian-speaking minorities inside their borders.[5]

On the whole, however, it is fair to say that the relative effectiveness of the first Stability Pact was mainly due to the 'golden carrot' of EU membership – that is, to its early overlap with the second approach: in other words, full integration and direct conditionality have mostly superseded (for the better) the initially more limited scope of the first approach – including that of CEFTA, which had by 1997 more or less achieved its goal of creating a tariff-free area for trade in industrial goods and which had constituted a starting point for the countries' accession to the Union's single market.

From 'Royaumont' to the Stability Pact for South-Eastern Europe

These considerations may help us understand why the so-called 'Royaumont Process' has had, instead, such a modest impact on the EU's immediate neighbourhood. At the suggestion of Brussels, and again based on a French initiative, a 'process of stability and good-neighbourly relations' in South-Eastern Europe was inaugurated at the Royaumont meeting, near Paris, in December 1995. It tried to take into account the experience of the previous Stability Pact and the latest developments in Bosnia-Herzegovina, but it lacked substance in that it failed to address the key issues (notably, borders and minorities) and limited itself to promoting dialogue and better understanding between governmental and non-governmental actors in the region. On top of that – but understandably so, at that time – the Process did not establish any link between policy change and future association to the EU, thus offering no 'carrots' whatsoever to the countries in question. Although the Union went as far as to appoint a special coordinator, in November 1997, the Royaumont Process never took off the ground.

Only in the summer of 1999 – in the wake of the fourth consecutive war of Yugoslav succession, so to speak, namely that over Kosovo – did the Union change its approach by offering a framework for economic and political cooperation between the EU (plus other international organizations) and the countries of South-Eastern Europe that put some solid carrots on the table. However, it stopped short of creating direct 'conditionality' – that is, an explicit link between compliance and good behaviour with the accession process. This is probably why the jury is still out on whether the Stability Pact for South-Eastern Europe (SPSEE) – in which the EU acts as a coordinator and facilitator – represents a fundamental policy shift as regards the membership prospects of the Balkan countries, and whether it will act as an effective means to stabilization and/or integration. On the one hand, the SPSEE encompasses countries – such as Bulgaria and Romania – that have already signed Europe Agreements and started accession negotiations, thus blurring the possible nature of the Pact as a more or less explicit antechamber of the Union.[6] On the other hand, since late 2000 the Union has independently set in motion a so-called Stabilization and Association Process (SAP) meant to foster peace, prosperity and democracy in the western Balkans: it sets out elements of a policy that – by resorting to a 'contractual' relationship between the EU and the five or six relevant states or entities (Albania, Croatia, Bosnia and Herzegovina, Macedonia, Serbia and Montenegro, plus Kosovo) – tries to bridge the gap between 'simple' stabilization and 'full' integration, and supplements this with an ad hoc programme called CARDS (Community Assistance for Reconstruction, Development and Stabilization).[7] To date, only two countries (Macedonia in 2001 and Croatia in 2002) have signed the so-called Stabilization and Association Agreements (SAA) with the EU; their successful implementation is a prerequisite for any further assessment of their respective prospects for accession (actually, in Croatia's case, a formal application for membership was made in February 2003). In other words, the maximum status the SAP can award is that of 'potential candidate'. Meanwhile, the EU has decided temporarily to 'freeze' the drafting of the fourth CFSP 'Common Strategy' envisaged after Amsterdam, notably as concerns the Balkan region.

Such ambivalence over the final outcome of the process is understandable, particularly in the light of the past instability of the region. It would be the first time, in fact, that certified failure, rather than prospective success, would have been rewarded with EU membership. At the same time, such ambivalence is partly due also to a fundamental uncertainty (and a certain degree of internal divisions) over the future geographical and functional scope of the European Union as such, for which the

Balkans are an important test case and a precedent – an uncertainty that deeply affects the policy of the EU towards its changing periphery.

The integration approach

By contrast, the second policy approach – based on integration as a goal and conditionality as a means – has been much more successful. Actually, enlarging the EC, and later the EU, has been, and still is, a quintessential security policy. It is a security policy by other means, so to speak, and a security policy in its own right. By other means, because extending the Union's norms, rules, opportunities and constraints to successive applicants has made instability and conflict on the continent ever less likely. And it is a security policy in its own right, too, because the entrants have brought in interests and skills that have broadened the scope of common policies and strengthened the EC/EU as an international actor.

This was the case with the first enlargement of the European Community, which incorporated the British (and partially Danish) overseas connections and also gradually stimulated an Anglo-Irish détente via Brussels. It was all the more the case with the southern enlargements of the 1980s, which paved the way for the successful completion of the post-authoritarian transitions to democracy in the countries concerned, provided a significant reinforcement of the EC's presence in the Mediterranean basin, and added an equally significant extension of European influence in the Americas. Finally, the 1995 enlargement of the newly created EU brought more stability to the Baltic 'rim' and strengthened the Union's drive to cooperate with the UN and the OSCE.

The current enlargement, however, is nothing like the previous ones. It is fundamentally different in size, scope and character: going from an EU of 15 to 25 member states – as decided at the Copenhagen European Council of December 2002[8] – will mean an increase in population of 20 per cent but an increase in GDP of only a few percentage points, coupled with an increase of 'small' members from the current 10 to 19. It is therefore likely to change radically the institutions, the policies, and even the very nature of the Union.[9] It will probably also affect the way in which the EU projects itself externally; though perhaps not so much in terms of its common foreign and defence policy, to which the current applicants are expected to add relatively little in terms of interests, inclinations and capabilities. However, its impact will be much greater in terms of neighbourhood (and to a certain extent security) policy, stretching from border issues (the issue of permeability as against control), the rights of transnational minorities, to the ultimate *finalité géographique* of the EU.[10]

It is worth noting here that the process finalized in Copenhagen in 2002 started out relatively early: PHARE was created in December 1989 to support the economic reform process in Poland and Hungary, and was subsequently extended and adjusted. The Europe [Association] Agreements were signed in early 1992 by the Visegrad countries (then Poland, Hungary and Czechoslovakia), soon followed by Romania and Bulgaria, the Baltic States and, finally, Slovenia. However, only at the Copenhagen European Council of June 1993 was the direct link between association and (future) membership made clear and explicit, thus giving the Agreements a wide-ranging and hitherto unique scope. This included 'conditionality', as spelt out in the so-called Copenhagen criteria, thus setting a series of benchmarks from the opening to the successful completion of entry negotiations. At that time, it was widely assumed that the next enlargement of the Union would be quite selective in the first instance, and the criteria served the purpose of drawing a relatively objective functional road map for EU membership. Therefore, it should have come as no particular surprise that the Luxembourg European Council in December 1997 earmarked only six applicants for the opening of accession negotiations: Poland, Hungary, the Czech Republic (the three countries which had been invited to join NATO a few months earlier), Estonia, Slovenia and Cyprus. Only two years later, under pressure from some member states, the Helsinki European Council extended the procedure to the five remaining applicants plus Malta and awarded Turkey (the longest-waiting associated country) the status of 'candidate', though one not yet ripe for opening accession negotiations.[11]

In the end, therefore, the integration/conditionality approach has fundamentally taken over as the dominant approach in most of East-Central Europe, not least because the tension and the potential contradiction with the stabilization/regionality approach were damaging the overarching security goal (stabilization) by triggering a 'beauty contest' among the applicants and fostering a dangerous sense of exclusion among those that lagged behind, and thus potentially undermining existing sub-regional cooperation. Actually, such a risk cannot be ruled out once and for all even now that the EU enlargement process has come full circle ('from Copenhagen to Copenhagen', so to speak). The recent controversies over the Hungarian law on Magyars living abroad, and especially the so-called 'Beneš decrees' in post-war Czechoslovakia, have shown that there remains a potential for sub-regional tension, if not open conflict (in particular over minority issues), that perhaps only the EU's norms and obligations can help overcome.[12] In addition, the fact that Romania and Bulgaria have missed – at least for the time being, given that in Copenhagen a target date (2007) has been set for their entry – the forthcoming wave of accessions may create some problems, especially if their eventual integration takes longer than foreseen, owing to the aftershock of the first wave inside the Union and the possible attendant repercussions on the two countries (now joined on the waiting list by Croatia, which formally applied for membership in February 2003). In this respect, Romania's and Bulgaria's inclusion in the other wave of enlargement, namely that of NATO – as decided at the Prague North Atlantic Council of November

2002, a few weeks before Copenhagen[13] – is expected to prevent such an eventuality from happening – or, perhaps more importantly, from having critically destabilizing effects. More generally, such problems will not necessarily go away even once the current enlargement process is completed and all the applicants have been brought into the EU fold. New minority and border issues are bound to emerge, this time with the new 'periphery' of the enlarged EU.

Between integration and partnership

The two approaches described so far have hardly corresponded to policies that were fully and/or thoroughly conceived from the outset. On the contrary, they have been more reactive than proactive, and a certain measure of ambiguity (however 'constructive') over the final outcome has always existed, fostered also by the existence of differing visions of enlargement among the current member states. Over time, however, it has become increasingly evident that such ambiguity or fuzziness has limits and may even be counter-productive. Unlike NATO with its Partnership for Peace programme, which has managed quite successfully to blur the difference between members and non-members and thus distribute security benefits across the entire continent without bearing significant institutional costs, the Union has serious problems in doing that effectively without clarifying (internally as well as externally) the ultimate goal of its partnerships and regional policies. Furthermore, unlike the OSCE and/or the Council of Europe, the EU cannot water down its nature and scope for the sake of extending its membership: it would lose its main strength and, consequently, its very appeal.[14]

Differentiation

To address this difficulty, the Union needs to assess how far it can stretch its present structure and policies, both geographically and functionally. This assessment may lead to the explicit introduction of forms of *internal* differentiation in order to accommodate potentially conflicting demands. The current institutional review process (the European Convention, followed by another intergovernmental conference) may well serve this purpose. In addition, a debate on the ultimate conceivable border of the wider Union – the *limes*, so to speak – may prove useful, if not conclusive. In fact, article 237 of the Treaty of Rome states that 'any European State' can apply to become a member of the EEC. Since the 1993 Copenhagen summit and the Treaty of Amsterdam (article 49 of the Treaty on European Union), 'European-ness' has been combined with conditionality. Since the Kosovo war in 1999, the prospect of EU membership has been floated in areas of the continent that had been hitherto ruled out, from the Balkans to Ukraine. Lately, even Russia, in the aftermath of its rapprochement with NATO, has been quoted as being a potential future candidate, although it is much more likely to remain an external (if possibly ever closer) partner. Perhaps it is high time the Union addressed the issue in a more stringent manner and devised coherent policies to resolve it.[15]

The EU should also conceive of forms of partnership and cooperation (bi- and/or multilateral) that may stop short of full eventual integration but nonetheless bring about a significant degree of cooperation and stabilization. The difficulty lies in the fact that the most effective regional policy tool at the disposal of the Union to this end has been conditionality; conditionality, however, really works only when eventual membership is at stake. When it is not, it proves a much weaker instrument, as the experience of the past decade has shown. Therefore, if membership is the 'golden carrot' but is not on offer, what 'silver' and/or 'bronze' carrots can be devised for the EU as a regional power to carry out effective policies in its (old and new) periphery? Probably a certain degree of *external* differentiation with respect to the various areas and countries involved has to be put in place: not a differentiation by accident and reactive improvisation, as displayed by the current array of diverse institutional and contractual relations (from the PCAs to the SAP, from Euromed to other formats), but one that takes adequately into account the peculiarities of the actors and issues involved.

The Turkish question

First of all, the Union will certainly have to sort out its collective attitude vis-à-vis Turkey. The constructive ambiguity that has dominated negotiations on both sides may have to be overcome sooner rather than later: either towards full membership, with a road map for negotiations and a tentative deadline, or towards a structured bilateral partnership without membership. The EU decision over Cyprus's entry may well become the initial catalyst for this. In Copenhagen, in fact, Turkey obtained a 'rendezvous for the rendezvous' in December 2004, at which point, after the current enlargement has been completed, Turkey's credentials will be thoroughly assessed and a clear decision (hopefully) taken. And it is worth recalling that, to date, all the countries that have started negotiations with the EC/EU – with the exception of Norway, as a result of its own autonomous national decision – have ended up as full members. The endgame is approaching, therefore, and its outcome will have repercussions on several counts. The European Conference that was invented in 1997 to accommodate Turkey's peculiar status has proved an empty shell, and the customs union with Ankara has not entirely got off the ground yet. At the same time, Turkey is an active NATO ally, is engaged on the ground in the Balkans, and is a crucial partner in the Middle East, the Gulf and the Caucasus. The structural imbalance between its strategic value and its economic weakness has to be addressed with instruments capable of meeting the specific (and at times contradictory) demands that come from both Turkey itself and the broader Eastern Mediterranean region. Meanwhile, the Turkish government elected in November 2002 has shown a readiness to change and compromise – from the status of Cyprus to the so-called 'Berlin-plus' arrangement between NATO and the EU – that bodes well for the crucial decision to be taken in 2004, provided that other sub-regional developments (Iraq) do not derail the whole process.[16]

Norway, Iceland and Switzerland

As regards Norway, Iceland and Switzerland, the decision between structured partnership and full membership lies exclusively with them. All three countries are already de facto members of the single market through the European Economic Area. Norway and Iceland are also part of 'Schengenland' through the Nordic Passport Union. Finally, acceptance of these countries by EU citizens is very high, as the Eurobarometer polls keep showing. In this particular case, in other words, there is nothing new to be put on the table: all the elements are there already. In the case of Norway, interest in joining the enlarged Union seems to be on the rise after Copenhagen and could well lead to a renewed attempt after the failures of 1972 and 1994.

The Balkans

As explained earlier, the jury is still out as far as the (remaining) Balkan countries are concerned, namely Serbia and Montenegro, Bosnia, Albania and Macedonia. Some of these are also candidates for NATO membership, and the expansion of the Alliance may influence EU policy towards them. However, the crucial issue here is whether and under what conditions full EU membership is both conceivable and acceptable on the Union's side. If it is conceivable (and all the countries in question meet the general 'European-ness' criterion), it has also to be made acceptable, first through a stringent scrutiny over the implementation of the SAP, then through a closely monitored road map to eventual accession. However, there will remain doubts as to whether the whole process can overcome the low acceptance of EU citizens towards most Balkan countries, an issue that may eventually play a decisive role. In fact, integrating countries whose social and economic development are lagging and marred by criminal networks, whose democratic credentials are unproven and whose administrative practices are pre-modern, is a daunting challenge. A possible fallback position could be either (in the event of accession) an ever-increasing internal differentiation in the enlarged Union – something very close to a multi-tier EU – or a very solid 'silver carrot', encompassing for example a brand new status of 'associate member', which would give both tangible benefits (customs union, economic and administrative assistance) and a European 'identity' (*photo de famille*, structured political partnership) without imposing the risks, for both sides, of an undesired or unaffordable membership. In a way, the choice is between further enlargement proper, with all its foreseeable costs on both sides, and a sort of enlargement 'by other means'. At the same time, again, it may be in the short-term interest of the Union's security policy to postpone such a choice as long as possible in order to exploit all the potential of the 'golden carrot'.

The Eastern 'new neighbours'

Once the current enlargement process is completed in 2004, the wider EU will automatically acquire some new neighbours, starting with Ukraine and Belarus and ending with Moldova. To a certain extent, some of the dilemmas illustrated above for the Balkan countries may apply also to the three westernmost members of the Commonwealth of Independent States (CIS). Much as they differ from one another in terms of history, size and potential problems, they are all 'European', at least geographically, but they are also all far behind on their path to 'Europeanization'. Furthermore, Ukraine and (though less explicitly) Moldova – but not Belarus – have expressed their interest in becoming, one day, EU members, although none of them has received any encouragement from Brussels.

In any event, the challenge for the Union is to try to disconnect its two main 'virtues' in the eyes of most of the neighbouring countries, namely its being both a vehicle for change and a potential end-goal. This implies conceiving an approach that conveys a sense of inclusion in 'Europe' separate from the end-state of full EU membership, while working to foster the kind of change that may make it conceivable at some point in the future, given appropriate circumstances, to consider this very membership. This means, in other words, a reversal of emphasis, stressing the process of adaptation to, rather than the end-goal of integration into, EU structures and policies. What the Union can sensibly do, in the meantime, is, first, increase the Eastern neighbours' awareness of the membership requirements, and, second, foster ever more decisively the process of democratization, state consolidation, administrative reform and economic liberalization – which will both contribute to stabilizing the Eastern 'rim' of the enlarged EU and facilitate its gradual entry into the European 'mainstream'.

That said, the peculiarity of the three Eastern 'new neighbours' – as distinct from all other potential members and partners – is their relationship with, and dependency on, Russia. This may shape a sort of 'Eastern dimension' of the EU, namely one based on a set of trilateral relations in which these countries represent, to varying degrees, an interface between Moscow and the Union as an explicit element of their direct bilateral partnership. In the case of Belarus, its likely eventual inclusion into the

Russian Federation would clearly simplify the current picture.[17] Moldova's Russian connection is mainly (but not exclusively) linked to the issue of secessionist Transdniestria but is matched by an equally delicate Romanian connection, which makes the country a particular test case for the enlarging EU.[18] As for Ukraine, its willingness to 'go West' is still not matched by consistent domestic reforms, while its strategic position in the energy supply market makes it a crucial partner for both Russia and the EU.[19] The EU could therefore envisage a neighbourhood policy to the East including two main components. One would be the reinforcement of links with each of the three countries, with due regard to their specificity. The other would be the development of a regional approach – an *Ostpolitik* in its own right – that would encompass all three and place them in the context of EU–Russia relations.[20] It is also predictable that the 'acceding' countries – as the candidates accepted in Copenhagen are now called – will push for the reinforcement of such an 'Eastern dimension' of the Union's policies: it is not by accident that in the run-up to Copenhagen, on 18 November 2002, the Council decided to launch a 'New Neighbours Initiative' focused on 'the need for the EU to formulate an ambitious, long-term and integrated approach towards each of these countries'. In the same vein, in March 2003 the Commission delivered a Communication on 'Wider Europe' that encompasses future relations with both Eastern and Southern neighbours, while Poland announced a policy non-paper on the 'Eastern Dimension' as limited to Russia, Belarus and Ukraine.[21]

The Barcelona Process

Finally, the Barcelona Process may have to be streamlined and redefined, to give a more realistic but also more tangible prospect of structured partnership for the Mediterranean countries, possibly including a certain degree of differentiation among them. Of the 12 partners in the Barcelona Process or Euro-Mediterranean Partnership (EMP), three are already involved in the current enlargement (Cyprus, Malta and Turkey), one tried – not long ago but in vain – to be accepted as a potential candidate (Morocco), and two are involved in a bilateral conflict (Israel and the Palestinian Authority) while being both important EU trade partners and aid recipients. In other words, the Euromed partners can hardly be considered a single and homogeneous unit: the Eastern Mediterranean (now part of the EU enlargement process proper), Israel/Palestine, the Mashreq (the eastern Arab lands), and the Maghreb are distinct sub-regional units, each with its own specific features. With this in mind, much can still be improved in terms of existing programmes and their implementation, including the extremely delicate security aspects. This is all the more important since, from 2005, the Barcelona Process may well end up encompassing only Israel and a whole set of Arab countries, with all the imaginable implications. Failing a shared and credible all-encompassing rationale, however, it may be wiser to envisage a set of targeted sub-regional programmes – silver and/or bronze carrots – aimed at addressing common as well as distinctive issues.[22]

The EU and its peripheries

A policy towards the periphery is an essential feature and requirement of any regional power, and the EU claims to be, or wishes to become, a fully-fledged one. At the same time, the Union conceives of itself also as an international/global actor, at least on the economic and (to a lesser extent) diplomatic front. That does not mean that it has the ambition to be a global power in its own right, or that it can and will operate worldwide across the board, especially as regards to military intervention and to strategic issues, such as non-proliferation and energy supply. On the contrary, if one looks for instance at the aid flows emanating from the EC/EU, it becomes clear that the range of its interests and partnerships is selective and corresponds to that of a regional power. with some clearly identifiable overseas interests. In 2000, for instance, out of the €12 billion of the Union's aid budget (EC plus European Development Fund), roughly €2 billion went to the East-Central European candidates, €1 billion to emergency humanitarian and food aid (mostly directed to Africa), €1 billion to the Mediterranean, and €500 million each to the CIS, Latin America and Asia. In so far as it is directed overseas, EU aid mostly ends up in ACP countries. And the picture is more or less the same, with marginal nuances, if one looks at the bilateral aid given by individual EU member states. This shows that the Union has a *geographical* periphery (the immediate neighbourhood) as well as a *historical/economic* periphery, which basically coincides with the post-colonial links and the preferential partnerships of its member states. As for security policy proper, the current provisions for the European Security and Defence Policy (ESDP) envisage a virtual geographical radius for EU military crisis management (up to approximately 4,000km from Brussels) that roughly covers the present immediate neighbourhood – starting with the Balkans but touching only lightly the CIS proper and the southern Mediterranean shore – but does not rule out, at least in principle, extension to the 'outer' periphery, as past discussions over deployment in the African Great Lakes or the UN mission in East Timor prove. Currently, the potential radius for purely humanitarian operations stretches as far as 10,000km from Brussels. Furthermore, soldiers and officials from EU individual member states are already engaged in multilateral peace support operations in the Balkans or in those parts of the wider world that embody some broader European and/or national interest.

In other words, there seems to be after all a discernible pattern and a substantial geographical overlap between the Union's various external policies: trade, aid, diplomacy, and crisis management proper. What is still lacking is a more streamlined and coherent approach, especially to the immediate periphery, after a decade of mostly reactive decisions and constructive ambiguities. To give just a practical example: does it make sense, once the current enlargement process is completed, to preserve the current rigid separation (also in bureaucratic and procedural terms) between the Interreg, PHARE, CARDS and TACIS programmes, thus perpetuating the tension between the two approaches analysed above?

The forthcoming enlargement, coupled with the growing demand for a more active foreign policy, should hopefully force the relevant policy-makers to adopt a more systematic approach. In terms of external policies, the enlargement will add next to nothing to the outer periphery – none of the applicants, with the partial exception of Turkey (the Middle East, the Caucasus and Central Asia), has an imperial past or extra-European linkages – but will add to the immediate periphery, of which these countries were a part in the past and with which they will be in close contact in the future. Indeed, the most important contribution of the new member states to the Union's policies is expected to be in this domain, especially as regards the 'Eastern dimension' and *Ostpolitik*: an interesting prospective test case was the controversy over the transit to and from the Kaliningrad enclave. As for the global dimension, finally, much will depend on the extent to which the CFSP/ESDP turns into a driver of European policy at large, and therefore commits the member states to pooling interests and capabilities that go well beyond – for some of them at least – the immediate periphery of the present (and foreseeable) Union.

Notes

1 For a tentative overview, see G. Edwards, 'The Potential and Limits of CFSP: The Yugoslav Example', in E. Regelsberger, P. de Schoutheete and W. Wessels (eds), *Foreign Policy of the European Union: From EPC to CFSP and Beyond*, Boulder, Colo.: Lynne Rienner, 1997, pp. 173–95.

2 In December 2000 the Secretary-General of the EU Council, and High Representative for the CFSP, Javier Solana, released an 'evaluation report' on the three 'Common Strategies' hitherto adopted by the Union that sounded fairly critical of the method and the substance of the exercise, which had been introduced with the Treaty of Amsterdam. See 'Common Strategies Report', reproduced in A. Missiroli (ed.), 'Coherence for European Security Policy: Debates – Cases – Assessments', WEU–ISS Occasional Paper 27, WEU–ISS, Paris, May 2001, Annex E, pp. 80–6 (www.iss-eu.org). Common Strategies are expected to be in force for five years. For specific evaluations, see G. Sasse, 'The EU Common Strategy on Ukraine: A Response to Ukraine's pro-European Choice?', in A. Lewis (ed.), *The EU and Ukraine: Neighbours, Friends, Partners?*, London: The Federal Trust, 2002, pp. 213–20; and H. Haukkala and S. Medvedev (eds), *The EU Common Strategy on Russia: Learning the Grammar of CFSP*, Helsinki and Berlin: FIIA and IEP, 2001.

3 See M. Maresceau and E. Lannon (eds), *The EU Enlargement and Mediterranean Strategies: A Comparative Analysis*, Basingstoke, UK: Palgrave, 2001.

4 On the CFSP machinery, see J. Monar, 'Political Dialogue with Third Coun-

tries and Regional Political Groupings: The Fifteen as an Attractive Interlocutor', in Regelsberger *et al.* (eds), *Foreign Policy of the European Union*, pp. 263–74. See also M. Holland, *The European Union and the Third World*, Basingstoke, UK: Palgrave, 2002; and, more generally, C. Piening, *Global Europe: The European Union in World Affairs*, Boulder, Colo.: Lynne Rienner, 1997.

5 On this phase, see K. E. Smith, *The Making of EU Foreign Policy: The Case of Eastern Europe*, New York: St Martin's Press, 1999; and P. Luif, 'The European Union's Projection of Security and Stability onto Central and Eastern Europe', in P. Luif (ed.), *Security in Central and Eastern Europe: Problems – Perceptions – Policies*, Vienna: Braumüller, 2001, pp. 307–42. For a broader approach and a thorough analysis of the various sub-regional groupings and initiatives, see A. Cottey (ed.), *Sub-regional Cooperation in the New Europe: Building Security, Prosperity and Solidarity from the Barents to the Black Sea*, New York: East–West Institute, 1999.

6 See R. Dimtcheva, 'La Bulgarie et la Roumanie dans le Pacte de stabilité', EU–ISS Occasional Paper, 41, EU–ISS, Paris, January 2001 (www.iss-eu.org).

7 For an overall assessment, see M. Brusis and N. Galer, 'South-Eastern Europe and the EU: Problems, Actors, Policies', in W. van Meurs (ed.), *Beyond EU Enlargement*, vol. 2, *The Agenda of Stabilisation for South-Eastern Europe*, Gütersloh: Bertelsmann Foundation, 2001, pp. 45–71.

8 Accordingly, Poland, Hungary, the Czech Republic, Slovakia, Slovenia, Estonia, Latvia, Lithuania, Malta and Cyprus signed the accession treaty in April 2003 and become full members from April 2004. For a first evaluation, see H. Grabbe, 'The Copenhagen Deal for Enlargement', Briefing Note, Centre for European Reform, London, 20 December 2002 (www.cer.org.uk); A. Missiroli, 'Two Enlargements and a Devolution', *EU–ISS Newsletter*, March 2003 (www.iss-eu.org).

9 For a general overview, see G. Avery and F. Cameron, *The Enlargement of the European Union*, Sheffield: Sheffield Academic Press, 1998.

10 See A. Missiroli (ed.), 'Bigger EU, Wider CFSP, Stronger ESDP? The View from Central Europe', EU–ISS Occasional Paper 34, EU–ISS, Paris, April 2002 (www.iss-eu.org). For a post-Copenhagen evaluation, see A. Missiroli, 'EU Enlargement and CFSP/ESDP', *European Integration*, 2003, vol. 25, no. 1: 1–16.

11 See U. Sedelmeyer and H. Wallace, 'Eastern Enlargement', in H. Wallace and W. Wallace (eds), *Policy-Making in the European Union*, Oxford: Oxford University Press, 2000, pp. 427–60.

12 See H. Grabbe, 'The Benes Decrees: Implications for EU Enlargement', Briefing Note, Centre for European Reform, London, June 2002 (www.cer.org.uk); 'A Spectre over Central Europe', *The Economist*, 17 August 2002, pp. 23–4. More generally, see E. Berg and W. van Meurs, 'Legacies of the Past, Ethnic and Territorial Conflict Potentials', in I. Kempe (ed.), *Beyond EU Enlargement*, vol. 1, *The Agenda of Direct Neighbourhood for Eastern Europe*, Gütersloh, Bertelsmann Foundation, 2001, pp. 129–63.

13 In Prague, the Atlantic Alliance decided to 'invite' Bulgaria, Romania, Slovenia, Slovakia, Estonia, Latvia and Lithuania to join the current 19 allies by May 2004. By then, therefore, NATO will have 26 members, 19 of which will also be EU members.

14 For comparisons between the different enlargements of European organizations over the past years, see S. Croft, J. Redmond, G. Wyn Rees and M. Webber, *The Enlargement of Europe*, Manchester: Manchester University Press, 1999; and A. Hyde-Price, 'The Antinomies of European Security: Dual Enlargement and the Reshaping of the European Order', *Contemporary Security Policy*, 2000, vol. 21, no. 3: 139–67.

15 For an interesting overview, see T. Christiansen, F. Petito and B. Tonra, 'Fuzzy Politics around Fuzzy Borders: The European Union's "Near Abroad"', *Cooperation and Conflict*, 2000, vol. 35, no. 4: 389–415.

16 A deal on 'Berlin-plus' was eventually struck in December 2002 in the wake of Copenhagen: it foresees *inter alia* that Malta and Cyprus will not participate in any EU operation conducted with NATO planning and logistical support. For an analysis of the issues involved, with particular emphasis on the military dimension, see A. Missiroli, 'EU–NATO Cooperation in Crisis Management: No Turkish Delight for ESDP', *Security Dialogue*, 2002, vol. 35, no. 1: 9–26.

17 See A. Lewis (ed.), *The EU and Belarus: Between Moscow and Brussels*, London: Federal Trust, 2002.

18 D. Lynch, 'Crisis in Moldova', *EU–ISS Newsletter*, Paris, February 2002 (www.iss-eu.org); and M. Bran, 'Les Moldaves et le passeport roumain', *Le Monde*, 29 November 2002, p. 17.

19 For example, T. Kuzio and J. D. P. Moroney, 'Ukraine and the West: Moving from Stability to Strategic Enlargement', *European Security*, 2001, vol. 10, no. 2: 111–26; O. Pavliuk, 'An Unfulfilling Partnership: Ukraine and the West 1991–2001', *European Security*, 2002, vol. 11, no. 1: 81–101; and Lewis (ed.), *The EU and Ukraine*.

20 See I. Kempe and W. van Meurs, 'Strategic Challenges and Risks of EU Eastern Enlargement', in I. Kempe (ed.), *Beyond EU Enlargement*, vol. 1, pp. 11–43; S. White, I. McAllister and M. Light, 'Enlargement and the New Outsiders', *Journal of Common Market Studies*, 2002, vol. 40, no. 1: 135–53; and C. Guicherd, 'The Enlarged EU's Eastern Border: Integrating Ukraine, Belarus and Moldova in the European Project', SWP-Studie 20, Stiftung Wissenschaft und Politik, Berlin, June 2002.

21 The relevant Council decision (doc. 14078/02) can be found in the Commission's Communication in www.europa.eu.int/comm/external_relations/we/doc/com_03_104_en.pdf. See also J. Reed, 'Poland Suggests New Eastern Policy for EU', *Financial Times*, 28 January 2003, p. 2.

22 See F. Tanner (ed.), *The European Union as a Security Actor in the Mediterranean*, Zürich: Zürcher Beiträge zur Sicherheitspolitik und Konfliktforschung, 2001; and M. Ortega, 'Military Dialogue in the Euro-Mediterranean Charter: An Unjustified Absence', *The International Spectator*, 2000, vol. 35, no. 1: 115–25. See also D. Schmid, 'Optimiser le processus de Barcelone', Occasional Paper 36, EU–ISS, Paris, July 2002 (www.iss-eu.org).

3 Strategy with fast-moving targets

East-Central Europe

Pál Dunay

> We must build the united Europe not only in the interest of the free nations, but also in order to admit the peoples of Eastern Europe into this community if, freed from the constraints under which they live, they want to join and seek our moral support. We owe them the example of a unified, fraternal Europe. Every step we take along this road will mean a new opportunity for them. They need our help with the transformation they have to achieve. It is our duty to be prepared.
>
> (Robert Schuman)[1]

These visionary words were not expressed at a time when the communist system was disintegrating in Eastern Europe and the socialist countries of East-Central Europe (ECE) were starting to consider a future on the 'other side' of the Iron Curtain. They were uttered in 1963 by one of the founding fathers of the European Community when the prospect of European reunification was decades away. As such, they point to the strategic vision of European integration that has existed from the very beginning of the European project.

The issue of whether the European Union (EU) has had an enlargement strategy since the end of the East–West conflict is important to answer not only in terms of intellectual curiosity but also for its continuing political relevance. Even though the enlargement process to ECE has reached an important juncture, with eight countries of the region to join the EU in 2004, this is not the end of the process. There are many other states that wish to join the Union. Two of them, Bulgaria and Romania, are pursuing accession negotiations; Croatia applied for EU membership in February 2003; and a large number of countries both in South-Eastern Europe and in the former Soviet Union also contemplate their future as being in the Union. So long as the EU continues to exist in the foreseeable future, and the aspiration of these states does not change, one can conceive of a major historical process that may result in the unification of Europe. This is a process of unprecedented importance and of historical proportions.

The issue has already generated a certain debate. Some scholars deny the existence of an enlargement strategy, mainly on the grounds that there has been no clear plan or identifiable thread that has run through the entire process. Those who regard strategy as a set of rigid rules and ideas may rightly draw such a conclusion.[2] However, if one starts from the premise that a political strategy cannot but be self-reflective and adaptable to changing reality, one can conclude that a political concept has underpinned the enlargement process. It is with this understanding that this chapter argues that the EU has had a strategy towards ECE. The strategy has not been static, has constantly adapted to changing reality and has even gone through a major change of emphasis, as Missiroli argues in this volume (Chapter 2) when he identifies two distinct EU approaches: one that aimed at the 'stabilization', and the other at the 'integration' of the immediate neighbourhood of the EU. This assessment is broadly correct, although further investigation may be required to determine the relationship between the two. Did the two aims of stabilization and integration coexist or did the former gradually give way to the latter? When and under what conditions did the change occur? Have residual stability concerns remained? It is clear, however, that Missiroli does subscribe to the view that there has been an EU strategy.

Those authors, more often than not from ECE, who criticize the enlargement strategy of the EU often implicitly recognize the existence of a strategy but simply see that strategy as having been wrong, and contrary to the genuine long-term interests of the Union.[3] This chapter does accept that the strategic conception was often overshadowed by the minutiae of detailed negotiations, particularly during the accession talks. It also accepts that the EU and its member states have short-term selfish interests that contributed to this. But neither of these critiques is sufficient for us to conclude either that the EU has lacked an enlargement strategy or that it has been an inappropriate or wrong strategy.

This chapter has four main sections. First, there is an account of the development and evolution of the commitment of the EU to ECE from the end of the Cold War. Second, there is an assessment of the nature of the political and economic transformation in ECE. Third, an analysis is provided of the problems and shortcomings of the enlargement process. Finally, the conditions and implications of the 2004 eastern enlargement are evaluated.

Evolution of the commitment to East-Central Europe

Prior to 1989, the European Community (EC) had only a strictly limited engagement with the Eastern Bloc, initiating low-intensity exchanges with the Council for Mutual Economic Assistance (CMEA) in the early 1970s and later signing a few bilateral trade agreements. But the fact that the EC had practically no links with the socialist countries did not mean that the continent was completely divided. EC member states pursued foreign policies with these countries, though their level of familiarity with them varied greatly. Generally speaking, the larger EC member states were more able to differentiate between the minor differences of Eastern Europe in their political course. Geographic vicinity also mattered. Germany and Italy, which are located closer to the region, had a better understanding of ECE than Spain, for example. France had a partial view based on its familiarity with some countries and not so much with others. The only EC member state that had a solid, detailed knowledge of ECE was the Federal Republic of Germany, the country that was obliged to have an active eastern policy, the *Ostpolitik*, from the end of the 1960s on.

Consequently, the whole story relevant for this study started in 1989. It was then that the EC noticed that there was a region adjacent to it that had started to change at breathtaking speed. In the light of the strictly limited knowledge of ECE, the initial and quite natural reaction was to gain an increased knowledge of the region. Caution was also dictated by the speed of events. It was not clear how stable and prosperous the newly established democratic regimes would be. The first years were thus a period of gaining familiarity with the East, accompanied by certain measures of practical cooperation. The PHARE project (see Chapter 2), which was gradually expanded to the reform countries of the region, was an illustration of this. The next major step in this process was the conclusion of so-called Europe Agreements between the EC and the most advanced candidate countries. The most important content of these agreements was to eliminate tariffs and non-tariff barriers between the Union and the candidate countries bilaterally, and primarily for industrial products. The agricultural sector, in which some ECE countries could have been competitive, was excluded from trade liberalization. Given the volume of EU trade, trade barriers were abolished asymmetrically, and full abolition was carried out by the end of 2001, as set out by the association agreements. The EU had to liberalize faster than the ECE countries throughout the process.[4]

During the negotiations over the first association agreements, the candidate countries raised the question whether the agreements should be viewed as part of a dynamic pre-accession strategy. At the time, the EC was reluctant to adopt clear language to this effect. Thus, the bilateral agreements stated that it was the objective of the candidate countries to become members of the EC but stopped short of declaring the same intention for the other side. For example, the association agreement with Hungary stated that 'the final objective of Hungary is to become a member of the Community and that this association, in the view of the Parties, will help to achieve this objective'.[5] In conclusion, the first phase of the development of relations between the EC and the more developed ECE countries can be characterized by the coexistence of three factors: first, the gaining of familiarity with the region through dialogue; second, the establishing of mutually advantageous economic cooperation; and third, the avoidance of any potentially risky strategic commitment in the region. The main objective was towards stabilization: ensuring that ECE did not undermine regional stability.

This approach primarily served the interests of the EC. It meant it could gain time and overcome the intellectual deficit it faced as a consequence of the unexpected and sudden change of the ECE's landscape. For the ECE reformers, who were implementing economic austerity measures in their countries in the hope of moving closer to the European institutions, the failure to offer the prospect of membership, even in a vague form, was painful. They noted that the EC was not necessarily 'acting in their favour'.[6] The EC also took no risks in its promotion of trade liberalization. This was evident in the significant trade surplus for the EU in the region throughout the 1990s. There was little justification to assume that the ECE countries would be in a position to dump their products onto EU markets. Indeed, the principal areas where some ECE countries have increased their competitiveness are those where Western companies, overwhelmingly firms of EU countries, invested heavily in the 1990s.[7]

This restrictive engagement only changed in 1992–3 when two European Councils decided to revise the underlying concept of eastward EU enlargement. The Edinburgh Council in 1992 confirmed that it 'accept[ed] the goal of eventual membership in the European Union for the countries of central and eastern Europe when they are able to satisfy the conditions required'.[8] The meeting did not specify the conditions for membership, which were only set six months later in Copenhagen, even if discussion about them was very limited. These conditions were as follows, with the aspirant ECE countries expected to have:

- stable institutions (guarantee of democracy, the rule of law, respect for human rights and minority rights);
- a functioning market;
- the capacity to cope with the competitive pressures inside the EC;
- the ability to adopt the *acquis* – that is, the accepted aims of political, economic and monetary union.

For its part, the only explicit condition for the EU was:

- its capacity to absorb new members without endangering the momentum of European integration.[9]

The list of criteria certainly represents an asymmetry, with four requirements listed for the candidates and only one for the Union. Bearing in mind this asymmetry and the difference in the economic strength of the two sides, the candidate countries not only had to live up to their side of the bargain but had to hope that the EU would in due course conclude that enlargement would not endanger the momentum of integration and fulfil its own requirement.[10] The setting of these criteria did, though, give first evidence of what was to follow, namely, that the whole accession process would more closely resemble admittance to a club where the existing members set the conditions for the candidates rather than engaging in negotiations on the basis of equality. Such asymmetries will only grow with further enlargements, since the enlarged EU of 2004 will be an entity of 25 member states with a population of 450 million and representing nearly one-quarter of the world's GDP.

In 1995 at the Essen Council, the EU adopted its White Paper *Preparation of the Associated Countries of Central and Eastern Europe for Integration into the Internal Market of the Union*. It followed the basic approach adopted at the Copenhagen Council, though was far more detailed and specific. The emphasis remained on the tasks the candidate countries had to fulfil. The Essen Council did, though, introduce two new elements. First, it underlined that candidate countries wishing to join the EU should not only have democratic credentials and respect human rights but must not bring unresolved problems concerning the treatment of minorities or frontier disputes into the EU. This can be regarded as the first direct encouragement by the Union to settle conflicts in the region as a precondition for membership.[11]

The second innovation was to list those 10 former socialist countries that could theoretically join the Union – these were Poland, Hungary, the Czech Republic, Slovakia, Slovenia, Bulgaria, Romania and the three Baltic States. For the successor states of the former Yugoslavia (except for Slovenia), this meant that their accession could be considered only after the ending of the violent conflict. For the Newly Independent States (NIS), the relationship was confined to another format: the Partnership and Cooperation Agreements. These decisions meant that the EU had delineated the geographical confines of eastern enlargement in a manner of lasting consequence.

In the summer of 1997 the moment of truth had seemed to arrive when the European Commission published *Agenda 2000*, its enlargement strategy, together with the first detailed assessment of the performance of the candidate countries. This involved a positive assessment for five of the candidate countries: Poland, Hungary, the Czech Republic, Estonia and Slovenia. As this report was published two weeks after the invitation was extended to the first former member states of the Warsaw Treaty Organization to negotiate their membership in the Atlantic Alliance, the ECE world appeared to have been divided into three parts. First was the 'double haves' of the Czech Republic, Hungary and Poland, which were invited to start negotiations for NATO membership and obtained a positive assessment from the European Commission. Second were the 'partial have-nots' of Estonia and Slovenia, which received a positive assessment from the Commission but were not invited to join NATO. And third were the 'double have-nots' which neither were invited to join NATO nor were assessed positively by the Commission. The countries falling into this camp were Bulgaria, Latvia, Lithuania, Romania and Slovakia. This had to be disappointing news for them. In reality, though, the positive assessments by the Commission were qualified by the unambiguous assertion that 'none of them fully satisfy all the criteria [for membership] at the present time' and that the favoured five would only satisfy 'the conditions of membership in the medium term if they maintain and strongly sustain their efforts of preparation'.[12]

Nevertheless, the European Council of December 1997 gave the green light to the Commission to begin accession talks with the five ECE countries that had received the more positive assessments. This was the formal end of the so-called regatta approach advocated by France, which was in favour of beginning negotiations with every candidate country but concluding such negotiations earlier with those that had more effectively prepared for membership. Paris wanted to postpone further 'the moment of truth' when it was made clear which countries had carried out a more successful transformation. It is not clear whether this was partly due to the revival of traditional sympathies with some candidate countries, such as Romania, whose performance was less convincing, or stemmed more from a wish to avoid engendering a sense of alienation in the excluded candidate countries.

It was clear, however, why the 'regatta approach' was not the favoured scenario for many of the candidate countries, the member states or the Commission. The more promising candidates exerted considerable pressure on the Union not to set up a negotiating framework in which they would have to wait for the weaker candidates to catch up. On a similar logic, some member states simply found it unnecessary to negotiate with states which could only at best join a decade later. Last but not least, the Commission was of the view that it could not manage effectively a dozen or more accession negotiations and that such an expansive framework would endanger the momentum of talks with the better-prepared ECE countries. These factors led to the rejection of the 'regatta approach' at this stage. Nevertheless, the approach was fairly speedily resurrected when, in December 1999 at the Helsinki European Council, agreement was reached that negotiations could be started with all the prospective ECE candidate countries.

A central feature of the negotiations that have taken place since 1998 has been the publication of annual reports on each of the candidate countries' progress towards accession.[13] It has been the intent of these reports to help the candidate countries meet accession criteria. These have generally been viewed as valuable and informative documents, providing a comprehensive overview of the economic and political progression of the candidate country concerned. Because they emanate from the EU's bureaucracy, a presumed 'meritocracy' and 'neutral observer', they have been respected in the candidate countries. It is for this reason that the reports have often been surrounded by controversy in domestic politics.

The opposition often refers to the reports to underline the poor performance of the government, whereas the government usually picks out those elements of the report that demonstrate the country's advance towards membership. As a consequence, the preparation of these reports has become a politicized process in which the candidate country, the member states and different interest groups attempt to influence the outcome of the report.

In terms of the substantive detail of the accession negotiations, the process is broken down into 31 chapters. The less complicated and controversial chapters are usually negotiated first and the most complex ones at a later stage, which means that the number of closed chapters does not necessarily say too much about the state of the negotiations. However, the main problem with these accession talks is that they are of great strategic importance, yet highly technical and complicated in their detail. As a consequence, it is difficult for the governments of the candidate countries to sustain public support for EU membership during the negotiation phase. This is one of the reasons why the governments of ECE have focused diplomatic attention, and emphasized to their public, the importance of determining the precise date for accession.

The date of accession as a political issue has three important features. First, it has real import for the accession countries, just as it has for the EU, and it is something easy to grasp for the broad strata of the population of these countries. Second, a date sets the state administration with a clear deadline to prepare for EU compatibility in the adoption and application of the *acquis*. Accession is not just a symbolic act but a real demonstration of the successful integration of the country into the West. And third, a specified date matters in identifying when the significant increases in flows of EU financial resources can be expected. The EU, though, has been reluctant to specify the date of accession, though some member countries have been more willing to speak about a date than others. It was only at the Göteborg Council in June 2001 that the EU presidency was ready to declare its hope that the first ECE candidate countries would 'participate in the European Parliament elections of 2004 as members'.[14]

At the Laeken European Council in December 2001, a list of countries was finally given for those eligible for early membership. The presidency conclusions declared that 'if the present rate of progress of the negotiations and reforms in the candidate states is maintained, Cyprus, Estonia, Hungary, Latvia, Lithuania, Malta, Poland, the Slovak Republic, the Czech Republic and Slovenia could be ready'.[15] This meant that eight ECE and two Mediterranean countries would gain membership at the same time. This so-called 'big bang' enlargement may not satisfy every candidate country but certainly serves some political and technical interests of the EU member states. First and foremost, 'big bang', even though unavoidably creating a sharp divide between those that gain membership and those that do not,[16] results in a relatively smaller number of frustrated political elites and disappointed peoples. As such, it represents an interesting and relatively generous recognition of both effort and achievement. There are certainly differences in the economic performance of the eight states, though these may look less important from the point of view of the rich Western member countries than from the more successful performers of the candidate countries. A 'big bang' enlargement also makes the ratification of accession protocols technically easier for the existing member states. The 10 protocols can be dealt with once in the 16 parliaments (the 15 member states and the European Parliament). Thus, the executive power of the member states will not have to keep going back to the legislatures with a few accession protocols every other year or so.

However, in light of the experience of the first eastern enlargement of NATO, the 'big bang' approach does also have a major disadvantage, namely, the danger that many problems will become visible only after accession, and countries that do not belong to this first group of eastern enlargement may consequently have to wait much longer than now anticipated. This may undermine long-term political stability in Romania and Bulgaria, which would be a most unwelcome development. In addition, there is the problem that the task for the EU to accommodate 10 countries, irrespective of their pre-accession preparation, will be an enormous one. The EU has never absorbed more than three countries at once. To move eight ECE and two Mediterranean states to the centre from the periphery of the EU (accession to the Schengen regime, the eurozone, completion of their 'phasing in' to the Common Agricultural Policy (CAP) and the regional and structural funds) will inevitably be extremely demanding. As a consequence, there might not be sufficient attention and resources left to complete the accession of those countries, primarily Bulgaria and Romania, which will not be part of 'big bang'. The EU seems to be aware of the potential problem, and at least the member of the Commission responsible for enlargement is seeking to guarantee, before the accession of the 10 new states, that resources will not dry up for the continuing process of integrating Romania and Bulgaria, which hopefully will be completed by 2008.

Overall, the record suggests that the European Union has had a strategy to integrate East-Central Europe, one that has been flexible and quite successful in representing both a commitment to the development and transformation of ECE and a promotion of the national interests of the member states. This strategy has been flexibly adapted several times and has proved to be responsive to the changes that have taken place in ECE. It requires further analysis to decide whether this mix of focusing on the vision, the future of the region adjacent to the EU, and on the self-interest of the EU and its member states has been adequate in terms of results.

Transform to integrate?

Immediately after the velvet revolutions in ECE, the countries of the region expressed their willingness to integrate into Western structures. This was hardly surprising, given that they were leaving a system that was, as regular uprisings and revolutions demonstrated, disliked by the population, imposed upon them and was in any case not viable economically. It should also not be forgotten that these are all small or medium-sized countries that can flourish only by belonging to larger entities in a globalizing world. In some senses, the size of these countries may be a more lasting inducement for integration than their past in the Soviet sphere of influence. They are aware that for them there is no alternative to integration and that it is a positive-sum game.

The resolve to integrate with the West consists of three major elements. First, the ECE countries have always felt they belong to European civilization, irrespective of how short-lived democracy was in the history of these countries. Most of them have no roots other than those connecting them to European civilization and (Western) Christianity. Second, Western Europe has always been economically more developed than ECE. Thus, the 'return to Europe' has been viewed as fostering economic development. Joining the EU also means joining the largest trading bloc in the world, which may provide the relatively small ECE countries with significant advantages. And third, the West both is highly institutionalized and has demonstrated stability for over 50 years since the Second World War. Part of this institutional network is an intensive security web, which also includes the world's strongest military power, the United States. All these factors contribute to the resolve of the ECE countries to join the West.

In response to this challenge, the countries of the East have reformed their political institutions and economic systems energetically and, at least initially, under disadvantageous conditions. They have been encouraged in their efforts by the West, although their perception has been for most of the time that the extent of Western support was less than they 'deserved'. This would not be a fair criticism if one works from the assumption that the countries of the region started with a clean slate and that it was up to the West to decide how it was to support its former adversaries. However, if one starts from the view, broadly held in ECE, that the West has a mission to reunite Europe and reintegrate those countries that belonged to the Soviet sphere of influence against their will, the criticism could be legitimate. That is especially the case if one also argues that the East–West conflict was due to failures of Western policy, such as the deal in Yalta or the opening of the second front on the Atlantic coast in 1944 rather than closer to ECE. I do not myself hold this view. It is a fact, though, that many ECE politicians are convinced of the historical responsibility of the West for ECE. Some have gone even further and expressed the view that the West 'owes' ECE an economic transformation, as in the form of a second Marshall plan.[17]

The East-Central European countries have certainly viewed EU integration as part of their symbolic 'return to Europe', but a more important goal has been to foster economic development. The statistics show that the depth of economic transformation has been quite dramatic. The most astonishing change may be trade diversion. The share of developed market economies (OECD member countries) in the total exports of ECE countries climbed from 35.7 per cent in 1980 to 49.5 per cent a decade later and further increased to 75.8 per cent by 1999. The share of exports to the Soviet Union declined from 27.1 per cent to 4.8 per cent in the same period.[18] In the total imports of ECE states, the proportion from OECD countries has risen from 38.7 per cent in 1980 to 72.1 per cent in 1999. Each ECE candidate country conducts more than 50 per cent of its foreign trade with the 15 EU member states. By 1998, the EU had secured a surplus of approximately €80 billion in its foreign trade with the candidate countries. Financial flows represent an even more explosive growth. In 1990, foreign direct investment (FDI) to the region was a mere US$479 million, whereas in 1999 it was US$17.2 billion. Since 1990, US$96.5 billion has been invested in East-Central Europe as FDI. Of the total amount, 75.6 per cent went to three countries: the Czech Republic, Hungary and Poland.[19] More generally, the region has been assessed by the Commission in 2001 as one capable of producing lasting high growth, although on a significantly lower GDP base per capita than Western Europe.[20]

The EU and its member states have contributed significantly to the development of the ECE region, serving the short-term and long-term interests of the West as well as those of the candidate countries. The candidate countries have, however, not developed in order to please the EU or the West at large, even though sometimes one might gain such an impression. They have modernized their society and economy primarily so that the peoples of these countries can have a better life. If this better life is easier to achieve through political stability and economic prosperity by the 'Westernizing' of these countries, and if it coincides with the interest of the West, this is a double advantage. However, the EU has certainly been an organization that has helped facilitate the transition countries to find their way towards economic transformation.

Problems and shortcomings

There are some who argue that Eastern Europe has become 'the European Union's major preoccupation – if not obsession' since the beginning of the 1990s.[21] It cannot be denied that the EU has been paying significant attention to the region. If it has done so at the expense of other regions on the periphery of the Union, such as North Africa or the Newly Independent States, this may have harmed the interests of these countries. One has to bear in mind, however, that ECE is currently the only region of the world that has both the right to apply for EU membership, given that the Treaty on European Union clearly states that 'any *European* state may apply to become a Member of the Union',[22] and with the realistic chance to join the organization reasonably soon. Moreover, the less successful the transformation in ECE, the more problems these countries will bring into the EU when they join, leaving a more demanding task for a later stage. After accession, this would to some extent be a common responsibility of the enlarged EU. It is for these reasons that the EU set its priority correctly when it paid much more attention to this region than to other parts of its immediate neighbourhood after the end of the Cold War.

The broader question of the extent to which the EU and its member states have influenced and guided the transition countries to prosperity and political stability is difficult to answer. No historian likes counterfactual questions such as 'What would have happened had this or that been done otherwise?' It is a fact, though, that no conflict between candidate countries has erupted into violence; there have been no *coups d'état* in the region; and, after some difficult years, the democratic system and market economy have gained mass popular support. But we do not know whether relations between Slovakia and Romania, on the one hand, and Hungary, on the other, would have developed as amicably as they did; or whether the early tensions between Poland and Lithuania would have been so speedily resolved; or whether the Russian Federation would have become a 'manageable' partner with its Baltic neighbours if the European institutions had not influenced Estonian and Latvian policies towards minorities in such a way as to accommodate Russian interests.

In addition, it would be methodologically incorrect to limit the analysis to one institution, the EU, over all the others. Even though the activities of the principal European institutions, such as NATO, the EU, the OSCE and the Council of Europe, were not coordinated closely, to say the least, they have set the ECE countries similar requirements, although their emphases have differed. Thus, the non-economic criteria set by the EU overlap with those of the Council of Europe and NATO, particularly after the EU requested the candidate countries not to have continuing unresolved territorial conflicts. As these Western organizations have all demanded the democratic legitimacy of government, the rule of law and respect for human rights in the candidate countries, it is problematic to assert that these conditions have been fulfilled because of one institution rather than the others.

However, it can still confidently be asserted that the behavioural pattern of the candidate countries has been significantly influenced by the demands made in anticipation of EU membership. Bearing in mind the fragility of the 'completed' transformation process in some ECE countries, it is necessary to emphasize that the criteria should be met permanently both before and after membership. It seems the EU has some limited means to guarantee that they will continue to be met beyond accession, at least in relation to major violations of freedom, democracy, human rights and the rule of law.[23] In terms of economic transition, the candidate countries have transformed their economies, principally to bring them in harmony with EU requirements. The extent and the depth of transformation were illustrated on p. 36. The association agreements between the EU and the candidate countries have significantly contributed to the process of trade liberalization. In fact, the existing EU member states gained their key goals of access to the ECE markets, companies, banks and economies through the association agreements, without needing to make a prior commitment to membership.[24] For the ECE countries seeking early membership, this initial commitment to trade liberalization might have been counter-productive, if other factors had not led the EU member states to fulfil their promises of membership.

Overall, it is fair to conclude that for the ECE, 'the *integration to the European economic space has become an accomplished fact* at the trade, financial, organizational and ownership levels alike'.[25] In many accession countries the proportion of private ownership is higher than in many EU member countries. The level of micro-economic integration is far advanced in many ECE countries. Such integration in the world economy has been important in order to import modern technology and increase productivity. Foreign ownership successfully contributes to the effective functioning of these mostly export-oriented economies. As most ECE countries are small, and the size of their domestic market is strictly limited, most firms that invest in these countries regard them as export production sites.[26] Overall, what one can say is that there has been a rapid integration of ECE into the world economy after the severe initial post-1989 decline.

On the more negative side, there is a strong sense, particularly for many ECE elites, of bad bargains being concluded, owing to the objective asymmetry between the parties. I was reminded of this in the office of an EU official when I pointed to some of the deals with the EU that had been disadvantageous for the candidate countries of ECE. The experienced official raised the ultimate counter-argument, 'Where else can these countries go? They will not join the Commonwealth of Independent States (CIS), will they?'[27] Even though the statement reflected reality, it is generally unwise to take advantage of a situation in this way. It is not surprising that certain ECE politicians react strongly to the way that the EU has often negotiated with the assumption that the candidate countries will accept practically any deal in order to gain membership of the Union.[28]

Nevertheless, the EU accession negotiations are a special case. As Graham Avery notes, 'the subject-matter is not so much a future pact between the parties as the way in which one party will apply the rules of the other party's club'.[29] This is especially the case when the asymmetry between the two sides, in both size and weight, is so great. In addition, as the EU absorbs more countries and further enriches the *acquis communautaire*, it becomes less willing to adapt its policies extensively to take account of enlargements.[30] Consequently, it is likely that the prescription according to which any enlargement should involve *mutual* adjustment, new items on the agenda and restructuring previous priorities will largely remain a plea.[31]

In this sense, it is a shortcoming of the EU's approach to the accession of ECE countries to treat it as 'just another enlargement', save for acknowledging that it will be more costly and demanding than any earlier enlargement. The Commission, which conducts the enlargement talks, is overwhelmed with harmonizing the position of 15 member states and carrying forward the negotiations properly. As a consequence, during the process there is little room for strategic engagement and far more for technical details. This is particularly the case in the end-phase of negotiations when the technocrats have completely taken over the accession process. This focus on the management of details has contributed to the impression that the EU has been acting without vision and without implementing a clear strategy. But this was perhaps understandable, as the strategic vision had been virtually fulfilled, with the candidates having become stable democracies and with full integration appearing only a matter of time.

Looking more into the future and beyond accession, it is necessary to highlight two issues that might represent more long-lasting problems in ECE's thinking towards European integration. The first relates to the underlying solidarity required between EU members to further the project of building an 'ever closer Union'. In reality, there have always been setbacks in this process, such as Margaret Thatcher's 'I want my money back' policy or the Spanish attitude to the financing of the development of those prospective ECE states. However, most ECE politicians see the EU as a body that will continue to contribute to the development of the economy of their country, principally through significant financial transfers. As the 'big bang' eastern enlargement will integrate countries with differing GDP levels, it may happen that one day a country from the region will be a net contributor to the EU budget. If Bulgaria and Romania were to join, this would almost certainly result in net contributor status for a country such as Slovenia. Many ECE politicians seem to be unable to cope with the prospect of such a situation. Some Slovenian experts speak about the EU as 'a new Yugoslavia' – an entity that takes money away from the country and redistributes it to others. The Hungarian conservative government went even further. When the finance minister received the new head of the EU mission in Budapest in March 2002, he informed the ambassador that it would be completely 'unacceptable for Hungary to be [a] net contributor [to] the EU budget after accession'.[32] In general, the feeling of solidarity, which offers concrete advantages to the accession countries now, and will offer even more after accession, has not become part of the thinking either of the establishment or of the general public. Accordingly, there is little understanding of the complexity of solidarity.

The second more lasting problem stems partly from an obvious short-coming of EU policy. The EU has been busy forging bilateral relations with all the candidate countries but has played little role in contributing to intra-regional integration and dynamics. As one ECE commentator has noted, the consequence is that the ECE leaders

> do not foresee the same integration with their immediate, equally poor or even poorer neighbours. In fact, they will be rather surprised to find that the parallel integration of neighbouring countries into the European centre automatically means close links with each other, too. They hardly understand that the integration efforts of adjacent countries might go – in principle – as far as common participation in a federation.[33]

Even though some regional cooperation frameworks have developed, they have been weak, temporary and not adequately institutionalized. Although there was encouragement from some EU members to foster such cooperation among the candidate countries, for example the Benelux–Visegrad group meetings, they were not determined or persistent enough and have thus achieved little. Those Western politicians who encouraged their counterparts to energize these processes regularly con-fronted the problem that the ECE countries did not want these frame-works to be seen as potentially substituting for integration into the West. The only exception, when the EU strongly encouraged ECE countries to cooperate with one another, was the so-called Stability Pact, which requested the parties to resolve some of their bilateral problems, most notably in terms of territorial claims and treatment of minorities, and sign bilateral treaties to this effect. Its minimalist objective was achieved, but it has not gone far enough.[34] It was practically the only attempt to encourage regional stability by the EU through the promise, or rather the prospect, of membership.

The situation is not much better if one looks further to the East and thus leaves the realm of candidate countries. One of the distinctive features of this enlargement is that it does not fill and incorporate a geo-graphical perimeter in the same way as did most of the earlier enlarge-ments, such as the UK and Ireland in 1973, Spain and Portugal in 1986, and, to some extent, Sweden and Finland in 1995. Instead, this eastward enlargement can be seen as a critical step that

> will bring in countries that can serve as links and lines of transit during the process of building up a pan-European economic system of rela-tions. So this enlargement has a basically different character, a differ-ent cost structure, and different efficiency and economic strategy implications.[35]

As recent developments demonstrate, particularly the introduction by ECE candidates years before their accession of visa obligations for the citizens of CIS countries, long-term strategic thinking is either absent on this matter or detrimental to the interests of the ECE states.

Finally, as accession draws closer, speculation has become more frequent as regards the political profile of the new members. Will they be cooperative European partners or troublemakers? Although it may be premature to draw conclusions, there are certain elements that are becoming increasingly clear. The new members will first have to act energetically to move from being peripheral to more central players within the EU. This will certainly dominate their agenda for the first years of membership. They will have to act in order to be eligible to join the eurozone, to upgrade their border facilities in order to participate in the Schengen regime, to gain the competence to present successful applications for structural funds, and to help their agricultural sector survive under conditions that can only be called discriminatory. In spite of the preparation for enlargement during the past decade, which has helped them gain some expertise in EU matters, it will still be a major challenge for the ECE state administrations, including the judiciary, to develop wide-ranging competence to apply the EU *acquis.* All in all, demanding years are still ahead of the accession countries after gaining membership.

Moreover, most of the accession countries are aware of their size and importance, and will not overemphasize their significance, as has already been seen with the three ECE countries that joined NATO in 1999. Thus, as far as the Common Foreign and Security Policy (CFSP) and the European Security and Defence Policy (ESDP) are concerned, ECE countries will try to avoid facing the difficult choice between their Atlantic and their European loyalties. This has proved impossible in the case of the Iraq crisis of 2003, when the accession countries without exception supported the Atlanticist line and upset some of the opponents of the US–UK position. Many of the accession countries indicated that they would have been happier not to have faced this choice. Even though they have proved loyal to the United States, in response to the strong US support for their membership of NATO and to their process of transformation, it is impossible to draw conclusions from this for the future. It is important to note that they faced this delicate choice because of the internal divisions of the EU. Moreover, the three countries that joined the Atlantic Alliance in 1999 have not yet joined the EU. Consequently, they have not arrived in the 'real world of schizophrenia', when loyalty may be expected from them on both sides of the Atlantic. This will come only when they gain membership in both organizations. It would be unfounded to assume that the ECE countries will consistently represent the position they took in the Iraqi case.

The 2004 eastward enlargement deal

Enlargement is the result of a compromise in which the accession countries feel they have made more concessions than the EU. This is fully understandable in the light of the structure of negotiations, as outlined in this chapter. Also, the conclusion of the talks took place during the Danish presidency, when Denmark's negotiations with each candidate country individually demonstrated a masterpiece of multilateral diplomacy. The Danes effectively sliced down the demands of the candidates.[36]

The end result is essentially enlargement 'on the cheap'. This is understandable, as enlargement is occurring at a moment when many current member states, including the largest contributor to the EU budget, Germany, face limited growth and have mounting budget deficits. During such times, it is difficult to be generous. It is 'cheap' in the sense that its total cost will be €40.83 billion for the first three years (2004–6), from which a significant amount will be returned by the new members as contributions to the common budget. It means that each EU citizen will pay only approximately €10 for the financing of enlargement every year. After 2007 the cost of enlargement will have to remain limited, as the new financial package (2007–13) will have to be approved by consensus. The interests of the 'new' members will be set against those of 'old' member states. Some of the latter will be determined not to increase their contribution to the budget (e.g. Germany), whereas some others will be determined not to lose current benefits (e.g. Spain). Last but not least, there will be net contributors that will insist on maintaining certain policies, such as the CAP in the case of France. Furthermore, the next wave of enlargement (Bulgaria, Romania and eventually Croatia) should then be around the corner. It will be critical that these two, or three, countries, with a combined population of 30 to 35 million people, should get sufficient assistance to be able to be adequately prepared for accession. Irrespective of how toughly the new member states negotiate, given the complexity of interests involved it can be assumed that eastern enlargement will have to continue 'on the cheap'.

As regards the more controversial issues regarding the enlargement negotiations, and the eventual compromises reached, these can be seen to be threefold. First, none of the new members will immediately become a net contributor to the EU budget, which is extremely important for them as part of selling the success of EU accession. They have been able to demonstrate their net beneficiary status. This will not be so important after accession, however, as it can be taken for granted that no later than after the next enlargement, preliminarily scheduled for 2007, some of the richer new members (most probably Cyprus and Slovenia) will become net payers.

Second, in certain critical areas the candidates had to accept extensive transitional phases. This included the issue of freedom of movement of labour, where a seven-year period of transition was introduced, though 'softened' by two important concessions. First, after the first three years, and then two years later, the EU will reassess whether the constraint should be maintained. Second, current member states can open their labour market bilaterally to the new members immediately after their accession. Approximately half of them, less exposed to migrant labour, have declared themselves ready to do this. It is unlikely, however, that they will attract significant amounts of foreign labour through this channel. This means that the EU compromise reflects the concerns of some of the current easternmost members of the Union, primarily those of Austria and Germany. Economic research does not validate their concerns. It does, though, help 'sell' eastern enlargement in Berlin and Vienna.

A further key set of concessions gained from the candidates concerned agriculture. There the 'compromise' is far more painful for some new members, primarily Poland, Lithuania and, to some extent, Hungary. Direct agricultural payments to these farmers will start in 2004 at only 25 per cent of the level provided to farmers of the 'old' members. This will gradually increase to 100 per cent over almost a decade. Even though the new member states will be permitted to supplement these subsidies from their own national budgetary resources, it is nevertheless the case that their agricultural sectors will have to be radically adapted to retain their competitiveness against the produce of the 'old', more heavily subsidized members.

The third controversial issue regarded structural and regional funds. After accession, the new members will have to compete for such funds along with some of the more experienced member states. It may happen that many of their applications will remain unsuccessful, and even where they are successful, the countries concerned may not be able to absorb the funds they would like to attract. For the period 2004–6, the deal with Poland was that structural funds for the country would be reduced by €1 billion but that this amount would be made available to Warsaw in 2005–6 without any conditions attached. The Czech Republic secured the same deal and will have €100 million freely available during the same years. Even though it may look a good deal, as access to these amounts is guaranteed, it is not necessarily the case that they obtained good solutions. Certainly the funds will help balance the budgets of the two countries, which may be necessary, particularly in the light of Poland's current budgetary situation. But on the other hand, the money will reduce the budgetary pressure on the two countries, although to differing degrees. It is doubtful whether this will make their governments more responsible. Perhaps it is more likely that they will be tempted to 'waste' this extra money won in the final phase of the talks.

In conclusion, though, it seems that the upcoming eastern enlargement has involved a reasonable compromise that has been broadly acceptable to both sides. Its success is likely, although it very much depends on how successful the governments and state authorities of the new members will be in their countries' post-accession adaptation. This is the most significant element of unpredictability for the future.

Conclusions

The European Union has been responsive and reflective to the changes brought about by the revolutions in East-Central Europe. Two aspects in particular had to be taken into consideration in the process: first, the national interests of the member states; and second, their willingness to contribute to the democratization and modernization of ECE based on the vision articulated by Robert Schuman, quoted at the start of the chapter. Since 1963, when this statement was made, the EU has developed enormously and its *acquis* has become far richer than one could have foreseen in the 1960s. One might therefore expect, rightly, that penny-wise calculations and a piecemeal approach to negotiations would determine the eastern enlargement process. Enlargement to a dozen countries that are less developed than the average EU country, and very often poorer than the poorest current member, impinges on the national interests of several member states and their citizens, at least as regards the financing of the new members and the indirect costs stemming from the relocation of industries. It is impossible to understand eastern enlargement without paying attention to both the strategic aspect and the 'penny-wise' calculations of the process. There was never any doubt, however, that in the end the vision of a unifying Europe through gradual enlargement would prevail. The decade or two that the accession of ECE to the EU has required is, in reality, an extremely short period of time in the broader sweep of history.

It would thus be incorrect to conclude that the EU failed to articulate a strategy in the face of this challenge. Those analysts who state that there has been no strategy impose their individual ivory-tower intellectual approach on the process and disregard the laws of politics. A political strategy is not a set of static ideas fixed for an unlimited period of time. This chapter has attempted to demonstrate that a strategy has existed and has been based on the common denominator of the position of the member states and the evolution of reality. A strategy evolves as a result of both the pressure of events and the influences of political interests. This has been the case with the EU strategy regarding the eastern enlargement of the EU.

It is a different matter whether this strategy that I have described was adequate in every detail and at every moment of the evolution of the process, and whether it could have evolved along somewhat different lines. No doubt it did not serve the interests of every actor in this process, and the candidate countries could particularly perceive its evolution as not serving their interests in every respect. It would be an exaggeration, however, to expect that the strategy of the EU could satisfy the interests of all the parties to the process. In addition, the closer enlargement gets, the more people become disappointed with the conduct of the process, in both the member states and the candidate countries. This is partly understandable, as decisions are now being taken on issues that directly affect various interest groups and differing strata of the population. Disappointment, not to mention disillusionment, could, however, be more limited if both sides keep sight of the strategic vision. A bit more empathy and flexibility on the part of the Union, more focus on the vision and less on the cost calculation and the nitty-gritty details, would have been welcome. This would, however, have required statesmanship instead of managerial skills, a quality we are short of – and not only in the candidate countries.

Notes

1 Quoted in Joschka Fischer, 'The Nation-State Is Irreplaceable', speech at Humboldt University, 12 May 2000. Online. Available http: <http://www. ellopos.net/politics/fischer.htm> (accessed 10 March 2003).
2 J. Zielonka, 'Policies without Strategy: The EU's Record in Eastern Europe', in J. Zielonka (ed.), *Paradoxes of European Foreign Policy*, The Hague: Kluwer Law International, 1998, p. 131.
3 It is sufficient to mention two well-known Hungarian economists in this respect. András Inotai is harshly critical of 'big bang' as enlargement strategy, whereas Péter Balázs emphasizes the dominance of short-term technical considerations in the enlargement process as factors undermining the prevalence of strategic considerations. See A. Inotai, 'Gondolatok az Európai Unió bővítési változatairól' (Views on the Enlargement Scenarios of the European Union), *Európa 2002*, 2001, vol. 2, no. 4: 5–18; and P. Balázs, *Európai egyesülés és modernizáció* (European Unification and Modernization), Budapest: Osiris, 2001, pp. 116–17.
4 There was one country that did not want to take advantage of this, Estonia, which agreed with the EU on parallel trade liberalization.
5 The Europe Agreement establishing an association between the European Communities and their member states and the Republic of Hungary. See European Communities, *Official Journal*, L 347, 31 December 1993, p. 3. Online. Available http: <http://www.europa.eu.int/smartapi/cgi/sga_doc?smartapi! celexapi!prod!CELEXnumdoc&1g=EN&numdoc=21993A1231(13)&model= guichett> (accessed 10 October 2002). After the Copenhagen Council of June 1993, the asymmetrical formulation was dropped from the negotiated association agreements.
6 A. Mayhew, *Recreating Europe: The European Union's Policy towards Central and Eastern Europe*, Cambridge: Cambridge University Press, 1998, p. 23.
7 Poland can be regarded an exception in this respect. The nearly 40 million population of the country made it interesting for investment aimed at selling products on the Polish domestic market.
8 Quoted in Mayhew, *Recreating Europe*, p. 26.
9 U. Sedelmeier and H. Wallace, 'Policies towards Central and Eastern Europe', in H. Wallace and W. Wallace (eds), *Policy-Making in the European Union*, Oxford: Oxford University Press, 1996, p. 374.
10 The EU did this at the Nice European Council in December 2000 and in the Nice Treaty, though only to the extent that was absolutely necessary.
11 The Essen Council lent support to the Stability Pact, which had grown out of

the so-called Balladur initiative. The same requirements appeared in the NATO Enlargement Study of September 1995.

12 'Agenda 2000: For a Stronger and Wider Union', *Bulletin of the European Union*, Supplement 5/97, p. 57.

13 In March 2003, three months after the conclusion of the accession talks, the EU presented the accession countries with a short letter listing those areas where they have to make further efforts in order to be adequately prepared by the date of accession. Further notifications will follow until six months before the projected accession date, i.e. 1 May 2004.

14 'Presidency Conclusions', Göteborg European Council, 15–16 June 2001, para. 9. SN200/1/01 REV 1.

15 'Presidency Conclusions', Laeken European Council, 14–15 December 2001, para. 8. SN300/1/01 REV 1.

16 In an effort to compensate for this divide, the EU expressed its determination to increase its contribution to the continuing transformation of Bulgaria and Romania and their preparation for membership by 2007. See 'Presidency Conclusions', Copenhagen European Council, 12–13 December 2002, paras 13–16. It is stated there that 'the Union endorses the Commission's communication on roadmaps for Bulgaria and Romania, including the proposals for a significant increase in pre-accession assistance' (para. 16).

17 In reality, as a colleague pointed out wittily, 'After World War II, Europe got the Marshall plan from the US whereas after the Cold War it got the Marshall Center in Garmisch-Partenkirchen.'

18 There is no space to address the changing basis of bilateral trade between the Soviet Union and other socialist countries from the transferable rouble to hard currency at the beginning of 1991. It is clear that the Soviet Union wanted to 'punish' its partners for the change of their political orientation under the assumption they would continue to rely on Soviet natural resources, whereas the Soviet Union would no longer be obliged to buy their low-quality industrial goods. This was partly true. In the end, however, it resulted in the ECE countries almost completely stopping buying Soviet goods, except for energy products, which caused trouble to some parts of the Soviet (post-Soviet) industry. More importantly, the Soviet step forced these countries to speed up their trade diversion from East to West. For details, see A. Köves, *Central and East European Economies in Transition: The International Dimension,* Boulder, Colo.: Westview Press, 1992, pp. 63–71.

19 For these data, see *Economic Survey of Europe, Statistical Appendix*, no. 1, 2000, pp. 234 and 240.

20 'Making a Success of Enlargement: Strategy Paper and Report of the European Commission on the progress towards accession by each of the candidate countries, Annex 2: Candidate countries: main statistical indicators (2000)', 13 November 2001. Online. Available http: <http://www.europa.eu.int/comm/enlargement/report2001/index.htm> (accessed 10 October 2002)

21 J. Zielonka, 'Policies without Strategy', p. 131.

22 'Treaty on European Union', Article O. In the consolidated version after the adoption of the Nice Treaty it is Article 49 of the Treaty. (Emphasis added.)

23 Ibid., articles 6 and 7.

24 A. Inotai, 'What Is Novel about Eastern Enlargement of the European Union?' in A. Inotai, *On the Way: Hungary and the European Union (Selected Studies)*, Budapest: Belvárosi Könyvkiadó and International Business School, 1998, p. 17.

25 L. Csaba, 'Ostpolitik and Enlargement of the EU: The Challenge of the Millennium', CEU Working Papers IRES, 2000, no. 2: 6. (Emphasis in the original.)

26 Poland is to some extent an exception in this respect.

27 Interview with an official of DGIA, Brussels, 18 December 1996. (On file with the author.)

28 One might mention former Hungarian Prime Minister Viktor Orbán, who said in spring 2000 that 'There is also life outside the European Union.' Even though I disagree with the message of this populist Hungarian politician, I do think it reflects his understandable bitterness after two years of accession talks with the EU.

29 G. Avery, 'The European Union's Enlargement Negotiations', *Oxford International Review*, 1994, vol. 5, no. 3: 28.

30 Heather Grabbe rightly points to the fact that the last time when countries less developed than the EC proper joined, it occurred before the single market programme and monetary union, so that 'they were joining a much less integrated and smaller EU market than the new applicants'. See H. Grabbe, *Profiting from EU Enlargement*, London: Centre for European Reform, 2001, p. 32.

31 W. Wallace, 'From the Atlantic to the Bug, from the Arctic to the Tigris? The Transformation of the EU and NATO', *International Affairs*, 2000, vol. 76, no. 3: 491.

32 See 'The visit of Jürgen Köppen at Mihály Varga', MTI (Hungarian News Agency), 6 March 2002. Later, similar statements were made in each East-Central European accession country.

33 P. Balázs, 'Strategies for the Eastern Enlargement of the EU: An Integration Theory Approach', in P.-H. Laurent and M. Maresceau (eds), *The State of the European Union*, vol. 4, *Deepening and Widening*, Boulder, Colo.: Lynne Rienner, 1998, pp. 71–2.

34 For details, see P. Dunay and W. Zellner, 'The Pact on Stability in Europe: A Diplomatic Episode or a Lasting Success?', in Institute for Peace Research and Security Policy (IFSH) (ed.), *OSCE Yearbook 1995/1996*, Baden-Baden: Nomos Verlagsgesellschaft, 1997, pp. 299–312.

35 Inotai, 'What Is Novel about Eastern Enlargement?', p. 24.

36 In Hungary such an approach is called 'salami politics', even though it has an extremely negative connotation. It refers back to the elimination of democratic parties in the late 1940s by the Communists.

4 The EU and Turkey

Between geopolitics and social engineering

Gilles Dorronsoro

In terms of nationalist rhetoric, Turkey likes to present itself as 'the bridge between East and West' or, more recently, 'the centre of the Turkic world'. Whether that is true or not, Turkey is certainly at the periphery of the Western world and has had less room for manoeuvre since the fall of the Soviet Union, owing to its financial dependence on Western countries and the global domination of the United States. Thus, the prediction made by Samuel Huntington that Turkey was going to redefine itself as a part of the Turkic world after the fall of the Soviet Union has clearly been proved false.[1] In fact, ever since the 1920s the discourse of the Turkish elite has been based on the Europeanization of Turkey as a means to gaining entry to the 'civilized world'.[2] Full membership of the European Union (EU) would be the culmination of this process, leading to integration with Turkey's Western neighbours but only at the price of a profound political and social change, which could be described as a new *Tanzimat*.[3] That is why the relationship with the EU is a central problem for the self-definition of the Turks and maybe the most important issue on the Turkish political agenda at the present time.[4]

For very differing reasons, Turkish membership could also be decisive for the EU. Turkey will have between 80 and 90 million citizens in less than a generation and will be the most populous country in Europe, excluding the Russian Federation. If Turkey were to be a full member, the EU would acquire a Middle Eastern dimension and external borders with Iraq, Iran and Syria. Moreover, Turkish membership would be a clear sign for Israel, Morocco and maybe some Caucasian states to apply for membership of the EU. The key question here concerns the frontiers of the EU. Since Europe is not a geographical but a political concept, there are no criteria to define 'objectively' what it constitutes. In addition, the cost of this new accession for the EU would exceed by far that of all earlier enlargements.

However, in spite of the importance of what is at stake for both sides, there is no clear European strategy, meaning an attempt to define a European interest in the realist tradition. The EU is nevertheless becoming a major actor in Turkey by inspiring a coherent project of in-depth reform of Turkish society. The EU is in practice deeply engaged in the internal dynamics of the countries at its periphery, even to the point of 'nation-building', which reflects the very process of the construction of the EU itself. In this process of 'Euro-globalization', Europe's institutions and style are spreading, potentially 'integrating' whole peripheral nations. As a consequence, the process of integration itself implies a deep change in Turkish foreign policy.[5]

This chapter first analyses the origins and development of Turkey's relationship with the European Community (EC), and later the EU. The somewhat contradictory results of the EU's support for reform of Turkish society are then assessed. Finally, the chapter concludes by highlighting how the enlargement of the EU places new light on some critical foreign and security issues that continue to be unresolved.

The origins of the Turkish candidacy

Since the post-World War II period, Turkey has been a member of a number of different European/Western organizations, most notably the Organization for European Economic Cooperation (OEEC), later the Organization for Economic Cooperation and Development (OECD) (1948), the Council of Europe (1949), and the North Atlantic Treaty Organization (NATO) (1952). Turkey's associate membership of the EEC began in 1963 and added a new dimension to its relationship with Europe. At that time, Walter Hallstein, President of the European Commission, declared that 'Turkey is part of Europe',[6] recognizing Turkey's vocation to become a full member. The Ankara agreement signed in 1963 included three phases to achieve full economic integration. After modification of this agreement in 1970,[7] a customs union came into effect on 31 December 1995.[8] Despite these developments, the Commission and the European Council have remained broadly negative about Turkish membership.[9] At the Luxembourg European Council Summit in December 1997, accession negotiations were opened to all applicant countries except Turkey. As a result of what was widely perceived as a national humiliation, the Turkish government refused to participate in the March 1998 European Confer ence in London. A compromise was finally worked out at the Cardiff Summit in June 1998. Turkey, unlike the East-Central European countries, was not considered for early membership, but the Commission offered proposals to assist Turkey's transition. Finally, the Helsinki meeting of the European Council on 10–11 December 1999 accepted Turkey as a candidate for full membership with the same requirements as the other countries. However, the Turkish government failed to obtain a negotiation schedule at the Copenhagen summit in December 2002 and was given a conditional date to start accession talks dependent on the outcome of a European Council meeting in December 2004.[10]

For the EU, acceptance of the Turkish application for candidacy is the result of a series of diplomatic compromises so as to avoid a crisis with a close ally. The United States, most notably with the Clinton administration, exerted a lot of pressure on the EU to accept the candidacy of Turkey for full membership as a means both to stabilize Turkey and to weaken the EU's political cohesion. Overall, the question of whether there exists an EU interest in Turkish full membership has never been addressed with consistency. For example, a special status for Turkey has never been officially proposed or even studied in detail.[11] In fact, one could argue that there is no clear economic interest for the EU to support Turkey's membership, given the existence of the customs agreement.[12] Since December 1995, Turkey's economic integration has been deepening, and the EU is the country's main economic partner, with 52 per cent of Turkey's exports and 49 per cent of its imports in 2000. Turkish membership would be an economic burden for the EU, since the Turkish GDP per capita is currently about 29 per cent of the EU figure. The gap between the EU and Turkey has not narrowed and maybe has even grown larger since 1995. The level of economic activity is less than 50 per cent in Turkey, and unemployment, officially around 9 per cent, is probably much greater (at around 25 per cent for the educated urban young). Inflation, largely a result of the fragility of the banking system and political clientelism, was around 45 per cent in 2002, an improvement from previous years due largely to the severe recession in economic activity since the crisis of November 2000 to March 2001.

The financial cost of preparing for Turkish membership will undoubtedly be heavy for both sides.[13] Turkish agriculture is not competitive on international markets, local small and medium-sized enterprises cannot easily adapt to European legislation, and regional disparities are extremely significant. Moreover, the EU has not provided much assistance to help accelerate the transformation of the Turkish economy, and the accession of the countries of East-Central Europe will put a strong constraint on the EU's financial capabilities for the next decade. Currently, Turkey has access to five different types of loans from the European Investment Bank (EIB), but only for €6.425 billion from 2000 to 2007,[14] which is far less than is needed to bridge the gap between the Turkish and the EU economic and social systems.

Politically, the Turkish candidacy is different from that of the other applicant countries. The Turkish accession to the EU will be hard to sell to European public opinion(s). The prospect of a free circulation of workers between Turkey and Europe is feared by a number of European governments. There is also evidence of an increase of illegal immigration through Turkey to the EU. The Turkish authorities have admitted to the presence of almost 100,000 illegal migrants on their territory in 2000 (as compared to only 11,362 in 1995), and the trend is upwards, with a significant increase in 2001. However, the August 2002 'Copenhagen homework' reform package passed by the Turkish parliament did include provisions for curbing illegal immigration. Even if the EU economies objectively need foreign workers, it is a political challenge to have this idea accepted by European public opinion. Moreover, the perception of cultural difference is increasingly used as an argument against Turkey's integration into the EU.[15] There is of course no clear definition of what is 'European', but Turks are generally not considered as such by a large number of EU citizens. There is also a growing anti-Muslim and anti-migrant prejudice in Europe, at least during the past decade, and some conservative politicians have clearly identified themselves as being against the accession of Turkey, notably Helmut Kohl, Valéry Giscard d'Estaing[16] and, more recently, Gerhard Stoiber during the 2002 German elections. Moreover, European social democrats are not necessarily in favour of full Turkish membership, with, for example, Helmut Schmidt publicly stating that the religious issue is an argument against Turkey joining the EU. The European People's Party, the largest political grouping in the European Parliament (232 deputies out of 626 seats), is also against Turkish membership and favours 'privileged partnerships' with countries such as Turkey and Russia that stop short of full membership.

The strategic advantages of Turkish accession are also limited for Europe, since the United States is the major player in the Middle East and has a strong and privileged relationship with Turkey. Strategically, there is no credible alternative for Ankara outside NATO and Turkey's Western allies. Turkey has a strong pro-US, pro-Israeli policy in the Middle East that is potentially at odds with EU policy, which tends to be more pro-Arab (especially in the case of France, Italy and Spain). The historically poor relations between Turkey and its Arab neighbours would be difficult to deal with inside the EU. There is a serious risk that Turkish accession would paralyse the EU as a strategic actor in the Middle East, since the EU would become part of the problem and would no longer appear as an impartial broker. In addition, the conflictual relationship between Greece and Turkey would pose serious problems for defining a common foreign and security policy. On the other hand, the accession of Turkey – and more generally the enlargement of the EU – is seen as a way to avoid the development of a more integrated and federal EU, notably by the UK government.

Overall, the process of Turkey's accession is not part of a coherent strategy of the EU, but rather the result of a diplomatic and bureaucratic process driven by economic interests. France, for example, was the first major investor in Turkey, in the late 1980s, after a period of political tensions earlier in the decade had subsided, and supported Turkey's candidacy in a large part to keep the country as a client. For France, as for other EU member states, the implicit idea and expectation was that Turkey would never be able to fulfil the requirements for full membership. The severe economic crisis since 1999 and the poor progress on human rights are clear indications that, contrary to statements by Turkish politicians, full membership is probably not on the European agenda before at best the next 10 or 15 years.[17] Turkey's candidacy has never been embraced with enthusiasm by EU member states and it was finally accepted at the Helsinki summit in December 1999 largely to avoid a political crisis. Even this decision can be seen as highly ambiguous. At the Nice summit of December 2000, Turkey's accession was not to be taken into consideration in determining the redistribution of the seats and posts in the European Commission for the next 12 years.

On the Turkish side, policy towards the EU was initially the result of geopolitical and economic interests, and not a will to merge in a European federation. Competition with Greece, the arch-enemy of Turkey, was a decisive factor. The Turkish government's initial application in July 1959 to become an associate member of the EC seems to have been largely a consequence of the Greek government's own application a few weeks before. After Greece's return to democracy in 1974, Greece's improved relationship with the EC culminated in full membership on 1 January 1981, and this process was a key factor in the Turkish policy at the same period, even though the Turkish application for membership was not accepted until 1987. Another significant factor promoting closer ties with the EC/EU was a desire, at certain times, for Turkey to distance itself from the United States. The initial Turkish candidacy was partly the product of a strained relationship with the United States in the 1960s at a time when US economic support had decreased significantly. As a consequence, the Turkish government looked to establish a more diversified set of international relations, leading to the rapprochement with the EC. The 1963 Ankara Agreement led to increased trade between Turkey and the EEC, to the detriment of the United States. The final explanation for Turkey's shift towards the EC/EU is economic, and is currently the most important source of popularity of the EU in a country facing a deep economic crisis. For a majority of Turks, accession to the EU is essentially an economic question. About half of the population are considering moving outside the country, and 1.5 million people tried to get a green card in 2002. Hence, whereas the EC/EU represented initially a geopolitical set of interests, it is becoming more and more perceived as a means by which to 'modernize' Turkish society.

The new *Tanzimat*

In the past few years, membership of the EU has been a major subject on the political agenda of Turkey, and the EU has become an increasingly important actor in Turkish politics. The EU has set a series of conditions that could lead to the starting of negotiations with Turkey over accession. In June 1993 the European Council in Copenhagen defined the standards that countries must meet in order to join the EU, notably a stable democracy, the presence of a state of law, and respect for minority rights.[18]

Turkish legislation has been significantly adapted, though in practice it is still far from what is required by the EU. Moreover, what is seen as growing interference by the EU in local politics has triggered a nationalist reaction.

'*Civil society*' *and* '*democratization*'

Even if liberalization of Turkish society has been evident since the beginning of the 1980s, the political system is still essentially different from that of Western democracies and represents an exception among NATO member states. The military is still a major political actor in Turkish politics. The National Security Council (MGK), which is dominated by the military, defines the broad lines of government policy. The Council put an end to the government of the Islamist Refah party in 1997 in defence of secularism. Since 1983, 21 political parties have been shut down by the Constitutional Court. Official Turkish government figures indicate that around 9,000 persons are in jail for crimes linked to freedom of conscience and expression. In a decision made on 14 December 2000, the Istanbul State Security Court forbade all publications showing Turkey 'in a state of weakness'. The Freedom to Publish Committee of the Turkish Publishers' Union stated that there were more books confiscated and writers and publishers accused and sentenced in 2002 than the year before.

The Turkish political system is nevertheless evolving in relation to the EU in three major ways: changes in Turkish legislation, the role of 'civil society', and appeals to the European Court of Justice. Now the major part of Turkish legislation is debated in terms of its conformity with EU regulations, the *acquis communautaire*. For example, the new law concerning the media and the media watchdog, RTÜK, was vetoed by President Sezer in June 2001 because it was not in conformity with European standards. On 19 March 2001 the Turkish government launched the Ulusal Program (national programme), which is a 523-page document that gives a detailed analysis of how Turkey must transform itself to meet the standards required by the EU. This programme will necessarily oblige the adaptation of a large part of Turkey's laws and administration. In this same period the Turkish government also created a General Secretary to the European Union under the responsibility of Mesut Yılmaz, the then Deputy Prime Minister, a member of the centre-right ANAP party.

The weight of EU recommendations is felt on a number of different subjects: the rights of women, the abolition of the death penalty, and the rights of minorities. On 3 October 2001 the 1982 Constitution was changed in relation to 34 articles, notably so as to ensure the prevention of torture, freedom of speech, freedom of association, and equality between men and women. The role and the composition of the MGK has been redefined, and the number of civilian members of the Council has been increased from five to nine. The government is invited to 'evaluate' its recommendations instead of giving them 'priority'. In August 2002 the Turkish parliament accepted, with a surprisingly large consensus, some major changes, most notably education in the Kurdish language and the abolition of the death penalty. The progressive liberalization of Turkey is in large part a result of EU influence. However, the practical implementation of these laws can still be authoritarian in numerous areas. Thus, the regulations legalizing Kurdish broadcasting on state television and radio (no private television broadcasts are allowed in Kurdish) are very restrictive: 2 hours a week on television, 4 hours a week on radio. In numerous cases the legal reforms are implemented in a way that casts doubt on the real capacity for change in the Turkish bureaucracy.

In this respect, the European Court of Human Rights is offering a way to get around Turkish jurisdiction. Over 4,000 individuals have filed cases in Strasbourg since Turkey recognized the Court's jurisdiction in 1990. Of 141 rulings, 131 went against Turkey. For example, imposing a heavy fine on the Turkish government, the European Court of Human Rights said that the 1993 decision by the Çiller government to dissolve the pro-Kurdish Democracy Party (*Demokrat Parti*, DEP) and disqualify 13 DEP Members of Parliament (MPs) had undermined the right to a fair election. The Strasbourg-based court ruled that Turkey had violated 'the very essence of the right to stand for election and to hold parliamentary office', adding that it had also 'infringed the unfettered discretion of the electorate which had elected the applicants'.

Another aspect of the European strategy to promote the democratization of Turkey is to strengthen Turkish 'civil society'. During the 1990s the emergence of an increasingly dynamic 'civil society' separate from the state was seen to promote a democratization of Turkish society.[19] For example, the EU media programme organized a music festival and a round table about multiculturalism in Diyarbakır on 25–27 May 2002. The Civil Society Platform, which was established by 175 civil society associations, issued a report supporting Turkish candidacy of the EU.[20] Turkey's most active employment institutes, worker organizations, disabled people's associations, environmentalists, leftists, rightists, press organs and universities are among these 175 NGOs.

The debate in Turkey: a nationalist reaction?

Accession to the EU is supported by a wide range of political and social actors in Turkey, beginning with big business, which has an interest in the integration of Turkey in the EU, knowing that it will lead to the opening up of new markets and assist the political and economic stabilization of Turkey. A number of other pressure groups also see the EU as a way to advance their cause. Europe has been more open to Kurdish and Alevi demands. Even if the Kurdish Workers' Party (PKK) has been forbidden in Germany and France for a number of years, Kurdish nationalist groups are well organized in Europe. Other Kurdish associations are also active and have played an important role in what can be described as a renaissance of Kurdish culture. Restrictions on civil liberties is leading a number of social actors to seek to play the supra-national structures of the EU against the Turkish state. In terms of the Turkish party system, the centre-right and centre-left parties are the most European in orientation. The Islamist movement was clearly opposed to the EU in the 1980s, but now different perspectives have developed and the movement is fragmented.

The EU is viewed by a part of Turkish society as a threat to the cultural identity and political independence of the country. Historically at least, the Turkish left is not very European in orientation. The National Action Party (MHP), which adopts a strongly nationalist stance, is opposed to what it sees as the potential loss of Turkish identity. The success of the nationalist movements and of the nationalist right at the 1999 elections was due to a strategy that gained the support of those Turks worried about the loss of national sovereignty. The MHP leader, Devlet Bahçeli, declared that abolishing the death sentence, broadcasting and education in Kurdish, and compromising over Cyprus were not an acceptable price to enter the EU. Indeed, while 70 per cent of Turkish citizens support Turkey's membership of the EU, there are 30 per cent who are against entry, because of fears of loss of national sovereignty.[21] The publication of the e-mails of the EU representative in Ankara, Karen Fogg, was part of a campaign against the EU. In addition, in 1987 the European Parliament adopted a resolution in which one of the conditions for Turkey's full membership was acknowledgement of the Armenian genocide. Even if this is not part of the Copenhagen criteria, this question is likely to constitute a source of tension.

The strategic relationship

The essential strategic partner of Turkey is, and will probably remain, the United States.[22] Since the end of the Cold War, US administrations have been careful to maintain good relations with Turkey. For example, Ankara had full US support in its confrontation with Syria in 1999, resulting in the Syrian president, Hafiz al-Assad, expelling Abdullah Öcalan from Syria. The interests of Turkey and the United States have differed over certain issues such as northern Iraq, however. US plans for the overthrow of Saddam Hussein were not generally well received in Ankara because the Turkish government was afraid of a possible independent Kurdish state in northern Iraq. Turkey's strategic alliance with Israel – underlined by an $800 million tank deal signed with Israel at the same time as Israeli military incursions onto Palestinian territory – has won Ankara important support in the US Congress and silenced complaints over its human rights record. The Israeli lobby has been making things easy for Turkey in

Washington and preventing the Greek and Armenian lobbies from imposing restrictions on US–Turkish relations.

For the EU's part, its role in Turkish foreign policy is more a result of
the membership process and the development of a common foreign and
military policy. The most critical issue is the relationship between Turkey
and Greece.[23] The two countries still have irreconcilable claims on
national air space and surrounding waters. Greece claims its national air
space to extend for 10 miles, which is not recognized by Turkey, and is
extending its territorial waters from 6 to 12 miles. Similarly, the status of
the 3,400 islets in the Aegean Sea is not legally determined between
Greece and Turkey, and there was a serious conflict in 1995 concerning
the Kardak/Imea islets. The EU Helsinki decisions of December 1999
require that the two countries reach a compromise before 2004 on this
issue, or, failing that, refer the issue to the International Court of Justice.
There is currently little indication that a compromise will be reached
before 2004. Directly linked to the Turkish–Greek relationship, there are
two major questions on the agenda: Cyprus and the European Security
and Defence Policy (ESDP). In these two cases, Turkey will be obliged to
comply with EU demands or renounce full membership.

The European Security and Defence Policy

Generally, Turkey has aligned its foreign policy to the EU communiqués
and has been associated with European common actions, especially in the
Balkans. In terms of ESDP, Turkey has cooperated in the 15 + 1 (EU
countries plus Turkey) and EU + 6 (European countries belonging to
NATO, but not to the EU) fora. Cooperation with the EU has sometimes
helped to ease tensions with Greece. The two governments are keeping
each other informed about military exercises in the Aegean Sea, and the
border areas will be cleared of mines. A direct phone line is functioning
between the two foreign ministries, but the mistrust between the two
countries still has a paralysing effect. In the June 2002 Seville meeting,
Turkey blocked a new EU deal on a rapid reaction force. In 2001, Turkey,
as a NATO member, had obtained a guarantee – in return for agreeing
that the 60,000-strong EU force could use NATO assets and equipment –
that EU forces would never be used in the Aegean Sea or Cyprus. The
agreement with Ankara was made without the consent of Greece, but,
after considerable pressure had been exerted by other European governments, Greece accepted a revised formulation of the agreement. However,
Turkey refused to accept this revision, and Turkish objections ruled out a
first EU mission in Macedonia, where the EU was supposed to take over
the NATO-led peacekeeping mission. At the Copenhagen summit in 2002,
a compromise between the EU and Turkey was finally reached over
ESDP.

Cyprus

Turkey has generally felt that the EU has been too influenced by Greece in its policy, notably over the Cyprus question. Despite all the encouraging signs on the EU side as regards Turkish membership, the resolution of the Cyprus question is a *sine qua non* condition for such membership. The Helsinki meeting of the European Council in 1999, at the insistence of the Greek government, included the condition that the Cyprus question should be resolved before Turkish membership. As a member of the EU, Greece will veto Turkey's membership unless Cyprus, divided between the internationally recognized Greek south and the Turkish-occupied north, is fully accepted in the EU. But if Cyprus joins the EU yet Turkish troops remain on the island, Turkey will be in a very contradictory situation: occupying militarily a part of EU territory while at the same time being an applicant for membership. In addition, the number of vetoes on the Council regarding Turkish accession would increase to two and, more generally, votes cast by Greece and Cyprus could lead to a deterioration in EU–Turkish relations in the future.

Since 1974, Turkish strategy towards Cyprus has been to legitimize the presence of the 35,000 troops on the island and to consolidate the independence of the North. The declaration of independence of a Turkish Republic of North Cyprus (TRNC) in 1987 was the outcome of this strategy, with the potential for a full annexation by Turkey. The integration of the Turkish part of the island with the mainland has been accelerated. As a de facto sovereign power, Turkey has tried to change the demographic equilibrium in northern Cyprus with the settlement of upwards of 70,000 Turks, thereby deeply affecting the political process. On the diplomatic front, the situation was pretty much frozen, as Turkish Cyprus only wanted negotiations that would lead to its recognition as a state. However, the attempt to legitimize the intervention has so far been a failure, since the TRNC has never been internationally recognized except by Turkey, and the EU has been very clear about the fact that the Turkish part of Cyprus is not a state.

Towards the end of the 1990s, the situation changed quickly, as Cyprus became an applicant country, with the prospect that such membership would be extended to the entire island. However, even if serious concessions seemed likely on the Turkish side, there were difficulties in moving to a new position in the negotiations. In 2001, Turkey backed Rauf Denktash in his decision to withdraw from the negotiations under the auspices of the UN and not to participate in the negotiations in New York in September 2001. At the same time, the National Security Council issued a communiqué which was adamant that recognition of Turkish Cyprus as a sovereign state was a *sine qua non* condition for negotiations. The 2002 elections in Turkey and the almost simultaneous EU summit in Copenhagen did, though, significantly change the dynamic, although the optimism generated was dissipated by the decisive failure in early 2003 of the UN-sponsored peace talks, which had focused on the so-called Annan Plan.

Copenhagen and the new Turkish administration

At a summit in Copenhagen in 2002, EU leaders agreed to enlarge the EU from 15 to 25 members. However, in spite of strong US pressures, the EU put off a decision on upgrading Turkey's applicant status until December 2004. One short-term consequence is that an enlarged EU will make Turkish candidacy dependent on the acquiescence of 25 rather than 15 countries. EU leaders agreed that so long as the Turks fulfilled certain conditions, negotiations could begin by December 2004. On the ESDP issue, a compromise was accepted stating that 'under no circumstances would the EU's force be used against a NATO ally' and that 'reciprocally' NATO would not use any action against the EU. It was agreed that the dispute with Greece over the Aegean must be settled by the end of 2004, while a solution for Cyprus had to be found by 28 February 2003. Overall, therefore, the 2003–4 period will be decisive for the Turkish candidacy, and a great challenge for the newly elected government in Ankara.

After its landslide victory in the November 2002 elections, the Justice and Development Party (AKP) appears relatively free to conduct its policy, having almost two-thirds of the deputies in the new parliament. The new government is trying to start negotiations in 2005 and, in a clear break with past governments, is prepared to make substantial concessions on Cyprus. Recep Tayyip Erdogan, the leader of the AKP, stated that 'I am not in favor of the continuation of the policy that has been maintained in Cyprus over the past 30 to 40 years'.[24] But Erdogan finds himself trapped between the demands of the EU and those of the nationalists, whose primary concern is to prevent the end of the TRNC, the removal of the 35,000 Turkish soldiers, and the return of some of the 70,000 colonists. The most strident opposition to Annan's proposals was articulated by the Chief of Staff Hilmi Özkök, supported in this issue by a large part of the political class. The failure of the negotiations in March 2003 was mostly due to the intransigence of Denktash, and Turkey could play a high price in future negotiations with the EU. Generally speaking, the reformist policy of the government is already weakened by the obstruction of the bureaucracy and the military establishment.

Conclusions

The EU is a coherent actor only in relation to the issues that are directly linked to the accession of Cyprus and the relationship between Greece and Turkey, these two issues being in any case closely linked. In general, the example of the Turkish–EU relationship reveals the style of the EU in dealing with its immediate environment. The EU tends to transform societies at its periphery, rather than projecting power in the realist tradition. The long-term effects are in a way more profound because the changes are deeper than a state-to-state alliance in the name of national interest, but the efficacy of the approach depends on the assumption that all the periphery is both willing and able to join the European model.

Two points should be underlined in this regard. First, the deep transformation of Turkey during the long process of accession will provoke internal tensions as the EU becomes more and more a part of Turkish politics. Second, the failure of Turkey to meet European demands would result in a deep political crisis. There is a real question whether the EU is ready to give enough support to Turkey to make it possible for the country to join in the not too distant future – that is, within 10–15 years. And the fact that Turkey will probably be the last, or one of the last, countries to join the EU is *per se* a problem. By the time Turkey is ready to join, it is likely that the EU will be considerably more integrated, with Turkey having to abandon most of its sovereignty but without having had any influence over the creation and formation of the institutional structures of the Union that it is joining.

Maybe the most important challenge for Turkish politicians is the very dynamic nature of the EU itself. The European institutions could be significantly different when Turkish full membership becomes a reality. The EU is probably moving towards a form of confederation, having achieved economic integration and now developing a more integrated foreign policy. The continuing crises in the EU and with the United States are part of this process. More importantly, the internal processes of decision-making within the EU are increasingly giving less possibility of vetoes by the governments of member states. Thus, the newcomers to the EU will lose a large part of their national sovereignty without being able to influence the making of the European Union.

Notes

1 S. N. Huntington, 'The Clash of Civilizations', *Foreign Affairs*, 1993, vol. 72: 22–49 at p. 42. Turkey nonetheless has played an important role in different regional organizations and is part of the Black Sea Economic Cooperation Council and the D8, a group of eight Muslim countries including Egypt, Nigeria, Malaysia and Central Asian states. However, none of those organizations offers an alternative to the EU.

2 L. McLaren, 'Turkey's Eventual Membership of the EU: Turkish Elite Perspectives on the Issue', *Journal of the Common Market Studies*, 2000, vol. 38: 117–39.

3 For a similar thesis highlighting the continuity between the policies of *Tanzimat*, Kemalist Westernization and Turkey's project of joining the EU, see W. Hale, *Turkish Foreign Policy, 1774–2000*, London: Frank Cass, 2000.

4 Discussions of a broad range of issues regarding Turkey's relations with the West, including the impact of domestic dynamics, can be found in V. Mastny

and R. C. Nation (eds), *Turkey between East and West: New Challenges for a Rising Regional Power*, Boulder, Colo.: Westview Press, 1996.

5 For a discussion of Turkey's post-Cold War relationships with Western European institutions, in particular the EU, NATO and the Western European Union, and the effects of these links on Turkey's definition of its identity, see G. Aybet, 'Turkey and European Institutions', *International Spectator*, 1999, vol. 34: 103–10.

6 J. Redmond, *The Next Mediterranean Enlargement of the European Community: Turkey, Cyprus and Malta?*, Aldershot, UK: Dartmouth, 1993, p. 23.

7 For the texts of the Association Agreement of 1963 and the Additional Protocol of 1970, see *Official Journal of the European Communities: Information and Notices*, vol. 16, C 113.

8 *Official Journal of the European Communities*, 'Decision 1/95 of the EC–Turkey Association Council of 22 December 1995', 13 February 1996, vol. 39, L 35.

9 See, for instance, the lukewarm 1989 Opinion of the Commission towards a general postponement of Turkey's membership issue in Commission des Communautés Européennes, sec. (89) 2290, 'Avis de la Commission sur la demande d'adhésion de la Turquie à la Communauté', Brussels, December 1989.

10 'If the European Council in December 2004, on the basis of a report and a recommendation from the Commission, decides that Turkey fulfills the Copenhagen Criteria, the European Union will open accession negotiations with Turkey without delay', Presidency Conclusions: Copenhagen European Council, 12–13 December 2002, p. 5. For further detail on the course of Turkey's relations with the EU, see A. Evin and G. Denton (eds), *Turkey and the European Community*, Opladen: Leske and Budrich, 1990; C. Balkir and M. A. Williams (eds), *Turkey and Europe*, London: Pinter, 1993; and M. Müftüler-Baç, 'The Never-Ending Story: Turkey and the European Union', *Middle Eastern Studies*, 1998, vol. 34, no. 4: 240–58.

11 However, it may be possible to discern the beginnings of such an approach in the so-called Matutes Package offering ideas for enhanced cooperation with Turkey but short of full accession. See Commission of the European Communities, 'Press Conference by Mr Matutes on the Membership of Turkey to the Communities', Brussels, December 1989: ref. BIC/89/393. See also C. Aktar, 'EU's new Turkey policy', *Turkish Daily News*, 25 December 2002. Online. Available http: <http://www.turkishdailynews.com/old_editions/12_25_02/feature.htm> (accessed 10 March 2003).

12 See M. Hiç, *Turkey's Customs Union with the European Union: Economic and Political Prospects*, Ebenhausen: Stiftung Wissenschaft und Politik, 1995.

13 Statistics in Turkey are not precise, which is a recurrent complaint from the EU, and it is therefore difficult to evaluate precisely the condition of the Turkish economy.

14 In 2000, the EIB had lent only €575 million for different projects in Turkey. Turkey is also eligible for the €8.5 billion special programme for the 13 applicant countries. There are also some special programmes, such as after the earthquake in August 1999 (TERRA, €600 million). In 2000, €209 million had been spent for assisting Turkey. The same year, ECHO gave €30 million more for emergency relief (the earthquake in August 1999). The EIB has also lent, as a part of its new Mediterranean policy, €545 million between 1992 and 1999.

15 G. Endruweit, 'Turkey and the European Union: A Question of Cultural Differences?', *Perceptions*, 1998: 54–72.

16 *Le Figaro*, 10 April 2000.

17 For an account that seeks to explain the ailments of Turkish democracy and the recent rise in ultra-nationalist and Islamist currents in terms of the country's

economic failures, see T. Demirel, 'Turkey's Troubled Democracy: Bringing the Socio-economic Factors Back In', *New Perspectives on Turkey*, 2000, vol. 24: 105–40. Another recent survey of Turkey's democratic development and political system can be found in E. Özbudun, *Contemporary Turkish Politics: Challenges to Democratic Consolidation*, London: Lynne Rienner, 2000.

18 Those principles have been reaffirmed at the December 2000 Nice summit.
19 This discourse and its political implications has been criticized at length, and Lacroix has shown the artificiality of the opposition between state and society. See J. Lacroix, 'Ordre politique et ordre social', in M. Grawitz and J. Leca (eds), *Traité de science politique*, Paris: Presses universitaire de France, 1985, pp. 469–565. On this debate, see also T. Mitchell, 'The Limits of the State: Beyond Statist Approaches and Their Critics', *American Political Science Review*, 1991, vol. 85: 77–96. For a discussion of Turkish civil society, see N. Göle, 'Towards an Autonomization of Politics and Civil Society in Turkey', in M. Heper and E. Ahmet (eds), *Politics in the Third Turkish Republic*, Boulder, Colo.: Westview Press, 1994. Also, see A. R. Norton (ed.), *Civil Society in the Middle East*, vol. 1, Leiden: Brill, 1995; B. Turner, 'Orientalism and the Problem of Civil Society in Islam', in A. Hussain, R. Olson and J. Qureishi (eds), *Orientalism, Islam and Islamists*, Brattleboro, Vt: Amana Books, 1984.
20 *Turkish Daily News*, 6 June 2002.
21 *Turkish Daily News*, 15 June 2002.
22 The Turkish elite is also becoming more and more influenced by US culture and the US way of life.
23 For an early evaluation of the new era of Greco–Turkey relations ushered in under the Simitis government, see E. Athanassopoulou, 'Greece, Turkey, Europe: Constantinos Simitis in Premiership Waters', *Mediterranean Politics*, 1996, vol. 1, no. 1.
24 *Anatolia News*, 3 January 2003.

5 South-Eastern Europe

The expanding EU role

Ettore Greco

From the late 1990s onwards, the political and economic weight of the European Union (EU) member states in South-Eastern Europe has grown steadily. They have taken on increased responsibilities for the conduct and direction of the international missions deployed in the region, as well as the coordination of their military and civilian aspects. They have acted under the aegis of various international organizations, but mostly through the EU, whose role in the region has become increasingly active and prominent. Indeed, the EU has committed itself to a demanding and ambitious long-term strategy of stabilization and integration of South-Eastern Europe which, in terms of political and economic resources invested, has arguably no parallel in other areas. Moreover, in South-Eastern Europe the EU is testing a series of newly acquired capabilities in the field of crisis management and post-conflict rehabilitation and reconstruction. For these reasons, the EU's performance in this area will, as it has done in the past, provide crucial indications about the EU's shortcomings and potential as an impending international actor.[1] Similarly, the European debate on the ways and means of making the Union's external policies more effective and consistent will continue to be influenced heavily by the 'Balkan lessons'.

The interests of the EU member states in South-Eastern Europe

The growing involvement of the EU in South-Eastern Europe reflects the consolidation of a wide spectrum of interests common to the member states. First of all, there is a shared perception that instability and conflict still present in the region can spill over into EU territory and negatively affect the societies of the individual member states. Insecurity emanating from South-Eastern Europe includes different forms of illegal trafficking involving drugs, arms and migrants. The links between criminal organizations based in the region and those in the EU countries remain a major source of concern. Especially in the aftermath of 11 September, the EU countries – as well as the United States – are increasingly worried that international terrorists can use the region as a safe haven or as a transit territory by exploiting the weaknesses of the local security structures. There is therefore a general European interest in helping the countries of South-Eastern Europe to build an institutional system capable of combating criminal groups and controlling their national frontiers and territories more effectively. This is a strong incentive for the Union's direct and extensive involvement in the institution-building efforts being promoted in the region.

South-Eastern Europe also offers the EU member states opportunities for economic expansion. Trade and investment in the region could grow considerably in the future if the stabilization and integration process were to be consolidated. Those that would benefit include a small group of EU countries, such as Germany, Italy and Greece, which already have a conspicuous economic presence in the area. Nevertheless, the integration of South-Eastern Europe into the EU will provide more than just economic benefits such as increased trade and investments. It will build a bridge between the Union and other areas, notably the Black Sea region and the Middle East, where the EU is interested in enhancing its presence. In view of this, the inclusion of the entire South-East European area into the pan-European infrastructure network is of crucial importance.

On a more general level, the EU's growing involvement in South-Eastern Europe is also dictated by a broader political interest in promoting the Union's role on the international scene. Since the early 1990s, the member states, generally with the support of their public opinions, have devoted considerable resources – both financial and human – to their efforts to stabilize the region. The failure of their ongoing stabilization plans would deal a serious blow to the EU's credibility and reputation. The future international standing of the Union will be inextricably linked with what it is able to achieve in South-Eastern Europe. Indeed, there is a widespread perception that the Union should take on special international responsibilities in neighbouring areas, where it has both consolidated interests and a good chance of influencing local actors through the wide spectrum of policy instruments available to it.

More than a decade after its launch, the Union's Common Foreign and Security Policy (CFSP) remains, in many respects, an embryonic reality. In particular, the Union's power of external projection remains still fairly limited. This provides a strong argument for the EU to concentrate its foreign policy initiatives on European soil and, more specifically, on those geographical areas, such as South-Eastern Europe, where it is in a better position to make synergic use of its diplomatic, economic and military capabilities.[2] Indeed, in South-Eastern Europe the EU has tried, with mixed results, to establish linkages between the Stabilization and Association Process (SAP), which mostly relies on the European Commission's structures and instruments, and the diplomatic and crisis management initiatives carried out by the High Representative for the CFSP and the local special representatives who are part of the structure of the Union's Council. Moreover, the EU's European Security and Defence Policy (ESDP) is for the first time being put to the test in South-Eastern Europe, which further increases the importance of the area for the definition of the EU's role as an international actor.

The EU member states are also vitally interested in the success of their common foreign policy initiatives in South-Eastern Europe as a way of fostering, and making more balanced, the partnership with the United States. Since the early 1990s the Europeans have emphasized their desire to become the central player in the area, a goal that is hardly attainable without the support of the United States. At the same time, US administrations have continuously encouraged the Europeans to assume greater political and military responsibilities in the area, provided that this happens in a way that does not conflict with their commitments within the context of NATO. The United States has gradually but steadily decreased its presence in the area and will certainly continue to do so in coming years. The process of US withdrawal may even accelerate as a result of its growing concentration in other – non-European – regions. The progressive Europeanization of the international missions in South-Eastern Europe therefore corresponds to a clearly stated US interest which is in tune with European ambitions. That is why the Union's action in the region must be seen as an integral part of a policy meant to keep the transatlantic partnership alive and vital on the basis of a sharing of burdens and responsibilities at a time when Americans and Europeans are at odds concerning the strategies to be adopted in other regions.[3]

Finally, it should not be forgotten that, in a longer-term perspective, South-Eastern Europe is of significant strategic military interest to the Union because of the EU's eventual projection towards adjacent areas, starting with the Middle East. It is notable that in the course of the conflict in Iraq in 2003, the United States asked for and obtained from almost all countries in the area various forms of logistical support for its troops and aircraft heading for the Gulf. A Union with the means and will needed to undertake interventions outside the European setting would naturally be interested in receiving the same kind of operational support in South-Eastern Europe.

South-Eastern Europe as a future part of the EU

The interests of the EU member states in South-Eastern Europe clearly differ in emphasis depending on geographic location and existing links with the individual countries of the area. There is, however, a general consensus that the entire Balkan peninsula should be integrated into the European Union sooner or later, even though it will take some countries a long time and, except for Bulgaria and Romania, no realistic time frame can be set for the moment. The debate which has developed during 2002–3 among European countries on the future boundaries of the Union – part of the wider debate on EU constitutional reform – has confirmed that the idea of a Union enlarged to include the entire Balkan area enjoys almost unanimous consensus agreement. The European leaders have expressed different views concerning the problem of whether Russia and other former Soviet states will eventually be able to join the Union. Isolated voices have even thrown into doubt the possibility of Turkey's integration, even though it is officially a candidate country. By contrast, the prospect of full integration of South-Eastern Europe is unchallenged.

There is a general feeling that the unification of Europe will be complete only after the accession of all the Balkan countries. As vague and fragmentary as the geopolitical vision upon which the EU is trying to develop its external projection may be, this seems to be a definitive acquisition. Above and beyond cultural affinities and a common historical heritage, the geographical continuity between what will be the territory of the Union after the accession of 10 new members in May 2004 and the Balkan peninsula provides a strong motivation for a policy of inclusion. The Union has frequently reiterated its commitment to giving all states in the region the prospect of membership, and gave substance to this in mid-1999 with the launch of the SAP.

The prospect of a gradual progression towards EU membership is the main political incentive that the countries of the region have been offered, both to deepen mutual cooperation and to develop individual national programmes of domestic reform. Institution-building and economic stabilization and reform are regarded as part and parcel of the road towards eventual membership into the EU. To this end, the new form of contractual relationship offered by the EU to the region's countries with the Stabilization and Association Agreements (SAAs) emphasizes the linkage between political stabilization – both internal and with regard to the relations with neighbouring countries – and domestic reform. A fundamental dimension of this was the EU's decision in autumn 2000 to establish a uniform system of trade preferences for the countries of the region and subsequently to incorporate this commitment into the SAAs. The signing of an SAA first with Macedonia and then with Croatia showed that, despite unresolved political problems, the EU seriously intended to take advantage of windows of opportunity offered in individual countries on their path to democratization and internal reform.[4]

The main financial instrument of the EU for the implementation of the stabilization and association process is the Community Assistance for Reconstruction, Development and Stabilization (CARDS) programme launched in 2000, which provides €4.65 billion for assistance to Albania, Bosnia and Herzegovina, Croatia, Macedonia, and Serbia and Montenegro in the period 2000–6.[5] In addition, an independent agency of the EU – the European Agency for Reconstruction – is responsible for the management of the CARDS programmes for Serbia, Montenegro and Kosovo, and for Macedonia.[6] It is worth noting that the focus of the EU's assistance has gradually shifted from reconstruction and rehabilitation – the most urgent tasks in the aftermath of the Yugoslav secessionist wars – to support for institution-building and economic reform. Especially since 2000, targeted technical assistance promoting approximation to EU standards and legislation has steadily grown in importance. In this way the EU has sought to establish a closer link between its financial commitments and the eventual political goal of granting membership to all countries of the region.[7] However, owing to persistent budgetary constraints and the planned increase in financial support for the 10 countries that are expected to join the EU in 2004, there is the risk that the Union will devote a decreasing amount of resources to the implementation of its programmes in the western Balkans. To avoid this risk, the European Commission has called for the incorporation in SAP of certain elements of the pre-accession process for candidate countries. This would require, as also proposed by the Commission, an increase in the CARDS budget.[8]

The stabilization and association strategy also includes the 'Stability Pact for South East Europe', the major regional cooperation initiative undertaken in the aftermath of the Kosovo war under the leadership of the EU. Its central political objective is to establish a cooperative environment conducive to regional integration as well as to the integration of the targeted countries into European and international structures. With its promise of comprehensive international support for those countries that embrace a consistent policy of regional cooperation and domestic reform, the Pact certainly contributed to the international isolation and eventual fall of the nationalistic governments in Croatia and the Former Republic of Yugoslavia (FRY). The collapse of Milošević's regime was indeed one of the immediate political goals of the decision to provide the countries of the region with a new set of political and economic incentives. The admission of the FRY to the Pact in late 2000 marked the successful completion of an effort to make possible the reopening of channels of cooperation with Belgrade. Arguably, the inability of the Pact's structures to prevent the eruption of a new conflict in Macedonia was a major blow to its credibility as a stability provider. However, as a post-conflict and long-term programme, the Pact is mostly aimed at establishing the structural conditions for the pacification of the area. It lacks specific conflict prevention and crisis management instruments of its own, hence short-term diplomatic and security measures fall outside its sphere of responsibilities.

The Pact has also proved useful to add a truly multilateral dimension to the multi-bilateral process of the SAP. By providing a unique forum of dialogue between international institutions and the targeted countries, the Pact's working tables, especially the economic one, have been instrumental in stimulating local leadership to go beyond strictly national logics and to embrace regional perspectives on a number of key issues. They have also served the purpose of establishing region-wide procedures for dialogue and negotiations as well as common standards for the implementation of domestic reform plans.

However, from the very beginning the Pact has suffered from a fundamental contradiction between its ambitious goals and the relatively small resources at its disposal. As a matter of fact, it has mostly acted as a mere instrument for the coordination of ongoing international programmes. A second major shortcoming of the Pact lies in the often disorderly multiplication of cooperation initiatives that have been placed under its aegis. The lack of adequate focus of the programmes launched has prevented an efficient use of the limited diplomatic and economic resources available. The systematic effort to add a regional dimension to the cooperation plans based on the involvement of international actors has been one of the most distinctive and commendable features of the Pact. Yet it has become increasingly evident that the reform and transformation processes should first and foremost take into account the specific needs and constraints existing at the national level. This applies, in particular, to such fields as economic liberalization and the fight against corruption and organized crime, where the Pact's standard-setting activity risks being futile unless accompanied by effective country-specific measures. As the root causes of a number of structural deficiencies that hinder the development of the countries of the region have a distinguishable national – rather than regional – origin, the Pact's broad regional programmes tend to have a limited impact.

In view of these difficulties, the EU has worked towards streamlining the Pact's activities, concentrating on a more limited set of programmes of key strategic value. These include transport infrastructures, environmental protection, energy, and such cross-border issues as organized crime and smuggling. It was also agreed that reform programmes aimed at transforming the economic and institutional setting of the individual countries can be promoted more effectively through bilateral cooperation mechanisms that take into account national specificities. This means, in practice, that most of the activities undertaken under the cover of the Pact tend to be absorbed by the SAP and to be managed as part of the accession programmes of the individual countries.[9]

The EU's growing role in crisis management and post-conflict resolution

In addition to pursuing a long-term strategy of bringing about the stabilization and integration of South-Eastern Europe, the EU member states – as well as the EU as such – have also assumed growing responsibilities in the direction and conduct of the international missions in the post-conflict areas. The European component of those missions – both military and civilian – is today much more important, at least in relative terms, than it was at their inception. This trend will continue in the coming years.

Indeed, there are plans for a further Europeanization of the international missions, mainly through the transfer of new operational responsibilities to the EU. What follows is a brief analysis of the most important EU engagements in the region and their possible future evolution.

Peace-making and mediation

The EU has played an increasingly active role in the conduct of peace-making efforts in South-Eastern Europe. This reflects the member states' growing capacity to intervene diplomatically with a single voice, mostly thanks to the initiatives undertaken by the High Representative for the CFSP. Another major factor has been the US acceptance of – and even encouragement for – the EU's efforts to take the lead to prevent further escalation of ongoing crises and to mediate between conflicting parties. The EU's action was instrumental, in coordination with the United States, in convincing the Macedonian authorities and the Albanian rebels to accept the Ohrid agreement of August 2001, which provided the basis for a peaceful settlement of the Macedonian conflict.

Subsequently, the EU has closely followed and encouraged the implementation of the new constitutional arrangements agreed upon for Macedonia. The Belgrade Agreement between Serbia and Montenegro of March 2002 was also sponsored by the EU (and then convincingly supported by the United States). The diplomatic scene in South-Eastern Europe is likely to be increasingly dominated by the EU's initiatives. However, it will remain essential that the overall direction of crisis management efforts involve all major powers, notably the United States and Russia. For this reason, ad hoc decision-making bodies such as the international Contact Group or the Peace Implementation Council (PIC) supervising the implementation of the Dayton agreement in Bosnia-Herzegovina remain vital.

Direction and coordination of civilian missions and institution-building

The structure of the international civilian missions in the region tend to be highly fragmented, which has often prevented effective direction and coordination. A telling example is the United Nations Interim Administration Mission in Kosovo (UNMIK), whose activities are divided into four different pillars, each with a different organization at the top. In this regard, a more or less gradual Europeanization of the civilian missions deployed in South-Eastern Europe may prove advantageous. Despite its persistent weaknesses, the EU is more cohesive than such loose organizations as the UN and the Organization for Security and Cooperation in Europe (OSCE), and can therefore provide stronger leadership. Furthermore, its competencies and capabilities cover a wide range of all areas of civilian missions. A recent sign of the EU's willingness to take over increased responsibilities in the direction and coordination of post-conflict civilian missions can be seen in the fusion in Bosnia-Herzegovina of the roles and functions of the Special Representative of the UN Secretary-General and the Special Representative of the EU. The EU already plays a central role in economic reconstruction and development in the region. In addition, its role in institution-building should be increased through its newly established Committee of the Civilian Aspects of Crisis Management (CIVCOM), which is entrusted with the task of establishing a pool of experts in civilian administration capable not only of providing technical assistance and training but also of performing, where needed, executive functions. In general, therefore, most of the state-building tasks in post-conflict areas of South-Eastern Europe could ultimately fall to the EU. An administrative handover from the UN to the EU can be envisaged in both Bosnia-Herzegovina and Kosovo.

The human dimension

The responsibility for the promotion of the human dimension in South-Eastern Europe, including the process of democratization, has been mostly assigned to the OSCE, which relies on a number of specialized instruments such as the Office for Democratic Institutions and Human Rights (ODIHR) and the High Commissioner for National Minorities (HCNM). The UN role in human rights promotion also continues to be important in specific sectors, notably through the actions of the UN High Commissioner for Refugees (UNHCR). However, the EU's role in the promotion of human dimension is far from negligible. In fact, its conditionality policy provides the most powerful stimulus for further development of the democratization process and for improvement of overall human rights conditions. Since the late 1990s the EU has closely watched key developments in the political life of the region's countries, contributing to various monitoring activities. The introduction of legislation implementing international standards for the respect of human rights, has also considerably benefited from the EU's advisory role. The EU's contribution to human rights promotion is likely to grow as a result not only of the deepening of integration and cooperative links with the individual countries, but also from the tendency of the OSCE to downsize its presence in the region, creating a void that is most likely to be filled by the Union.

Law and order

In general, the principal international actors have shown an almost complete lack of preparedness in performing police functions, which, as has become increasingly evident, are key to the success of post-conflict reconstruction and rehabilitation process. Serious problems emerged with the recruitment of an adequate number of professional personnel capable of performing police duties in both Bosnia-Herzegovina and Kosovo. In June 2000 the Feira European Council undertook a major initiative to remedy these shortcomings in promoting law and order by approving a plan to provide the EU with specific capabilities in this field. The EU member states committed themselves, in particular, to earmark 5,000 police staff for international missions by 2003. About 1,000 of them are to be deployable within 30 days. The Union is also developing a standing capacity to contribute to re-establishing and reforming judicial systems in conflict-torn areas, including the setting up of a rapid-response group of legal specialists. This effort, which is coordinated by the aforementioned CIVCOM, is likely to lead to a growing EU role in the direction and management of the law and order aspects of the international intervention in the Balkans and elsewhere. In February 2002 the EU foreign ministers accepted High Representative Javier Solana's proposal that an EU police force take over from the UN International Police Task Force (IPTF) deployed in Bosnia-Herzegovina. The new EU-led police mission started to operate in January 2003 when the IPTF's mandate expired. The establishment of the mission confronted the EU with unprecedented organizational and financing problems. However, the EU police force, like its UN predecessor, is very limited in size and does not engage in executive policing; rather, it helps to build and monitor the local police force.

Military tasks

After the failure of the UN peacekeeping missions in Croatia and Bosnia-Herzegovina, the central military tasks were assumed by NATO – with the notable exception of the operation in Albania in 1997. In the post-conflict military missions that were established in the context of NATO – as in Kosovo and Macedonia – or through an ad hoc coalition of the willing – as in Albania – the Europeans took over central command responsibilities. This already indicated a pronounced trend towards the Europeanization of the international military presence in South-Eastern Europe. The decision at the Laeken summit (December 2001) to declare the ESDP operational was expected to lead to further involvement in military tasks in South-Eastern Europe. At the Barcelona summit (15–16 March 2002) the EU countries declared their intention to take over from NATO in Macedonia, providing security for the EU and OSCE personnel monitoring the implementation of the Ohrid Agreement. Following an agreement between the EU and NATO in March 2003, ensuring the EU's access to NATO planning assets (the so-called Berlin-plus agreement), the EU-led Operation Concordia – the first military mission under ESDP – was deployed in Macedonia. Given the volatility of the political and security situation in Macedonia, the mission may represent a serious test for the EU's ESDP. There is also a general consensus that the EU will also take over – possibly from 2004 – from NATO's Stabilization Force (SFOR) in Bosnia. In the longer run, if European defence plans make further progress and the military missions in Bosnia and Macedonia go well, a EU military mission could also be established in Kosovo.

Pending regional challenges

Since the late 1990s the stabilization of South-Eastern Europe has made impressive progress. The fall of the authoritarian and nationalistic regimes first in Zagreb and then in Belgrade was a crucial watershed. It created a qualitatively new regional environment in which the initiatives of international actors have met with considerably less resistance than in the past, or have even received active cooperation and support from the new local leaderships. A steady movement towards reconciliation, democratization and institutional reform has been evident in several countries and areas.

However, major unsolved political issues remain which continue to hinder the completion of these processes and could give rise to new conflicts in the future. The Macedonian crisis in 2001 was a stark reminder that conflictual dynamics could take root even in areas that had until then remained relatively calm. More generally, the ethnic tensions between the Albanian and the Slav populations remain a major source of concern on the regional scale. Moreover, quite independently of the ethnic factors, the persistent weaknesses of state institutions and the fragility of democratic practices in several countries also make the eruption of new domestic crises possible. What follows is a brief overview of the region's major pending issues, illustrating the major challenges that the EU will continue to face in its efforts to implement its stabilization and integration plans.

The constitutional design for **Bosnia-Herzegovina** agreed on in Dayton (1995), based on a carefully balanced power-sharing arrangement, has been implemented precariously and only partially. The new institutional structures, which largely depend upon cooperation between the different ethnic groups, are extremely fragile. They are not able to ensure territorial control and the management of many social problems. Coexistence between the different ethnic groups remains problematic, requiring the continued presence of an international military force. Radical ethnically based groups continue to dominate the political landscape, although their action has been effectively countered, on many occasions, by the international actors. These groups are still capable of preventing the implementation of several key aspects of the Dayton agreement. The aid and development policies of international organizations and external donors have been largely unsuccessful. While they were designed to stimulate a local growth capacity, economic life in Bosnia-Herzegovina continues to depend heavily on foreign assistance.[10] The Office of the High Representative (OHR) has continuously resorted to its coercive powers to ensure central administrative functions, especially in the past few years.

However, this has hardly encouraged local ownership of the institution-building process. In sum, not only does Bosnia-Herzegovina appear to be far from reaching a state of self-sustainability, but the local political dynamics make it unlikely that this objective can be reached in the near future.

In **Kosovo** the post-conflict reconstruction efforts have achieved notable results and the security situation has gradually improved, although it remains problematic. Recent international action has focused on improving the population's living conditions, while also enabling the provisional local institutions for self-government to take over growing responsibilities for everyday administration and the implementation of the reform process. Since the deployment of NATO forces in mid-1999, however, there has been very little progress towards inter-ethnic coexistence. Most non-Albanians continue to live in a state of insecurity and under the protection of the NATO Kosovo Force (KFOR) mission. Only a very limited number of Serbs and refugees of other ethnic groups have come back to their homes, although their return was a central objective of the international action. The participation of Serb representatives in the newly established institutions remains highly problematic. The issue of the region's final status also remains unsolved. Despite the pro-Western stance of the Serbian government and the repeated electoral defeats of the more radical militant Albanian groups, no room for a compromise over the final status question has emerged, so that even the prospect of opening talks between Belgrade and Priština under an international framework – as required by the United Nations Security Council Resolution 1244 – continues to be viewed widely with much scepticism. Nor is any key international actor willing to endorse the Albanians' secessionist claim, which would mean throwing into question the principle stated in Resolution 1244 that Kosovo should be granted self-government rights but not full independence.[11]

With the signing of the EU-sponsored Berlin Agreement in March 2002, the risk of a traumatic separation between **Serbia and Montenegro** was averted. In keeping with the agreement, the Federal Republic of Yugoslavia was replaced by the loose union of Serbia and Montenegro. But the new political entity appears extremely fragile. It is, in many respects, an artificial construction, which was imposed mainly from outside and only grudgingly accepted by the leaderships and populations of the two countries. In fact, the constitutional arrangement on which the union is based is subject to a possible revision after three years. The continued rise of pro-independence political groups in Montenegro is likely to result in renewed secessionist drives even before the three-year moratorium expires. More generally, there remains considerable uncertainty surrounding the institutional and political future of both Serbia and Montenegro as separate entities.[12] The assassination of Serbian prime minister Zoran Djindjić in March 2003 showed how strong the legacy of the past regime remains. In fact, consolidation of the current Serbian democratic leadership cannot be taken for granted, especially in view of the difficulties that its reform efforts continue to encounter. In Montenegro the weakness of institutional structures is compounded by widespread criminal activities, which allegedly implicate and involve the governing authorities.

In **Macedonia** the implementation of the Ohrid Framework Agreement that put an end to the internal conflict of 2001 has generally proceeded smoothly. Indeed, the country has moved steadily towards a growing normalization. An attitude of compromise and cooperation has prevailed among both Albanian and Slav Macedonians. The parties representing the two ethnic groups in the government have so far kept their commitment to promoting the peace process and have convincingly reiterated their intention to do so in the future. The general elections of September 2002 took place without the controversies and reciprocal accusations of the past, which indicates that the democratization process has a good chance of success. However, significant long-term structural factors could jeopardize the country's stability in the future. There continues to be a marked social separation and a climate of mistrust between the two ethnic groups. This represents a constant source of tension, which may be exploited by ethnically based radical political groups. In addition, the demographic balance is changing in favour of the Albanians, which complicates the establishment of fair and stable power-sharing arrangements.[13]

Albania appears to be much more stable than it was at the time of the 1997 crisis, which was prevented from degenerating into a civil war only by international intervention. The country has since experienced other internal political crises but, especially since 2000, the democratization and reform processes have made considerable progress. The Albanian government has also managed to develop cooperative relations with all the neighbouring countries despite problems affecting the ethnically Albanian population in some of them. However, Albania's institutions still suffer many shortcomings. Indeed, their performance remains well below Western standards. Owing to the widespread power of criminal groups and the weaknesses of the judicial system, the rule of law is far from guaranteed. Coupled with the persistent tendency of political competition to become radicalized and extreme, the country continues to face the risk of future internal crises, which could in turn interrupt or reverse the country's integration path.[14]

Policy dilemmas facing the European Union

In the light of the regional challenges sketched out above, it can hardly be said that the 'Balkan anomaly' – that is, the set of factors, often interrelated, that have delayed and considerably complicated the region's integration into the European sphere – has been completely overcome. In most countries of the region, internal and external factors of insecurity have continued to impact strongly on the evolution of the internal political systems. Reform of these systems has developed at a considerably slower pace than in the former communist states of East-Central Europe. As a result, the countries of South-Eastern Europe still have to pass a number of critical tests before they can participate fully in the European cooperation and integration process.

Given these specificities, the European Union has adopted a two-track strategy, based on the one hand on a set of stabilization measures and, on the other, on a policy of gradual – step-by-step – integration. These two tracks are considered mutually reinforcing. The stabilization of the governments of the individual nations, of the inter-ethnic relations within them, and of their external relations with neighbouring countries are prerequisites for proceeding successfully towards integration. Conversely, the prospect of integration is the most powerful incentive that the EU can utilize to induce responsible and cooperative behaviour among the local political leadership. The key element of this strategy is encouragement and support for regional cooperation. In fact, political cooperation has increased progressively at the regional level. While regional cooperation has been a prime aim of the EU's conditionality policy, it has also found fertile terrain in the mind-sets of the new Balkan leaderships and has rapidly become one of their foreign policy priorities.

The dual strategy of stabilization and integration adopted by the EU towards South-Eastern Europe has, therefore, produced promising results so far and should be continued. Nevertheless, within this broad strategy the Union is confronted with critical policy dilemmas. The answers it will find for them will have a profound impact on its relationship with the region. The general principle underlying the Union's action is that any meaningful association path requires a reasonable degree of stability. Yet application of this principle is often problematic. The issue of whether and when to promote deeper integration with countries that were formerly involved in major conflicts and have only recently become stable implies a complex assessment of the long-term sustainability of the likely results. The case of Macedonia is a good illustration of this dilemma. The crisis that broke out in 2001 rudely interrupted Skopje's approach to the Union, which had only months earlier made a significant step forward with the signing of a Stabilization Association Agreement (SAA). In retrospect, as the Commission itself has acknowledged, it is clear that the positive assessment on developments in Macedonia which had led to the signing of the agreement was hurried and had failed to take into account the risks emanating from the region's conflictual dynamics. This integration dilemma applies especially to newly formed states, such as Macedonia, which lack solid historical and political foundations and are therefore more susceptible to internal and external crises.

A second dilemma concerns the application of the EU's policy of conditionality, which involves granting openings and concessions to partner countries once they have fulfilled the defined political requirements.[15] The most controversial question is how flexibly the policy should be implemented. This can be illustrated by the example of Croatia, which, with the encouragement of the EU institutions, submitted an application for EU membership in February 2003 (when its SAA with the Union still had to be ratified). The rapid integration of Croatia, a central regional player, would have a long-term beneficial effect on the other countries in the region and would represent an important signal of encouragement for them. In fact, Croatia has already attained a notable degree of economic stability and trade diversification, especially if compared with the other countries in the region, and delaying the further steps of integration could have negative domestic effects. On the other hand, Croatia still has to satisfy certain fundamental political demands set by the EU and the other international actors, such as active cooperation with the International Criminal Tribunal for the Former Yugoslavia (ICTFY), introduction of a policy allowing for the return of refugees and, more generally, the integration of the Serbian minority within the country. If the Union were to cave in on those requests, it would lose credibility in the eyes of the other regional actors, which would eventually reduce its influence and leverage. This kind of dilemma could also easily emerge with other actors in the region, starting with Serbia, that were heavily involved in the Yugoslav secessionist wars and have not yet solved some key problems deriving from them.[16]

A third major political dilemma facing the EU is whether it should concentrate its efforts on the implementation of the peace and constitutional agreements it has promoted and sponsored, even where they have revealed clear deficiencies and continue to meet structural obstacles, or work instead towards their revision. The incomplete and still strongly resisted implementation of the Dayton agreement is the most evident example of this dilemma. It is hard to imagine that the arrangement laid down in Dayton for Bosnia-Herzegovina is ultimately sustainable. It might, therefore, be advisable to reopen the diplomatic game to pursue a more stable solution with greater chances of success, even if this were to mean rethinking some of the fundamental principles of international action in the area, such as the refusal to redraw borders. Associated are the problems related to maintaining an international presence, the costs of which could become increasingly difficult to sustain, especially if the risk factors continue to multiply in other parts of the world. Nevertheless, the risks inherent in adopting an approach aimed at reviewing the existing agreements are no less evident. The most serious risk is that this could reopen the Pandora's box of opposing demands or foment a broader, regional revisionism. From this point of view, it could be better to continue to support the imperfect solutions which, despite their flaws, did make it possible to end the armed conflict and to ensure a certain degree of stability and international control of the crisis areas. Furthermore, there is the hope that the international initiatives will in time generate a real process of pacification. Then again, to stay with the case of Bosnia-Herzegovina, no convincing alternative solutions to the Dayton arrangements have as yet emerged, and each of the proposals put forward has inherent risks that cannot be overlooked.

The problem of whether the EU should undertake new diplomatic initiatives to seek more stable political arrangements also points to other regional questions. The agreement that gave rise to the Union of Serbia and Montenegro has only begun to be implemented, and any action that could throw it into doubt therefore appears to be premature, all the more so because the risk of armed conflict seems remote. The fact remains, however, that the fictitious nature of the new political entity could call for new diplomatic mediation on the part of the major international actors, notably the EU. In any case, in 2005 the Belgrade agreement will be up for revision, and the Union will have to prepare itself properly for that eventuality.

In Kosovo, international action continues to concentrate on improving the everyday living conditions in key sectors such as public services, security, employment, enabling the return of refugees, and bringing about the progressive adjustment of the provisional institutions of self-government to a set of benchmarks which would permit the remaining competencies to be transferred to them. But it is unlikely that in the absence of a solution to the problem of the final status, the institutional framework can be consolidated. As long as the region's future remains undefined, the local actors will continue to be tempted to undertake actions challenging or actively opposing the international plans aimed at stabilization and institution-building.

Conclusion: a road map for South-Eastern Europe?

In general, the EU's diplomatic action in South-Eastern Europe has tended to focus on conflict containment rather than on working pro-actively in the search for more stable solutions. This could result in a prolonged waiting game based on the principle that secessionist drives should always be resisted, as they represent a major factor of instability. Because of the EU's internal divisions, this approach often represents the minimum common denominator among member states.

The Stabilization and Association Process is by definition a long-term process whose fundamental objective is the economic and institutional development of the targeted countries. However, it is unlikely that it will be successful if the EU does not work out a more decisive strategy to deal with the conflicts that are still unresolved. The challenge facing the EU is not only to act as a political force of attraction and engine for regional integration, but also to prove itself an effective actor not only in managing but also in resolving conflicts.

The answer to the dilemmas described above could be the definition of a more precise road map for the Balkans that takes account of the need, once the stabilization process has reached a certain stage of maturation, to settle the underlying conflicts that have not been fully resolved.

Some priorities already seem to be sufficiently defined. In the coming years, the EU will have to take over responsibilities for the direct management of the more unstable areas – first Bosnia-Herzegovina and then probably Kosovo – and, in the meantime, will have to continue with the integration of those countries which, like Croatia, have attained a significant degree of stability and in which the reform processes are accelerating. As the integration process moves ahead in these countries, it should hopefully create a political setting that is more conducive to consensual agreements on the key pending issues involving the main regional actors. It is essential that these governments be reliable interlocutors for negotiations, with democratic credentials, not subject to nationalistic excess and with European integration as the overarching goal of their external and internal policies.

If these conditions were met, it is likely that an enlarged – pan-Balkan – negotiating framework could emerge and a stable solution could be found to both the Kosovo issue and the revision of the Dayton agreement. The idea of a Balkan conference – that is, a forum for the discussion by all parties of unsolved regional problems – could once again come to the fore. The fundamental objective of such a diplomatic endeavour would be to establish effective international and regional guarantees for the new political arrangements set down in any agreement. The promotion and implementation of such an initiative would be a considerable step ahead for the EU's external projection in that it would consolidate not only its role in the region but also its credibility as an international actor able to intervene in a proactive way, at least in the areas of its primary responsibility.

Notes

1 For a comprehensive analysis of the EU's role on the international scene, see R. Balfour and E. Greco, *Il ruolo internazionale dell'Unione Europea*, Gaeta: Artistic and Publishing Company, 2002 (English version, 2003, forthcoming).
2 On this aspect, see S. Everts, *Shaping a Credible EU Foreign Policy*, London: Centre for European Reform, 2001.
3 The importance of South-Eastern Europe as a testing ground for the transatlantic relationship was recently emphasised by M. Abramovic and H. Hurlburt, 'Can the EU Hack the Balkans?', *Foreign Affairs*, September/October 2002, vol. 81, no. 5: 2–7.
4 For an overall assessment of the EU's stabilization and association strategy, see W. van Meurs and A. Yannis, 'The European Union and the Balkans: From Stabilisation Process to Southeastern Enlargement', joint paper by the Hellenic Foundation for European and Foreign Policy (ELIAMEP) and the Bertelsmann Stiftung und Centrum für angewandte Politikforschung (CAP), September 2002.

5 Council Regulation 2666/2000.

6 Council Regulation 2667/2000.

7 A critical assessment of this change of priorities is provided in European Stability Initiative, *Western Balkans 2004: Assistance, Cohesion and the New Boundaries of Europe: A Call for Policy Reform*, ESI: Berlin, Brussels and Sarajevo, 3 November 2002.

8 'Communication from the Commission to the Council and the European Parliament. The Western Balkans and European Integration', 21 May 2003.

9 The recent developments and future prospects of SAP are examined in European Stability Initiative, *The Road to Thessaloniki: Cohesion and the Western Balkans*, Berlin: ESI, 11 March 2003.

10 On this aspect see International Crisis Group, *Bosnia's Precarious Economy: Still Not Open for Business*, Sarajevo and Brussels: ICG, 7 August 2001.

11 For recent analyses of the final status question, see J. Bugajski, R. B. Hitchen and P. Williams, *Achieving a Final Status Settlement for Kosovo*, Washington, DC: CSIS, April 2003; and United States Institute of Peace, *Simulating Kosovo. Lessons for Final Status Negotiations*, Washington, DC: USIP, Special Report 95, November 2002.

12 For an overall evaluation of the prospects of the agreement between Serbia and Montenegro and the role of the EU, see International Crisis Group, *Still Buying Time: Montenegro, Serbia and the European Union*, Balkans Report 129, Podgorica, Belgrade and Brussels: ICG, 7 May 2002.

13 The persistent risks of new conflicts in Macedonia are examined by R. Stefanova, 'New Security Challenges in the Balkans', *Security Dialogue*, 2003, vol. 34, no. 2: 165–78.

14 See International Crisis Group, *Albania: State of the Nation 2003*, Tirana and Brussels: ICG, March 2003.

15 See *General Affairs Council Conclusions*, 29–30 April 1997.

16 For an in-depth analysis of the problems of the EU conditionality, see O. Anastasakis and D. Bechev, *EU Conditionality in South-East Europe: Bringing Commitment to the Process,* a report by the South East Europe Studies Programme, St Antony's College, University of Oxford, April 2003.

6 Policies towards Russia, Ukraine, Moldova and Belarus

Andrei Zagorski

Relations between the European Union (EU) and the Soviet successor states, including the four countries covered in this chapter, developed from the early 1990s in parallel with the development of the Common Foreign and Security Policy (CFSP). They have evolved on the basis of the Partnership and Cooperation Agreements (PCAs) concluded with the countries concerned in the mid-1990s, as well as, in some cases, on the basis of CFSP Common Strategies towards individual countries, and/or decisions by the Council of Ministers. In most cases, relations were, and predominantly, remain within the domain of the European Commission, and only recently the EU's CFSP institutions have started getting more actively involved in pursuing cooperation with some of the countries in the region. This Union engagement is particularly true with regard to the evolving 'strategic partnership' of the EU with Russia. Nevertheless, EU policy towards the countries concerned, as with the CFSP in general, is as yet far from representing a single policy of a single actor. Policymaking is not only evolving from the mutual adjustments of different national policies on the basis of a common denominator, but also gradually emerging through the development of 'binding orientations' and 'the increased coherence of EU and Member States' action'.[1]

For the EU, managing and supporting the economic and political transformation of the Newly Independent States (NIS) by promoting the market, democracy and the rule of law has represented a series of challenges. This is especially true for the western Newly Independent States that are prospective new direct neighbours of an enlarged EU: Belarus, Moldova, Russia and Ukraine. However, this dimension of the Union's policy has never enjoyed the highest priority. The internal institutional reforms and developments of the EU, as well as the management of the eastward enlargement process, have been and remain the immediate preoccupations of the EU and its member states. From the mid-1990s, stabilization and peace-building in the western Balkans shifted the focus of EU policy further away from the NIS. This is reflected in the significant redirection of assistance funds. Within the CARDS assistance programme for the western Balkans, the EU has allocated €4.65 billion for the period from 2000 to 2006. For the same period of time, it has allocated €3.14 billion for the TACIS assistance programme which seeks to address the problems of the Soviet successor states and Mongolia.[2]

For this and other reasons, EU policy towards the NIS was, and remains, a work in progress, both for the EU itself and for the CFSP. In the early 1990s the underlying assumption of EU policy towards the NIS was based on the expectation that the Soviet successor states would form a relatively coherent group of countries around Russia within the framework of the Commonwealth of Independent States (CIS). This was why in 1991, when defining the criteria for recognition of the NIS, the EU urged that close economic links with Russia be maintained and why it has never considered offering any of the NIS either membership or any sort of formal association. This approach still remains the foundation stone of EU policy towards the NIS. However, developments over the past decade have shown that the initial expectation that the CIS states would remain a cohesive group was wrong. Not only did the CIS fail to develop as a viable framework for regional cooperation, but there was also increasing differentiation among the NIS, with distinctive and diverging perspectives as to the future of relations with the European Union. The western NIS, such as Moldova and Ukraine, particularly sought to keep open the option of eventual membership.

Though gradually differentiating its policies towards individual NIS, the member states of the EU, and therefore the EU itself, were not at all responsive to such membership aspirations. Although EU representatives emphasize that they do not wish to see an 'exclusion syndrome' to develop on the EU's eastern borders, or to set up new dividing lines across the continent,[3] they have mainly been concerned with the lack of progress towards economic and political transformation, and with the 'soft' security threats emanating from their future new neighbours, such as nuclear safety, organized crime, drug trafficking and illegal immigration, and the spread of diseases and environmental pollution.[4] This gap in mutual expectations between the EU and those NIS that have clearly articulated their desire for membership has become the source of mutual frustration and controversy. This is especially true with regard to Ukraine.[5]

This chapter examines the evolution of the EU's common policy towards four NIS: Russia, Ukraine, Moldova and Belarus. It starts with a review of the major instruments of this policy, mainly focusing on the PCAs concluded by the EU with the respective individual countries. This review is followed by an examination of the four cases of the EU's policy towards the four countries. The concluding part of the chapter focuses on the lessons that can be drawn from the EU common policies towards these specific cases.

General frameworks

After the collapse of the Soviet Union, the EU offered the NIS a new instrument called 'Partnership and Cooperation Agreements'. The PCAs were to replace the 1989 agreement regulating trade with the Soviet Union. The first NIS to sign the PCAs with the EU in 1994 were Ukraine (in force from 1998), Russia (in force from 1997) and Moldova (in force from 1998); these were followed by Belarus in 1995 (not yet in force) and with other countries from 1996 onwards.

All PCAs were negotiated individually, so their terms vary in points of detail. However, the basic objectives of all PCAs were:

- to establish a new trade regime with the NIS, partially extending to them 'most- favoured-nation' (MFN) arrangements (trade in several sectors was treated through separate agreements, however).
- to institutionalize political relations, including political dialogue, in order to address relevant issues as well as to provide for the opportunity to further improve and expand cooperation. This dialogue developed within the Cooperation Councils, the Cooperation Committees and the Parliamentary Cooperation Committees established with each individual country, as well as at the working level.
- to ensure that EU cooperation and assistance is conditional upon the progress of the countries concerned in terms of political and economic reform.

The PCAs offered neither prospective membership, nor any sort of association with the EU. The most they had to offer was, dependent on substantial progress in economic transition, the establishment of free trade with the Union. These provisions clearly distinguished the PCAs from the Europe Agreements with the aspirant countries of East-Central Europe (ECE), and they differ in this respect from the Stabilization and Association Agreements (SAAs) considered for the western Balkans. EU technical assistance to the NIS (TACIS), implemented and administered by the European Commission since 1991, was intended to support the goals of the PCAs and help the transformation of the NIS societies and economies. Indeed, the EU became the largest provider of external assistance to those countries over the past decade, in the hope of supporting the conditionality provisions established within the PCA framework. The EU is also either the largest (Russia) or the second largest (Ukraine, Belarus) trade partner of those countries. Therefore, questions of trade do play an important role in its relationship with them and provides a certain degree of leverage for the EU.

Given the increasing differentiation among the NIS and the differing objectives of the EU itself towards these countries, the EU gradually sought to differentiate its policies with regard to the individual NIS, particularly by adopting CFSP 'common strategies' towards some of them.

The Common Strategy on Russia was adopted on 4 June 1999 in Cologne and was complemented, in December 2001, by the EU Country Strategy Paper on Russia, which specified the objectives and priorities of EU policy for 2002–6. The Common Strategy on Ukraine was adopted on 11 December 1999 in Helsinki. Meanwhile, the EU is considering another common strategy to be developed with regard to the other three countries: Belarus, Moldova and Ukraine. Drawing from the provisions of the PCAs, these strategies have sought to specify more clearly the goals of the European Union with regard to individual countries, identify particular areas of cooperation and mutual interest, and focus the instruments available to the Union on those goals and areas. Through being more specific and targeted, as well as seeking to acknowledge the perspectives and the interests of the partners, the country-specific strategies of the EU may prove a more efficient instrument. They also increase the cohesiveness of the policies of individual EU members with regard to the NIS.

The evolving EU policies towards the western NIS have been updated and consolidated in the European Commission's Communication of 11 March 2003, which offered a new long-term approach to enhancing relations with the forthcoming eastern neighbours of the EU, as well as the southern Mediterranean countries. Building on previous experience, progress and failures, the Commission has offered the countries concerned 'the prospect of a stake in the EU's Internal Market and further integration and liberalization to promote the free movement of persons, goods, services and capital'.[6]

Regular meetings held at the level of presidencies, and at the senior government level within the Cooperation Councils, which are part of the 'mechanism for dialogue' provided by the PCAs, function as the most important forums for the ongoing adjustment of the mutual policies of the EU and its partner countries, for the definition of common objectives, and for the identification of the main avenues for cooperation. The dialogue conducted between the EU and Russia and Ukraine since 1999, after the respective CFSP common strategies had been adopted, has made considerable progress and is close to identifying the modalities of their relationship for the near future. This may result, in the end, not only in a more specific but also in a more realistic approach on both sides, abandoning excessive ambitions and laying the ground for a more solid, productive and efficient collaboration.

The 1990s, however, also revealed the limits and deficiencies of the EU common policy towards the NIS. As compared to the ECE countries, which have directed their efforts over the past decade to meeting the Copenhagen criteria and preparing to adopt the *acquis communautaire*, the transformation policies in the NIS have been predominantly driven by domestic considerations and by consensus-building among the relevant domestic interest groups. Hence the PCAs have clearly failed to provide any stronger incentive or rationale for those countries to accelerate reforms, and they have not provided instruments with which to prevent setbacks or even to stop, in some countries, the reversal of reforms. Similarly, the EU's technical assistance to the NIS was initially guided by the rather broadly defined goals of the PCAs and was not directed to achieving clearly measurable progress. As a result, it could have only a marginal effect on domestic developments. Although many projects have been implemented successfully, the TACIS programme has failed to help produce any serious systemic effect on the reforms in the countries concerned.

The NIS also had to learn that the EU is a rather complicated bureaucratic counterpart. The problem for Moscow, Kiev or Chisinau was not only to learn the complex, lengthy and often non-transparent way decisions are taken in Brussels, but also to understand the complex interplay of national and Union authorities. The EU has proved to be a reliable partner for the implementation of policies with agreed terms of reference. However, should those terms be changed, or a countervailing political decision be taken, in most cases lobbying in Brussels has proved to be much less helpful than acting in the capital cities of influential member states.

For these and other reasons, the instruments of conditionality developed and applied by the EU towards the NIS have generally not proved to be efficient. In many cases the EU was unable to use its leverage to make a difference in the region, especially when developments in the NIS went wrong. In particular, the linkage between democratization, cooperation and technical assistance from the EU, which was built into the concept of the PCAs, has not worked as well as was initially hoped.

The case of Russia

The declared objectives of EU policy towards Russia include fostering political and economic stability; contributing to the strengthening of the rule of law through the development of efficient institutions as well as effective legislative, executive and judicial systems; supporting measures for a better investment climate in Russia; enhancing legislative harmonization with the EU; and cooperating in combating 'soft' security threats.[7] Political dialogue between the EU and Russia involves the most institutionalized framework for cooperation among all the NIS. It includes regular meetings at the level of the presidencies, between the Russian prime minister and the president of the European Commission. The work of the Cooperation Council, the Cooperation Committee and the Parliamentary Cooperation Committee is complemented by a dense network of consultations at the level of ambassadors and experts, and is supported by a number of high-level task forces. The infrastructure of the EU–Russia dialogue goes much beyond the initial provisions of the PCA and extends to the discussion of CFSP and European Security and

Defence Policy (ESDP) issues with the High Representative and other relevant bodies of the European Union.

The EU's policy towards Russia has also undergone some important evolution over the past decade. Initially guided by the vague idea of providing support for Russia's systemic transformation, it lacked any specific focus. It picked up on the 'Washington consensus' philosophy in the expectation that liberalization and privatization would be at the core of the transformations to the market, and sought to support this development. Later on, the EU recognized the limits of this approach and the deficiencies of the instruments applied. In 1999, the country programme evaluation for Russia clearly highlighted the limited impact the EU assistance has had on the regulatory and policy framework in Russia. Thus, the normative approach of the EU policy has gradually shifted from the vague idea of a market transformation towards emphasizing the idea of a 'partnership', or of a 'strategic partnership', with Russia in a number of areas including energy, the development of a Common European Economic Area, and European security issues.[8]

Both the EU and Russia proceed on the understanding that their future relations will evolve on the contractual basis provided by the 1994 PCA.[9] Eventual membership by Russia of the EU is not an issue on the agenda. Moscow clearly pursues a policy of non-integration into the EU in order to maintain freedom of action, or, as expressed in the language of the Russian documents, in order to 'retain its freedom to determine and implement its domestic and foreign policies, its status and advantages as an Euro-Asian state and the largest country of the CIS, and the independence of its positions and activities in international organizations'.[10] Instead of membership, Russia and the EU both seek to develop a strategic partnership which, at least as far as European security is concerned, is based on the concept of shared responsibilities. As expressed in the EU Common Strategy,

> Russia and the Union have strategic interests and exercise particular responsibilities in the maintenance of stability and security in Europe, and in other parts of the world. The Union considers Russia an essential partner in achieving that objective and is determined to cooperate with her.[11]

Both the Russian and the EU strategies envisage, as a mid-term goal, progress towards the establishment of a free trade area, which, in the understanding of the EU, will be preceded by Russian accession to the World Trade Organization (WTO).[12] Furthermore, the EU–Russian summit held in Brussels in October 2001 agreed that their medium- and long-term economic strategy shall be aimed at the creation of a Common European Economic Area (CEEA).[13] The CEEA concept largely mirrors the ideas in the EU strategy on Russia, which focuses on the progressive approximation of legislation and standards between Russia and the EU. This is largely the mandate of the EU–Russia High-Level Group established by the summit and charged with elaborating the concept of a CEEA:

> The task of the High-Level Group is to elaborate a concept for a closer economic relationship between Russia and the EU, based on the wider goal of bringing the EU and Russia closer together. The High-Level Group will consider the opportunities offered by greater economic integration and legislative approximation and assess options for further work. It will also identify means and mechanisms to achieve common objectives and consider the time-scale for implementation.[14]

The agenda of approximation of legislation and standards is to be complemented by the exploration of concrete opportunities for cooperation in 'areas of established Russian expertise', such as science, aircraft, space and energy.[15]

Should the High-Level Group succeed in elaborating a jointly accepted road map for the harmonization of legislation and standards, it could herald an important new beginning in EU–Russian relations, largely overcoming the limitations of the less focused approach of the PCA. In the case of the aspirant countries, the task was clear though not easy: they were supposed to take over the entire *acquis communautaire*. The mandate of the High-Level Group is more difficult. It has to identify the extent to which the *acquis* needs to be taken over by a country not seeking membership but interested in benefiting from participation in a common economic space. Should the group successfully complete its task and come up with the list of particular areas that require harmonization, as well as with respective work plans, this could greatly help the setting up of clear priorities for the TACIS programme and help in allocating its resources in a much better targeted way than before.

Two other issues have also been a central focus of developing the 'strategic partnership' between the EU and Russia: developing an 'energy dialogue' and partnership; and exploring possibilities for closer cooperation in the field of security and defence policy. Both projects were launched at the EU–Russia summit meeting in Paris in October 2000[16] and remain the subject of discussions. In both areas, however, the substantive content remains vague. The ability of Russia to contribute significantly to the 'energy security' of the EU largely depends on Russia's capacity, and the necessary investment, to be able drastically to increase energy supplies to Europe. As regards partnership in European security, this largely depends on the evolution and maturing of the ESDP of the European Union. It also remains an open question the extent to which Russia will be able to share responsibilities with the EU in terms of maintaining European security.

It should be acknowledged that both the EU and Russia have demonstrated a pragmatic approach in developing mutual cooperation. The 'strategic partnership' approach corresponds to the Russian self-perception as a regional power that does not want to be fully integrated into the multilateral framework of the EU but, at the same time, needs to develop closer cooperation with it. The EU, for its part, appears to have learned the limits of its impact on Russian developments and has now basically accommodated itself to the idea of a partnership which helps to make cooperation in specific areas more operational and more focused. The limits of the initial concept of conditionality implied in the PCA have become more apparent. It largely did not work in the relationship with Russia, mainly for the reason that incentives, such as the prospect of joining the EU, were not offered to the Russian side.[17] Thus, the attempt by the EU to persuade Moscow, in the late 1990s, to stop the second war in Chechnya by freezing the implementation of many TACIS programmes has had only a limited effect.

Nevertheless, Russia and the EU have made use of the tools provided by the PCA to engage in an intensive dialogue over the past few years so as to identify common goals for a partnership. By the beginning of 2003 they were close to reaching certain concepts as far as the CEEA and, probably, the energy partnership are concerned. The challenges ahead are likely to reside less in the lack of agreement concerning the goals and rather more in the willingness and the ability of either side to implement joint decisions.

The case of Ukraine

The 1999 EU common strategy on Ukraine spells out a number of broadly defined 'strategic goals':

- to contribute to the emergence of a stable, open and pluralistic democracy in Ukraine, governed by the rule of law and underpinning a stable, functioning market economy that will benefit all the people of Ukraine;
- to cooperate with Ukraine in the maintenance of stability and security in Europe and the wider world and in finding effective responses to common challenges facing the continent; and
- to increase economic, political and cultural cooperation with Ukraine as well as cooperation in the field of justice and home affairs.[18]

As in the case of Russia, the EU common strategy speaks of a 'strategic partnership' with Ukraine.[19] While seeking to please the partner in Kiev by spelling out these far-reaching and ambitious goals, the institutions of the EU have concentrated on the task of 'bringing Ukraine in line with the legal frameworks of the single European market and the GATT/WTO system', and with a prospective option of establishing a free trade regime.[20] The particular objectives spelled out in the presidency's work plans focus on:

- helping Ukraine to consolidate a full, stable and pluralist democracy governed by the rule of law and respect for human rights;
- supporting the process of economic and social reform in Ukraine and helping in the creation of the conditions for an efficient market economy that will enable the country to be integrated into the world economy;
- promoting co-operation in the field of justice and home affairs;
- promoting rapprochement between the Union and Ukraine, including continuing efforts to secure gradual approximation of EU and Ukrainian legislation;
- continuing co-operation and dialogue in the field of the Union's common foreign and security policy; and
- strengthening co-operation on non-proliferation and disarmament and in the fields of environment, energy and nuclear safety.[21]

Despite the fact that the EU is the largest international donor to Ukraine, it has as yet been unable, through the instruments of the PCA, to persuade the Ukrainian government to introduce deep systemic changes. The European Commission has had to acknowledge that

> Ukraine still needs to continue reform of the energy sector, privatization, and improve tax collection. It is also necessary to press ahead with reform of the judiciary and financial institutions in order to improve the business environment and attract foreign investment, much needed for the modernization of the Ukrainian economy's obsolescent infrastructure and technological standards.[22]

This reflects the strong argument of the EU that the priority in EU–Ukrainian relations should be the implementation of the PCA, particularly in the fields of trade, investment and the approximation of legislation. Developing cooperation in the field of justice and home affairs (combating illegal migration and transnational organized crime, including trafficking in drugs and human beings) reflects the concerns of the EU and member states with regard to the 'soft security' threats emerging from the forthcoming enlargement of the EU.

EU–Ukrainian cooperation can hardly be seen as a success story, and not just because of the poor progress and limited systemic effect of this cooperation. The EU–Ukraine 'strategic partnership' is an unfortunate example of a relationship between two sides pursuing very different agendas, with Ukraine's aspirations being much more ambitious than the EU is prepared to accept. The 'Strategy of Ukraine's Integration to the

European Union', approved by President Leonid Kuchma on 11 June 1998, launched Kiev's politico-diplomatic offensive with the declared goal of fully fledged EU membership. This strategy sought to

> ensure the involvement of Ukraine in the European political (including spheres of foreign and security policy), economic and legal space. The main foreign policy priority of Ukraine in the medium-term is to acquire the status of an EU associated member which would be obtained at the same time as the candidate countries with common borders with Ukraine acquire fully-fledged membership status.[23]

Kiev has further specified its ambitions in a road map included in a document defining a conception for the socio-economic development of the country for the period 2002–11.[24] This envisaged that by 2004, Ukraine would finalize the negotiation of an association agreement with the EU to replace the PCA of 1994 and would complete negotiations on the introduction of free trade. By 2007 the domestic legislation of Ukraine in key areas would be harmonized with EU requirements and a customs union would be established. In the years 2007–11, the association agreement would be fully implemented, and Ukraine should then meet the Copenhagen criteria, thus becoming ripe for full EU membership. Kiev admits that Ukraine's transition record is not yet sufficiently impressive for it to start accession negotiations. However, it wants Brussels to send an explicit message that Ukraine will be considered eligible for membership once it meets the Copenhagen criteria. Foreign minister Anatoly Zlenko pledges, along with many other Ukrainian leaders, that a clear commitment to prospective membership for Ukraine would be an important motivation to boost domestic reforms: 'we speak about a clear landmark to which Ukraine could direct its efforts now'.[25]

While realizing that membership of Ukraine in the EU is not something to be resolved by the current presidency, and probably not during the lifetime of the next political generation, Kiev looks for the type of association agreement concluded by Turkey in 1961. And having launched the 'membership offensive', Ukraine not only has largely distorted the agenda of its relations with the EU but also seems to have partially reversed the logic of the conditionality initially applied by the EU. In this reversed logic, progress in Ukraine's transition is conditional on the readiness of the EU to grant Ukraine an 'upgraded' status by promising future membership. At the very least, this strategy has helped Kiev partially to escape the pressure of the conditionalities which the EU has sought to impose by the PCA.

For all sorts of reasons, Brussels is reluctant even to discuss, let alone commit itself to, eventual membership for Ukraine. The public debate over the issue, however, has to a great extent distorted the agenda of the relationship between Brussels and Kiev. It has also greatly limited the serious consideration of what needs to be done to achieve real progress. The politicized summit meetings have partially degenerated into a diplomatic language exercise, with Kiev seeking to score points on the accession issue and Brussels seeking to obfuscate any clear position through the language of 'positive ambiguity'. Thus, the the EU strategy on Ukraine 'acknowledges Ukraine's European aspirations and welcomes Ukraine's pro-European choice'.[26] The Joint Statement of the Yalta EU–Ukrainian summit meeting of 11 September 2001 reinforces their 'strategic partnership, aimed at further *rapprochement of Ukraine to the EU*'.[27] For the time being, the EU–Ukrainian partnership appears handicapped by the diverging interpretations of those 'positive ambiguities' on either side.

The attempt by the EU to find a way out of this impasse by further diversifying its relations with the western NIS by considering offering Belarus, Moldova and Ukraine a status of 'special neighbours', as proposed by the United Kingdom at the EU summit meeting in Luxembourg on 15 April 2002, has only emphasized the concentration of the EU's attention on its 'soft security' concerns and is unlikely to put an end to the continuing debate over membership. Ukraine wants the EU to adopt a new strategy, but definitely not one that would put Kiev into the same basket as Minsk and Chisinau. As one report from Kiev summarizes:

> The 'neighbour' status, as proposed in Luxembourg, is not a step forward in the EU eastern policy. It is rather a groundless attempt to simplify the nature of relations with the new neighbours by reducing common interests only to problems of migration, trade, and international crime.[28]

The new Neighbourhood Policy communicated by the European Commission in March 2003 has, in that respect, definitely fallen far short of Ukraine's expectations. While it continues to encourage further approximation, development of free trade and the promotion of the four freedoms (the free movement of persons, goods, services and capital), it has put an end to the continued ambiguity of the EU's statements with regard to the final objectives of its policy towards the western NIS. The Communication of the Commission, for the first time, clearly states that 'the aim of the new Neighbourhood Policy is ... to provide a framework for the development of a new relationship which would not, in the medium-term, include a perspective of membership or a role in the Union's institutions'.[29]

The case of Moldova

EU policy towards Moldova over the past decade may be a good example of both confusion and conspicuous progress. This small country has never been a focus of attention for Brussels and has often been confusingly neglected. In 1994, Moldova was among the first NIS to sign a PCA that applied the standard framework for cooperation with the EU offered to all Soviet successor states. Later on, however, Moldova was admitted to the framework of the Stability Pact for South-Eastern Europe, which might have raised the expectations of a potentially different future relationship with the EU since membership in the Stability Pact, at least theoretically, could imply Moldova's eligibility to sign a Stabilization and Association Agreement with the European Union and thus make Moldova eligible for membership in the distant future. This could only be welcome in Chisinau, the government of which considers integration into the EU 'a strategic objective of the foreign policy of the Republic of Moldova'.[30]

The proposal put forward in spring 2002 for developing an EU CFSP common strategy towards the three western NIS – Belarus, Moldova and Ukraine – and to offer them a 'special neighbours' status after the enlargement of the EU may help to clarify the category of countries into which the EU places Moldova. With this background of such fluctuations in the position of Brussels, it does not appear surprising that, at the time of writing, the official Web site of the European Union explains the purposes of the PCA concluded in 1994 by using merely the text pasted from the site dealing with the EU–Ukrainian relations. This document explains that the PCA concluded with Moldova is supposed to be instrumental 'in bringing Ukraine [*sic*] in line with the legal framework of the single European market'.[31]

Relations with Moldova have so far not been the subject of any CFSP common policy. Although the frozen domestic conflict concerning the status of the Transdniestr region within the Moldovan 'common state' is an issue for the CFSP, the EU has never sought any direct involvement in conflict resolution, especially since it has not wanted to displace the Organization for Security and Cooperation in Europe (OSCE), which has been involved in this issue since the early 1990s. Brussels therefore has limited itself to including the issue of the conflict in Moldova on the agenda of political consultations with Moscow and to supporting engagement with the OSCE. Thus, the development and the implementation of the EU's policy towards Moldova have been predominantly the domain of the European Commission.

Despite this frozen conflict, the overwhelming social and economic problems facing the second poorest country of the former Soviet Union (FSU), and the need for further economic reforms, the progress in relations between the EU and Moldova is surprisingly good – in any case, it seems to be much better than with any other country of the FSU. Despite its declared membership aspirations, the Moldovan government has never made this a prominent issue with Brussels. At the same time, Moldova has benefited from the EU assistance provided through different channels and from the EC General Preference System. According to EU evaluations, not only are EU–Moldovan relations 'good in both political and economic areas', but also the Moldovan government 'has demonstrated steady progress' in the implementation of the PCA. Furthermore, after joining the WTO in 2001, Moldova became the first country of the FSU to initiate joint studies with the EU on the feasibility of a free trade area, which resulted in the acknowledgement of the need to improve the legal and administrative framework for business in Moldova before a free trade area could be created.[32]

Thus, Moldova can be regarded as a relatively good example of the implementation of the PCAs, and, as such, a partial success for EU policy. However, this does not guarantee the successful completion of the transition in Moldova, a country that is facing growing socio-economic and political problems.

The case of Belarus

Since the late 1990s, the evolution of relations between the EU and Belarus has been the most important test of the viability of the EU's policy towards non-aspirant countries, and the most explicit proof of the limits of the Union's projection of its common policy.

Belarus is certainly a special case. Domestic developments in the country, which were accompanied by setbacks in reforms and increasingly authoritarian rule by President Alexander Lukashenka, have brought about a significant distortion in EU–Belarus relations. In the aftermath of the flawed 1996 referendum, which resulted in a revision of the 1994 Constitution and an extension of the period of office of the president, the EU Council of Ministers decided upon a number of sanctions against Belarus. The ratification process of the PCA signed in 1995 was frozen and the interim agreement not enacted. Bilateral relations at the ministerial level were suspended. The EU technical assistance programmes were frozen, with the exception of humanitarian aid, regional programmes and programmes aimed at supporting civil society in Belarus. In 1999 the EU adopted a stick and carrot approach to Belarus whereby sanctions were to be gradually lifted pending fulfilment of the four benchmarks set by the OSCE: return of substantial powers to the Parliament; opposition representation in electoral commissions; fair access to the state media for the opposition; and electoral legislation conforming to international standards.[33]

With encouraging signs of moderate changes in the Belarusian regime,[34] the EU continued to put pressure on the regime with the approach of the parliamentary (2000) and presidential (2001) elections in the country. EU Commissioner Chris Patten noted in summer 2001 that

> The EU has a clear position – as long as the present intolerable situation remains, we cannot consider closer economic or political relations. Unless and until there are significant improvements, our financial assistance will remain limited to direct help to those involved in promoting civil society and humanitarian assistance where needed.[35]

Finding itself isolated among the European community of states, the Lukashenka regime was forced to manoeuvre. However, it has managed to survive both elections, and without giving in on the principal issues at stake. In this particular case, the linkage between evidence of progress in domestic reforms and increased cooperation with the EU (including the provision of technical assistance) has failed to yield fruits. The stakes were too high for the Belarusian regime. President Lukashenka continued along his path despite the crucial importance of Belarusian trade with the EU. The EU (and Germany within the EU) is not only the second biggest trade partner but the main source of hard currency income and the principal support for the modernization of Belarusian industrial enterprises.[36]

The outcome of the two elections has produced an ambiguous situation in EU–Belarusian relations. Although neither election is recognized as meeting the democratic standards of the OSCE, the EU, along with other international institutions, will have to live with the Lukashenka regime at least until 2005. The available policy options are limited to either continuing the isolation of the country (unless it collapses economically), or to change strategy and engage the regime more actively. The problem is that there appears no credible political alternative to Lukashenka. For its part, Belarus, which is increasingly dependent on bilateral cooperation with Russia (with the latter largely keeping it afloat), does not have a wide set of policy choices either. Its agenda is currently reduced to preserving a 'neighbourhood belt'[37] (Ukraine, Poland and Lithuania as well as Russia favour a more positive engagement with the Minsk regime), and to seeking the normalization of relations with the EU, the Council of Europe and the OSCE Parliamentary Assembly. Especially taking into consideration the forthcoming extension of the EU, the Minsk authorities emphasize the need for a rapprochement with the EU. They emphasize that they are prepared to go as far towards seeking a rapprochement as the EU is prepared to go.[38]

The peculiarity of EU–Belarusian relations implies, however, that the distortion in this relationship since 1996 has liberated both sides from the need to take any decision concerning the long-term policy options for Belarus in Europe. The authoritarian regime of Lukashenka is a good excuse for the EU not to deal with the question of whether or not an eventual European (EU) vocation for Belarus, which would be logical in the context of its geographic location, should be given serious consideration. Belarusian authorities and experts also realize that such a question is premature in a medium-term perspective.[39] This issue, however, has only been postponed as a consequence of the rule of Lukashenka. It is by no means off the agenda, and once Lukashenka is gone, it is going to reappear as an issue in EU–Belarusian relations. Even President Lukashenka has hinted at this vocation, as in this statement from 1999:

Our people and our country belong to European civilization, and we should not stay outside the process of European integration. Therefore, today, I responsibly declare the readiness of Belarus not only to normalize relations with the European countries, with the Council of Europe, but to take decisive steps towards participation in pan-European integration.... I believe nobody doubts that, due to its intellectual and cultural potential, Belarus is capable to be a full-fledged member of the family of European peoples, a member of the European Union.[40]

This statement may be taken as one of Lukashenka's many intimidation attempts addressed to the Russian leadership, or as another unpredictable escapade of his. It is more difficult to ignore, however, that 'associated membership in, and a prospective accession to the European Union', remains a proclaimed 'long-term strategic goal of Belarus'.[41]

It is hard to believe the current Minsk leadership seriously believes in this. However, it certainly reflects the views of the Belarusian opposition. Any 'third force' likely to succeed Lukashenka would objectively come back to invoking a European vocation for Belarus similar to that of the current Ukrainian government. The contemporary deviation of Belarus from that path would then appear only as a brief aberration in modern Belarusian history. The EU, however, appears no better prepared for such a development than it is for dealing with the European vocation of Ukraine.

Conclusions

This review of the European Union's policies towards the four Soviet successor states reveals four differing cases. While the slowly evolving 'strategic partnership' with Russia may stand for an increasingly pragmatic framework based on a contractual relationship and on cooperation in areas of common interest, the Ukrainian drive for recognition of prospective membership of the EU most explicitly demonstrates the ambiguous nature of the evolving Common Foreign and Security Policy, which avoids setting clear end-goals. The case of Belarus most explicitly reveals the weakness of the instruments so far available to the CFSP, while the case of Moldova may be regarded as a sort of relative success. Taking into consideration the differences in these various cases suggests that developing one single common strategy covering the EU's policy towards the NIS situated to the west of Russia may miss the distinct problems that should be addressed for each individual country.

At the same time, all those cases demonstrate a gradual, though slow, evolution of the EU's East European policy, which increasingly is differentiating between individual countries. And, especially in its relations with Russia and Ukraine, the EU is increasingly resorting to the instruments of the CFSP for developing a political and security dialogue. Indeed, the negative critique often expressed in many NIS towards the EU should not necessarily mean a failure of the CFSP or the lack of a EU policy. Brussels should not be blamed for having started its relations with the NIS from the false proposition that they would stay together as a cohesive group of countries. Most Western states made the same mistake. Brussels should not be blamed either for the lack of a clear vision as to the future direction of its relations with individual post Soviet countries. The EU member states have no such vision either. Moreover, there is no reason to blame Brussels for being unable to live up to the expectations of its forthcoming direct neighbours. It is politically legitimate for the EU to concentrate, in the first instance, on its own immediate concerns. It is only natural, which is also true with regard to any individual country's policy.

It is true that Brussels could do a better job and develop a better inter-face with the partner countries if it streamlined decision-making within existing institutions and made the process less bureaucratic. There is much room for improvement even within the limits of a policy that is intergov-ernmental in nature. More generally, the lessons that the EU may learn from a decade-long testing of its common policies vis-à-vis the Newly Independent States are twofold. First, the economic and financial strength of the EU is not easily translated into political leverage. The instruments of the EU, including the method of conditionality, have not yet yielded tangible results. They have not been sufficient to stop the war in Chech-nya, to ease Lukashenka's authoritarian rule, or to persuade the Ukrainian government to engage in really deep political, economic and social reform. Thus, the EU has yet to identify ways and instruments to increase the effi-ciency of its common policies.

Second, the ability of the EU to translate its economic strength into significant political leverage evidently depends on the stakes involved, and on the ability to identify common interests with the respective partners. For those countries that aspire to it, the really big stake is EU member-ship. This probably explains why the accession process of the East-Central European countries was the most successful project of EU policy in the 1990s. The 'common interest' approach may work when membership is not at stake, but the EU and the respective partner state do need to share common interests, even if they are asymmetric in nature. The gradual improvement of the dialogue between Russia and the EU may prove the validity of this proposition. However, it would not be conditionality but rather the common interest, principally in the energy dialogue and also with the engagement of Russia in the European security concert, that would increase the viability of the relationship.

Finally, if these lessons are right, conditionality will not be the most effi-cient tool for dealing with Ukraine unless the EU decides to grant Kiev a prospective membership option. The alternative is that the EU should be encouraged to engage in a sincere dialogue with Ukraine in order to identify common interests beyond the verbal commitment to shared values and to cooperation in addressing the soft security challenges. These lessons would also imply that the EU's objectives vis-à-vis Belarus will hardly be obtainable until the regime changes, or unless the EU is ready to pursue a policy of regime change. The latter is, however, a highly improbable scenario.

Notes

1 Country Strategy Paper 2002–2006 and National Indicative Programme 2002–2003', Russian Federation, 27 December 2001, p. 3. Online. Available http: <http://www.europa.eu.int/comm/external_relations/russia/csp/index.htm> (accessed 10 October 2002).

2 See Commission of the European Communities, 'The EU's Relationship with the Countries of Eastern Europe and Central Asia'. Online. Available http: <http://www.europa.eu.int/comm/external_relations/ceeca/index.htm> (accessed 10 October 2002): and Commission of the European Communities, 'The EU's Relations with South Eastern Europe'. Online. Available http: <http://www.europa.eu.int/comm/external_relations/cee/news/ip01_1464.htm> (accessed 10 October 2002).

3 Speech by R. Prodi, president of the European Commission, 'What the 21st Century Holds for the EU–Russia Relationship', European Business Club (EBC) dinner, Moscow, 28 May 2002. Online. Available http: <http://www. europa.eu.int/comm/external_relations/russia/summit_05_02/sp02_237.htm> (accessed 10 October 2002).

4 J. Dempsey, 'Enlarged EU agrees new ties with neighbours – Moldova, Ukraine, Belarus', 17 April 2002. Online. Available http: <http://www.europa. yam.ro/articles/2002/aprilie/17/1.html> (accessed 10 October 2002).

5 For example, see O. Pavliuk, *The European Union and Ukraine: The Need for a New Vision*, Kiev: East–West Institute, 1999.

6 Commission of the European Communities, 'Communication from the Commission to the Council and the European Parliament. Wider Europe – Neighbourhood: A New Framework for Relations with our Eastern and Southern Neighbours', COM (2003) 104.

7 Commission of the European Communities, 'The EU's relations with Russia'. Online. Available http: <http://www.europa.eu.int/comm/external_relations/ russia/intro/index.htm> (accessed 10 October 2002).

8 For example, see I. Kempe, 'Die Europäische Union und Russland nach dem 11. September', *Europäische Rundschau*, 2002, vol. 30, no. 2: 113–14.

9 This corresponds not only to the EU vision but also to the Russian strategy approved in 1999 and reconfirmed by President Putin in 2000. See I. Ivanov, 'Medium-term Strategy for Development of Relations between the Russian Federation and the European Union (2000–2010)', in *Novaya Rossiyskaya Diplomatiya: Desyat' Let Vneshney Politiki Strany* (A New Russian Diplomacy: Ten Years of the Country's Foreign Policy), Moscow: OLMA-Press, 2002, p. 279.

10 Ibid.

11 'Common Strategy of the European Union of 4 June 1999 on Russia' (1999/414/CFSP), L 157/2.

12 'Medium-term Strategy for Development of Relations between the Russian Federation and the European Union (2000–2010)', p. 279; 'Common Strategy of the European Union of 4 June 1999 on Russia', L 157/2.

13 'Joint Statement', EU–Russia Summit, 3 October 2001. Online. Available http:

<http://europa.eu.int/comm/external_relations/russia/summit_10_01/dc_en.htm> (accessed 10 October 2002)

14 Ibid.

15 'Common Strategy of the European Union of 4 June 1999 on Russia', L 157/5.

16 'Joint Statement', EU–Russia Summit, 30 September 2000. Online. Available http: <http://europa.eu.int/comm/external_relations/russia/summit_30_10_00/statement_en.htm> and <http://europa.eu.int/comm/external_relations/russia/summit_30_10_00/stat_secu_en.htm> (accessed 10 October 2002).

17 See also Kempe, 'Die Europäische Union und Russland', p.114.

18 'European Council Common Strategy of 11 December 1999 on Ukraine' (1999/877/CFSP), L 331/1.

19 Ibid.

20 Commission of the European Communities, 'The EU's Relations with Ukraine'. Online. Available http: <http://europa.eu.int/comm/external_relations/ukraine/intro/index.htm> (accessed 10 October 2002)

21 General Affairs Council, 'Relations with Ukraine', 28 January 2002. Online. Available http: <http://europa.eu.int/comm/external_relations/ukraine/intro/gac.htm> (accessed 10 October 2002).

22 Commission of the European Communities, 'The EU's Relations with Ukraine', p. 7.

23 Government of Ukraine, 'Strategy of Ukraine's Integration to the European Union' (unofficial translation). Online. Available http: <http://www.mfa.gov.ua/eng/diplomacy/?ua-eu> (accessed 10 October 2002).

24 'Poslannya Presidenta Ukraini do Verkhovnoy Radi Ukraini. Evropeiskii vibir: kontseptualni zasadi strategii ekonomichnogo ta sotsialnogo rozvitku Ukraini na 2002–2011 roki' (The Address of the President of Ukraine to the Supreme Rada of Ukraine. The European Vocation: The conceptual basis of the strategy of the social-economic development of Ukraine in 2002–2011). Online. Available http: <http://www.kuchma.gov.ua/main/?sp/index> (accessed 10 October 2002).

25 Statement of A. Zlenko, Minister for Foreign Affairs of Ukraine, 'The European Home Is a Home for Ukraine', Conference of the East–West Institute, Kiev, 27 April, 2002. Online. Available http: <http://www.mfa.gov.ua/eng/information/card.shtml?speech/2002/04/2701.html> (accessed 10 October 2002).

26 'European Council Common Strategy of 11 December 1999 on Ukraine', L 331/2.

27 'Joint Statement', Ukraine–European Union Summit in Yalta, 11 September 2001, p.1 (emphasis added).

28 *Ukrainian Monitor*, Policy Paper 8, May 2002, p. 3.

29 Commission of the European Communities, 'Communication from the Commission to the Council and the European Parliament. Wider Europe – Neighbourhood: A New Framework for Relations with Our Eastern and Southern Neighbours', COM (2003) 104, p. 5.

30 Ministry of Foreign Affairs of Moldova, 'The Foreign Policy Guidelines for the period 1998–2000'. Online. Available http: <http://www.moldova.md/ro/government/oll/FOREIGN/en/DIREC_POL_en.htm> (accessed 10 October 2002).

31 See the Commission of the European Communities, 'The EU's relations with Moldova'. Online. Available http: <http://europa.eu.int/comm/external_relations/moldova/intro/index.htm> (accessed 10 October 2002).

32 Ibid.

33 Commission of the European Communities, 'The EU's relations with Belarus'. Online. Available http: <http://europa.eu.int/comm/external_relations/belarus/intro/index.htm> (accessed 10 October 2002).

34 The EU has lifted travel restrictions for senior government representatives of Belarus, and has extended until 2004 the agreement on trade with textile products while raising the import quotas from Belarus – an issue considered crucial by the Minsk authorities.

35 C. Patten, 'Commission Statements in Urgency Debates', European Parliament, Strasbourg, 5 September 2001. Online. Available http: <http://europa. eu.int/comm/external_relations/news/patten/sp01_331.htm> (accessed 10 October 2002).

36 T. Alekseyeva, A. Gordeychik and E. Dostanko, 'Vzaimodeystviye Respubliki Belarus s vedushchimi evropeyskimi organizatsiyami v kontse 1990kh godov' (The Interaction of the Republic of Belarus with the Leading European Organizations in the late 1990s), in *Belorusskiy Zhurnal Mezhdunarodnogo Prava i Mezhdunarodnykh Otnosheniy* (Belarusian Journal of International Law and International Relations), Minsk, 2000. Online. Available http: <http://www.cenunst.unibel.by/journal/2000.2/algordos.shtml> (accessed 10 October 2002).

37 See the interview with the head of the European Department of the Belarusian Foreign Ministry, Victor Shikha, *Respublika* (Minsk), 16 April 2002.

38 For example, see statement from the Belarusian Foreign Ministry. Online. Available http: <http://www.mfa.gov.by/cgi-bin/policy.pl?file=005.txt> (accessed 10 October 2002).

39 T. Alekseyeva *et al.*, 'Vzaimodeystviye Respubliki Belarus'.

40 *Belorusskiy rynok* (The Belarusian Market), Minsk, 1999, no. 26. Online. Available http: <http://www.br.minsk.by/archive/1999–26/bk6929.stm> (accessed 10 October 2002).

41 Ministry of Foreign Affairs of Belarus. Online. Available http: <http://www.mfa.gov.by/cgi-bin/policy.pl?file=005.txt> (accessed 10 October 2002).

7 The Northern Dimension

A presence and four liabilities?

Hiski Haukkala

Introduction

The Northern Dimension (ND) of the European Union's policies[1] has its roots in the early 1990s when three Nordic countries – Finland, Norway and Sweden – were negotiating their accession into the European Union (EU). It is fair to say that with the accession of Finland and Sweden at the beginning of 1995,[2] the EU acquired an entirely new 'northern dimension', as what had previously been a predominantly Western and Southern European entity was introduced to a host of new geographical realities. This was reflected, first of all, in the much harsher climate, Arctic agriculture, low population density and long distances to be found in the two Nordic member states. A striking example of this is the fact that with the accession of Finland and Sweden the land area of EU grew by 33.3 per cent whereas the population grew by only a meagre 4 per cent (see Table 7.1 for more comparisons). The new dimension was not only a list of obstacles and hardships: new northern member states were also seen as highly developed market economies, as well as representing positive Nordic values such as equality, transparency and the welfare state.

The 'northern dimension' brought new flavours in terms of more strategic issues as well. Finland and Sweden were well-known Cold War neutrals – a stance that raised eyebrows in some of the older member states.

Table 7.1 Some peculiarities of the 'northern dimension' compared to EU-12.

	Finland	*Sweden*	*EU-12*
Land area	338,000 square km	450,000 square km	2,368,000 square km
Population	5.2 million	8.9 million	353.1 million
Population density	15/square km	20/square km	150/square km
GDP per capita	19,360 euros	20,800 euros	17,960 euros
Agricultural growth period	110–180 days	110–220 days	230–340 days

Sources: Eurostat and the Finnish Ministry of Agriculture and Forestry. Statistical year 1995.

The beginning of the accession negotiations in 1993 coincided with the ratification process of the Treaty of Maastricht, which had introduced a Common Foreign and Security Policy (CFSP) into the EU. The neutrality, or non-alignment as it was soon to be known, of Finland and Sweden[3] was seen as a potential liability for the further development of the CFSP.[4] Combined with the Danish opt-out from the common defence policy, agreed in the aftermath of the failed referendum in 1992, it can be said that the emerging northern dimension was also viewed as including rather awkward partners in the development of the security dimension of the EU.

After nearly a decade of Finland and Sweden's membership, it is evident that the worst fears of the EU-12 have not materialized. If anything, it has been the new Nordic members themselves that have expressed a certain measure of disappointment with the lack of efficient and coherent European foreign policy making. Moreover, Finland and Sweden have shown a good deal of creativity in devising initiatives and proposals that can be seen as having foreign and politico-security significance. Their activism has, however, tended to emphasize the 'soft' end of the security spectrum, which has been reflected in, for example, the joint proposal for the inclusion of the so-called Petersberg tasks into the Amsterdam Treaty in 1996–7. They have also shown initiative in developing the Union's Russian policy. Indeed, the Finnish initiative for a Northern Dimension can be seen as an embodiment of these two tracks: seeking to bring the attention of the whole Union to the challenges and opportunities that Russia presents, while stressing the primacy of soft security threats and the role of multilateral cooperation in combating them.

This chapter is based on a two-pronged analysis of the Northern Dimension. First, it gives an overview of the development and the content of the specific EU policy tailored for Northern Europe. Second, it analyses the impact of the European Union and its policies in Northern Europe by first examining the increase in *presence* that the EU has acquired and developed in the course of the past decade in the region and then asking the question, to what extent has this increased presence been translated into strategic *actorness*?[5] The argument in this chapter is that increased presence can turn into a liability if it does not result in a corresponding increase in the EU's capabilities as an actor over the longer term.

The chapter is divided into three parts. The first part introduces both the short history of the Northern Dimension as well as its main content and achievements so far. The second part analyses the role that the EU and its Northern Dimension have assumed in the ongoing multilevel game that is being played in the region, while the third and last part draws some conclusions.

The emergence of a 'northern dimension' into the European Union

The term 'northern dimension' emerged during the accession negotiations when the Finnish team of negotiators in particular used it in order to highlight the fact that the EU was about to have new member states with drastically different conditions compared to the West European members. But the accession of Finland and Sweden had external repercussions for the EU as well. It brought the Union for the very first time into direct contact with the turbulent Russian Federation in the form of a 1,300-kilometre Finnish–Russian border. This 'exposure' is bound to grow larger still with the ongoing enlargement process.

With his initiative in 1997, Prime Minister Paavo Lipponen linked the slogan with the EU's external relations. Indeed, the Finnish initiative for the Northern Dimension has always made a clear distinction between the internal and the external, placing it exclusively in the realm of EU external relations. This basic distinction reflects a clear choice of a 'marketing strategy' devised for the initiative, as the Finns have from the start consciously sought to avoid entangling it with the internal power struggles for scarce financial resources in the EU, including the Common Agricultural Policy (CAP) and structural funds.[6] Therefore the initiative was carefully crafted, emphasizing the wider EU interest while downplaying the significance of parochial Nordic interests.

The Finnish initiative

Prime Minister Lipponen made his initiative in September 1997. In a speech entitled 'The European Union needs a policy for the Northern Dimension', he argued that the Union and its member states share vital common interests in Northern Europe and that those interests should translate into a new EU policy.[7] Lipponen's original approach to the initiative was quite ambitious, as he linked the initiative with making the Union a more effective global actor. Moreover, in a letter sent to the then president of the Commission, Jacques Santer, in April the same year, Lipponen stressed the strategic qualities of the Northern Dimension, proposing that it 'should define what are the economic, political and security interests of the Union in this area, especially in the long-term'.[8]

Geographically, Lipponen's original vision was rather Russia-centric, but it also included a wider interpretation of the scope of the initiative, which included the United States and Canada. The main emphasis was, however, related to a host of different threats emanating mainly from the north-western parts of Russia, such as the poor standard of the environment, including the burning question of nuclear safety. Another set of challenges was derived from the existence of, arguably, one of the steepest welfare gaps in the world on the Finnish–Russian border, with the associated fear of uncontrolled immigration together with the danger of rampant transmissible diseases, such as HIV and drug-resistant forms of tuberculosis. These threats are indeed a legitimate source of concern, as the north-western parts of Russia, and the Kola Peninsula and the Kaliningrad region in particular, represent some of the most toxic and dangerous environmental hotspots on the planet.[9]

Furthermore, the region is not void of hard security problems. The Kaliningrad enclave remains of significant military importance to Russia, although its strategic usefulness will be further undermined when it is surrounded by NATO countries in the coming years. Moreover, the Kola Peninsula still acts as the principal base for Russia's decaying Northern Fleet and is the main launching area for a good deal of Russia's still formidable armoury of intercontinental ballistic missiles (ICBMs). It is, however, important to note that issues with military significance were explicitly excluded from the initiative.

Lipponen's speech was not only a list of obstacles and hardships. The 'positive' side of the initiative was based on the idea that in the future the EU will be increasingly dependent on imported energy and that there are vast reserves of these resources in the north-western parts of Russia. However, in order to exploit these reserves, the region needs an immense amount of investment in basic infrastructure, including rail and road connections, harbours, airports, border crossing facilities as well as improved telecommunication systems. These are all things that, according to Lipponen, the ND could help to provide. In sum, the ND envisaged by the prime minister and later realized by the European Commission is a hybrid policy for the EU's eastern periphery that contains elements of both stabilization and integration.[10]

As can be seen, the high level of ambition in the original thinking concerning the initiative is equally matched by the number and scale of the challenges that the Northern Dimension should tackle. Therefore, it is somewhat surprising that the ways of delivering the envisaged initiative were painted with a very broad brush. Lipponen's approach can be summed up as 'no new money, no new institutions', as it explicitly made clear that benefits to be derived from the ND would come from a better coordination of already existing policies and instruments. However, this emphasis also reflected the strategic undertone of the initiative, which was that the ND was to be achieved through an identification of clear priorities for future actions.

It is here that the initiative reveals some of its internal paradoxes. Lipponen's claim that the ND could basically be funded by means of the better use of existing funds seems ludicrous when compared to the ambitious objectives he had just enumerated. This statement does, however, become more understandable when it is seen as a crucial part of the Finnish marketing strategy: it is easy to see that a Northern Dimension explicitly asking for vast amounts of EU funding would never have flown.

But although perhaps a necessary choice, it has had the negative consequence of limiting the future scope of the initiative, especially when it comes to funding, and thus hampering the efforts at making the initiative more concrete. However, the approach has its merits, too. The idea that the policy would be implemented via the existing organizational frameworks, such as the Council of the Baltic Sea States (CBSS), the Barents Euro–Arctic Council (BEAC) and the Arctic Council (AC) makes especial sense, as even by 1997 the problem was that the proliferation of regional cooperation schemes in Northern Europe had reached such a level that the organizations were stepping on each other's toes. This will be discussed in more detail later on.

Lipponen's speech was met with a generally positive reaction from various member states. For example, the prime minister of Portugal, António Guterres, and the British minister for European affairs, Douglas Henderson, rushed to express their approval.[11] As a result, the initiative's elevation on the EU agenda was rather swift: it sailed through the European Councils of Luxembourg (1997) and Cardiff (1998), and landed in Vienna in December 1998, where the Commission presented its views on the topic in the form of an interim report. In this report, much like Prime Minister Lipponen's original speech, the actual content of the Northern Dimension was described mainly as a list of negations – that is, what it was not supposed to be: no new institutions, no more money, and no new form of regionally based cooperation in Northern Europe. Instead, the central notion was the 'added value' that the ND should bring, mainly through increased coordination of existing actions in the North. The report also clarified the geographical scope of the initiative, giving it a much more regional focus, as the global dimensions of the United States and Canada were excluded. Instead, the Northern Dimension would consist of EU member states together with the so-called partner countries Estonia, Iceland, Latvia, Lithuania, Norway, Poland and Russia.[12]

The usefulness of the concept has, however, been diminished by the fact that despite Prime Minister Lipponen's original intentions, the Northern Dimension has not been devised along strategic lines whereby certain issue-areas would be given priority over others. Also, the ways and means by which the goals were to be reached have remained largely undefined. This is particularly well illustrated in the interim report, which emerged as a vague declaration in which every problem, threat and remote economic prospect in the region were enumerated, while concrete proposals for the realization of these goals were almost entirely neglected.

The Vienna European Council invited the Council to identify, on the basis of the Commission's interim report, guidelines for action in 'the relevant fields'.[13] In turn, the General Affairs Council in May 1999 set its own guidelines for the implementation of the Northern Dimension, mainly along the earlier lines of the Commission, as the 'added value' in the initiative would come solely from the increased synergies of better coordination and complementarity of the Community and member state actions in Northern Europe.[14] The Cologne European Council in June 1999 noted the Council's earlier guidelines and invited the partner countries to take part in the Foreign Ministers' Conference on the Northern Dimension, which was to be arranged in Helsinki during the Finnish presidency in November the same year.[15] Originally, making the ND more concrete with the Foreign Ministers' Conference was supposed to be among the highlights of the Finnish presidency. Unfortunately, the timing, which so far had been on the Finns' side, was turning against them, as the year preceding the presidency was an exceptionally unfortunate one for the initiative's prospects.

First, the financial and political crisis in Russia of August 1998 evaporated European hopes for a rapid transformation of the Russian economy. Second, the war in Kosovo in the first half of 1999 turned the gaze of the EU southwards just at the time when it was supposed to be focused on the North. And finally, the second Chechnya war, which began in earnest in October 1999, crippled the EU–Russian relationship. Both the Northern Dimension and the Foreign Ministers' Conference fell victim to these three events and thus it was no surprise that there was a failure to agree on almost anything substantively new, other than that the Helsinki European Council should decide on drafting an action plan for the Northern Dimension.[16] Indeed, the Helsinki European Council did then invite the Commission to prepare an action plan.[17]

The action plan

An important milestone for the initiative was reached in June 2000 when the Feira European Council adopted the first action plan. The document simultaneously represented an important milestone and a source of further disappointment and even disillusionment with the Northern Dimension. It was undeniably the final breakthrough for the initiative, as the existence of an action plan consolidated its place on the EU agenda. But the actual content of the document can be described as falling short of the mark, as it failed to develop a truly strategic approach to the concept and make it more concrete. In certain respects it actually managed to dilute some of the more ambitious features to be found in the original Finnish approach.

The action plan, initially adopted for the years 2000–3, is divided into two sections. The first, horizontal, section lays out the framework for the Northern Dimension. The main idea, and limitation, of the dimension is spelled out very clearly at the beginning, where the action plan states that the added value is to be gained 'through reinforced coordination and complementarity in EU and Member States' programmes and enhanced collaboration between the countries in Northern Europe' and that 'the Northern Dimension is an on-going process without a specific budgetary appropriation'.[18] Otherwise, the horizontal section is almost identical to the earlier Commission report as it goes through the most important sectors in the initiative.

The role of the action plan in actually guiding the actions of the member states is set out in rather careful wording, as the document is called a 'political recommendation to be taken into account by relevant actors whenever appropriate'.[19] As a political obligation, this is of the weakest kind. Moreover, it is indeed in the realm of 'relevant actors' that the biggest setbacks in terms of the content of the initiative can be identified. The role of the three most important regional councils – the CBSS, BEAC and AC – which in the original initiative had played a central role in the implementation of the Northern Dimension, has been reduced to a vaguely worded statement that they 'may assume a significant role in consultation with the Council of the EU in identifying common interests of the Northern Dimension region'.[20] The role of other, mainly sub-regional actors, such as the Nordic and the Baltic Councils of Ministers, has been reduced even further: they 'may also be consulted in accordance with EU internal rules and procedures when implementing the Action Plan'.[21]

The second, operational part of the action plan gives an in-depth account of different sectors ranging from infrastructure and environment to public health and justice and home affairs.[22] The list is once again quite exhaustive, but the action plan fails to bring significant new 'added value' in terms of clear priorities that would in turn easily yield concrete proposals or actions to be taken during the first four-year term.

Although the official documents do not reflect any clear strategy and prioritization of actions in different issue areas, the implementation phase of the Northern Dimension has yielded some results. When one examines the actual work done under the auspices of the initiative, three sectors seem to be of special importance: the environment, combating organized crime, and cooperation in information technology (IT). All these three issue-areas have their own special initiatives, such as the Northern Dimension Environmental Partnership (NDEP), Northern *e*Dimension and the CBSS Task Force for Organized Crime. In addition, all these initiatives have been centred largely on the north-western parts of Russia – to such an extent that it has almost become the sole geographical focus of ND.

The European Union's increasing presence in Northern Europe

The Northern Dimension has not had a visible impact on making the EU a more strategic actor in the North. This is largely due to the fact that it has been based on an inadequate prioritization of aims as well as a largely insufficient allocation of means for the realization of the broad range of objectives enumerated under the aegis of the initiative. Yet it is important to keep in mind that this fact has not prevented the EU from having a considerable impact on the events in the region. However, the question that this raises is to what extent the results achieved so far have been intentional (i.e. reflecting 'strategic thinking') or whether they just reflect accidental and arbitrary outcomes of the contacts and exchanges taking place within the dense network of overlapping actors and policies in the North.

What does seem clear is that the elevation of the Northern Dimension on the EU agenda during the latter part of the 1990s reflects the growing importance of the Union in Northern Europe in two important and largely interrelated respects. First, the memberships of Finland and Sweden cemented the EU's presence in the region, and consequently brought the EU to the attention of the North.[23] This is largely due to the fact that the direct presence of the Union in the region has exposed it to new conditions and opportunities – but also challenges and threats – to which it has had to try to find appropriate responses. Second, and largely flowing from the first point, these attempts, such as the adoption of the Northern Dimension policy, have in their turn increased the EU's presence in the region, tying it closely into the ongoing and largely overlapping multi-level game that is being played in the northern reaches of Europe. This has resulted in a somewhat self-sustaining dynamic where there are growing pressures for an ever-increasing EU presence and the need for more coherent policies and increased funding for cooperation in Northern Europe. This dynamism is likely to grow only stronger with the ongoing eastern enlargement.

Instead of considering whether or not the EU has become a more strategic actor in the North, it might be wiser to look at the other avenues through which the EU has managed to have an impact on the events in Northern Europe. Accordingly, studying the EU's growing presence in the North could be a more viable starting point for the analysis. As David Allen and Michael Smith have suggested, presence is a useful approach, especially in the case of the EU, as it does not make so rigid and essentially statist assumptions of coherence and capabilities as the term 'actor' does.[24] Studying presence gives us a way of getting around the problem of the largely 'unstrategic' nature of the EU's policies in the region.

The problem in assessing the EU's presence in the North is that it is at times hard to distinguish such a presence from those of other actors and fora at work in the region. This especially applies to the Northern Dimension, as it is hard to pinpoint exactly what would be missing from the scene if the initiative did not exist. However, maybe there is no need to do this, as we can also examine to what extent the sub-regional actors are actually implementing the EU agenda. As Allen and Smith have suggested, the impact of a presence can be discerned from the place it occupies in the perceptions and expectations of policymakers, its credentials and legitimacy, and the capacity to act and mobilize resources.[25]

Northern Europe provides a good environment for the EU's presence. No one can doubt the EU's legitimacy or its capacity to mobilize resources in the region. The EU also occupies a central place in the perceptions of all the relevant political players in the North.[26] Moreover, the wide spectrum of opportunities and challenges that the EU faces, as discussed in the first part of this chapter, is matched by the diversity of different institutional mechanisms that have been devised in order to tackle these problems. Indeed, the post-Cold War Northern Europe has been a laboratory of innovative thinking resulting in a dense network of often overlapping regional arrangements all aimed at bridging the former East–West divide. Consequently, and as Pertti Joenniemi has noted, the North has become one of the most regionalized parts of Europe.[27]

As a result, the North has an extensive and multi-layered network of overlapping organizations in which the EU is at least partially involved, either directly through the Commission or indirectly through its member states. First, there are the already mentioned three regional councils, ranging from the high North to the southern shores of the Baltic Sea: the Arctic Council, the Barents Euro-Arctic Council and the Council of the Baltic Sea States. In addition to these three, there are other councils with a more limited membership, such as the Nordic Council, the Nordic Council of Ministers and the Baltic Council. As a consequence, there is considerable overlap in the regional councils in terms of both their geographical scope and their thematic interests.[28] There are also new forms of subregional cooperation whereby sub-state actors, such as administrative regions, chambers of commerce, universities, cities and even small towns and municipalities are networking and fostering cooperation.

The problem for the EU and its Northern Dimension is that it does not exercise authority over these diverse actors in the North, with all of them acting independently of the EU and not being obliged to take heed of the ND agenda. A striking example of the lack of rather basic coordination between the EU and the regional organizations can be found in the 2002 annual progress report on the implementation of the action plan. The report is based on information provided solely by the Commission and does not contain any information about the actions of the other partners and organizations which, according to the action plan, were supposed to be central to the implementation of the initiative. To be fair, this handicap is also acknowledged by the report, which admits that 'it would certainly be helpful if partners could provide such information with a view to preparing a more comprehensive report [in the future]'.[29] In the future, the EU would, however, seem to have one instrument through which it can influence the actors' behaviour in the North: money. Many of these organizations are increasingly looking towards the EU and its Northern Dimension for funding.

Member state policies in the North

In addition to the direct presence that the EU enjoys in different councils, individual member states of course have their own policies for the region.

For example, Finland, in addition to actively promoting a EU-wide approach, has also devised its own policy for Northern Europe. Since 1990 Finland has had a special 'Neighbouring Areas Policy' for bilateral cooperation, through which it has channelled almost €1 billion in aid to the areas adjacent to Finland (north-west Russia, the three Baltic countries and Kaliningrad).[30] More recently, Finland has, however, sought to align this policy closely with the Northern Dimension, seeing it as a national instrument to be used for the implementation of the initiative.[31]

Finland is by no means the only northern member state with its own independent approaches and policies. Sweden had a high profile in the Baltic Sea region throughout the 1990s. Sweden has been especially active in the development of the CBSS, using, among other things, its presidency in 1996 to deepen political cooperation by engaging the prime ministers in the Council's work.[32] But Sweden has sought to consolidate its position also on the bilateral level. A concrete manifestation of this has been the so-called 'Baltic Billion Fund'. The first programme period (1996–8) allocated 1 billion Swedish crones (approximately €110 million) especially in the areas of food, energy systems, exchange of know-how, infrastructure and the environment, so as also to stimulate trade and investment.[33] In the second fund, covering the period 1999–2003, another billion crones have been allocated. The fund is motivated by Swedish self-interest, as its objective is 'to stimulate economic exchange, growth and employment in Sweden and the Baltic region, and to strengthen the position of Swedish companies in the region'.[34]

Therefore, there is not only cooperation but also a natural element of competition between the EU member states. This is so on the general level of activities, where not only governments but also businesses, regions and even municipalities compete for influence, standing and markets in the region. This seems also to be the case of the Northern Dimension, where the member states appear to have diverging interests and expectations on where the emphasis should be in terms of the actual content of the initiative. When one compares the different interpretations given by Sweden and Denmark in their EU presidency programmes with the view put forward originally by Finland, one can easily discern some clear differences. Whereas Finland emphasized the role of the north-western parts of Russia, Sweden gave a much more southerly interpretation, stressing the importance of the Baltic Sea region and especially Kaliningrad.[35] By contrast, the first version of the Danish programme placed its emphasis once again on the North but with a different twist compared to Finland: the Danes speak of an 'Arctic window' with Greenland playing a major role.[36] The waters can be, however, muddied even further, as the Northern Dimension is not the only initiative of its kind in the region. In fact, since its inception the ND has had its almost identical counterpart in the form of the US 'Northern European Initiative'.

The US Northern European initiative

The birth of the Northern European Initiative (NEI) coincided with the Northern Dimension, as Assistant Secretary of State Marc Grossman introduced the NEI to the Nordic and Baltic foreign ministers in Bergen, Norway, in September 1997.[37] It has, however, at no point achieved the same level of publicity, or academic interest, as its EU counterpart.

Whereas the Northern Dimension explicitly excludes security policy from its agenda, the NEI largely has its origins in issues of security of the hardest kind. It is often seen as a response to the perceived impossibility of extending NATO membership to the three Baltic countries during the first round of NATO enlargement in 1997–9. The NEI is, however, based on a different logic as compared with traditional alliance formation, as it stresses the soft spectrum of security and promotes cooperative security through growing integration and cross-border networking as a means to achieve security.[38] In this respect, the similarities between the NEI and the ND are striking. Like its EU counterpart, the NEI stresses the role of increased coordination in bringing the desired benefits. In addition, the NEI has identified six priority areas for action: business and trade, law enforcement, civil society, energy, the environment, and public health[39] – all identical to, or compatible with, the objectives of the ND discussed earlier in the chapter.

The NEI has been seen as a testing ground for the United States in developing entirely new approaches to international relations, aimed at transcending power politics and promoting regional integration. Indeed, those few scholars who have been engaged in doing research on the initiative have been eager to read many 'post-modern' qualities into the US approach.[40] This interpretation has also been given some support by US officials. This was especially the case during the Clinton presidency, when on numerous occasions the qualitatively new role of the NEI in abolishing the 'most failed principle of international politics . . . which is the balance of power itself' – as one official put it[41] – was repeatedly emphasized.

With the Bush administration, the continuation of the NEI has been put into question. The apparent increase in US unilateralism has been seen as boding ill for the concept. Despite the fact that the new administration has continued to pay some lip service to the concept,[42] even a superficial glance at the Web pages dedicated to the NEI reveals how the situation has changed from the Clinton era as the amount of material available concerning the initiative has experienced a dramatic drop.[43] It seems logical that the NEI now faces the risk of being sidelined by the ongoing NATO enlargement – the very process it was originally meant to replace.

Despite its relatively modest manifestations so far, the NEI has not been an easy thing for the EU to manage. As Christopher Browning has pointed out, negative perceptions or a total lack of interest in the NEI has been apparent on the EU side.[44] According to David Arter, part of the 'blame' for this state of affairs belongs to the French, who have been suspicious of US actions in the region.[45] Also, the Commission has been less than enthusiastic about the NEI, preferring to keep the ND as an EU-only exercise. However, the EU is not without divisions on this, as the Nordic member states seem to support a stronger US role in the region. For example, Lipponen's original initiative made the links to the United States, and to a lesser extent to Canada, explicit. In addition, Lipponen has continued to emphasize the role of the United States and the NEI in the Northern Dimension.[46] Also, Sweden views the continued US presence as beneficial for the region.[47] It is, however, important to note that this emphasis does not necessarily have anything to do with the soft security dimensions spelled out in the Northern Dimension, but rather is closely related to the two non-aligned countries' wish to balance the predominance of Russian military power in the region.[48]

The Northern Dimension and the triple challenge of dimensionalization, externalization and pillarization

On a more general note, the Northern Dimension has highlighted three problems in the way the EU conducts its external relations. First, it has revealed a growth of what might be called 'dimensionalization'. It is perhaps too simplistic to argue that there is a clear-cut North–South divide within the Union, but it is evident that the previous enlargements, together with the impending one for 2004, have brought increased diversity into the Union. This is unavoidable, and in a sense natural, as the member states, both old and new, do of course bring their own priorities and national interests to the common table. The question that does emerge, however, is how these different sets of priorities can be made to fit together in the future to merit the label of a 'European foreign policy'.

In this respect, the Northern Dimension represents only one of the different dimensions that the EU has and will have. The other, already well-established one is the 'southern dimension', which includes the Mediterranean, North Africa as well as the Middle East.[49] This dimension already has its own mechanisms in the form of the so-called Barcelona Process and the MEDA fund. In addition, there is also an emerging 'eastern dimension', where the new neighbours that the EU will soon have – Belarus, Moldova, Ukraine, and also, increasingly, Russia – will require special attention in the future.[50] For example, Poland has already made clear that it intends to advocate a policy for this 'eastern dimension'.[51] At the beginning of 2003, well before its actual date of likely EU accession in May 2004, the Polish government presented its future EU partners with a background paper outlining the content of the 'eastern dimension'. According to news sources, the Poles argued in the paper for a new dimension by using vocabulary essentially borrowed from the ND: the aim of the initiative would be to 'eradicate divisions between the enlarged Union and its eastern neighbours' by promoting stability, security and prosperity in Ukraine, Belarus, Moldova and Russia. The main aim of the new dimension would be to find a suitable compromise that would meet the new neighbours' demands for closer ties with the EU while ensuring that actual EU membership would not be on the cards.[52]

The proces of 'dimensionalization' does not by any means stop there. In fact, it is to be foreseen that the membership of Bulgaria and Romania would result in a 'south-eastern dimension' in which the Black Sea would become significant. One can also already discern a 'south-western dimension' in which the Balkans can be seen as presenting the EU with a specific set of challenges. Moreover, the possible membership of Turkey would present the EU with a host of new geographical dimensions, as the EU would not only come to share a common border with such countries as Armenia, Georgia, Iran, Iraq and Syria but also become more directly engaged in the 'Great Game' over the resources of the Caspian Sea and the conflicts in the Caucasus.

One of the biggest issues behind the divergence in member states' interest between these different dimensions will be the competition for scarce (financial) resources in the external relations of the EU. There already seems to be a certain North/East–South divide whereby the northern member states are eager to increase spending in the North and East, whereas the southern member states are naturally concerned about being sidelined in terms of future funds, particularly after the next round of enlargement.[53] In addition, according to a study conducted by the Trans-European Policy Studies Association (TEPSA) in 1998, the southern member states perceive the existence of a Northern Dimension as a potential threat to their own national interests.[54] One consequence is that the southern member states have an interest, although an obstructive one, in relation to the ND: their main priority is in limiting the importance of northern issues on the European agenda as compared to the relative importance of the 'southern dimension'. This tendency was highlighted at the NDEP pledging conference in July 2002, when the only member states giving money for the fund were northern: Finland, Denmark, the Netherlands and Sweden all pledged €10 million for the fund, with promises of future assistance coming from France and the United Kingdom.[55]

Second, the Northern Dimension has blurred the clear demarcation between inside and outside in policy formulation and implementation within the EU. The partner-orientated approach in the ND has meant that the EU has been required to allow the views of outsiders ('the partner countries') to affect policymaking in the North.[56] This 'externalization' of EU policymaking has proved to be problematic. On the one hand, it has not been greeted with enthusiasm within the EU, as it runs largely counter to the standard EU approach to external and foreign relations, an approach in which, especially for the second pillar, the EU shows little willingness to prepare its policies in cooperation with its intended 'objects'.[57] The gradually diminishing role of the regional councils in the implementation of the ND can be seen as a symptom of the pervasiveness of this thinking. On the other hand, there are also increasing signs that the EU door is not sufficiently open to satisfy the outsiders either. In particular, Russia has repeatedly voiced its frustration over its inability to influence policymaking in the Northern Dimension.[58]

Third, the Northern Dimension injects EU external relations with an entirely new logic, which requires a vastly increased degree of internal coherence and coordination between different programmes and policies. In order to be implemented successfully, the ND therefore requires a multi-level approach, in which not only the EU and its member states but also other existing actors in the North must play a significant role.[59] Moreover, the ND requires horizontal coordination and cooperation within the EU across previously separate programmes, pillars and initiatives.[60] Although there have been some attempts at bringing about increased coordination and complementarity of the existing instruments, such as two inventories on current activities[61] and the guide on how to combine Interreg and TACIS funding,[62] the results have so far been fairly modest. Indeed, overcoming the sectoral and pillarized logic of the Union has proved to be an extremely difficult challenge for the Northern Dimension, which seems to be effectively bogged down in the infighting of the Brussels bureaucracy.[63]

Conclusions

The Northern Dimension is an ambitious political initiative. It has sought to raise the EU's awareness of the peculiarities of Northern Europe while promoting a change in the way it conducts its foreign policy. It has also placed a special emphasis on the EU's relations with Russia, seeking avenues through which increased cooperation and even modest integration between the two could take place.

Yet despite its ambitions – or perhaps because of them – the ND has been only a partial success. It has managed to raise awareness of the North in the EU in general, and the very fact that it has managed to secure its place on EU's highly competitive agenda can be considered a victory in itself. But instead of changing the rules of the game, it has only managed to highlight the various bottlenecks and internal contradictions that confront the EU as an international actor. As an EU policy, the ND has itself become a victim of these weaknesses. So far, it has suffered from a lack of a truly strategic perspective that would allow the EU to devise an action plan with clearly established priorities and guidelines. Instead, it often seems that the ND has lost most of its momentum, owing to the bureaucratic inertia inside the Commission. Also, the horizontal coordination between the different programmes has proved to be problematic.

The fact that the EU is not the only relevant player in the implementation of the ND makes matters even more complicated. There are a host of regional and sub-regional actors in the North, and the element of competition between these actors often yields sub-optimal results, unnecessary duplication and wasted resources. What is more, and as was illustrated in the 2002 annual progress report on the implementation of the action plan, there is often a lack of basic knowledge concerning the actions of other actors.

At first sight, the Northern Dimension appears a laudable idea that should serve a good purpose as the 'organizing principle' for cooperation in the North. However, the realization of this objective has proved to be very difficult: mere presence is clearly not enough. In fact, the presence approach reveals the very constraints that the EU faces in using power in the region. Despite its supremacy in terms of financial and political resources combined with its institutional finesse, the EU has not been able to impose its will on either the regional organizations or the main 'target' of the Northern Dimension, Russia. Instead, there seems to be an ongoing debate concerning the ends and the means of the initiative, and it is a debate that is increasingly being conducted in a polemical and even confrontational fashion. This is true in the context of the EU–Russian relationship, but it also has relevance on the level of regional councils, which are growing increasingly frustrated at the lack of concrete projects bearing the ND label.

As a consequence, although the successive rounds of enlargement have increased the EU's presence in the region, this has not automatically translated into increased 'actorness'. Herein lies the problem, as the EU has been exposed to a host of new demands, challenges and threats that if left unanswered can become serious liabilities in the future. In a way, the situation in the North is Christopher Hill's 'capability–expectations gap' revisited.[64]

Nevertheless, the current situation creates both an opening and a demand for the EU to take the lead in Northern Europe. For this to happen, two prerequisites have to be met. First, the EU has to be willing to assume this role. This means that the EU and its member states have to come to an agreement about the importance of the North for the EU in general and what it wants to achieve in the region in particular. Second, this requires the devising of a more coherent strategy for the region. This strategy would have to entail a clear set of goals and priorities as well as a list of concrete steps that the EU proposes to take in order to achieve these goals. In this respect, the Northern Dimension can be seen as a good start – but nothing more. It remains too vague and underfunded as it is.

There is, however, a paradoxical 'danger' that the increase in the EU's presence in the region could ultimately be the undoing of the Northern Dimension. As the new century advances, dealings with the Baltic countries and Poland will become part of the EU's internal dynamics. As a consequence, Russia will soon be the main 'partner country' in the North, accompanied by the small countries Iceland and Norway, and even they have a more important forum for discussions with the EU in the form of the European Economic Area.[65] Therefore, there is a risk that the most ambitious, as well as most problematic, features of the ND will lose their relevance as it potentially becomes a mere regional component of the EU's policy on Russia.

This should not be seen in entirely bleak terms. It is possible that the Northern Dimension could reach its apex in a more subordinated role. If realized, its stated emphasis on concrete projects could complement the EU's otherwise non-existent Russian strategy very well. What is more, the ND could act as a model for the other emerging 'dimensions' in the post-enlargement EU: fostering positive mutual interdependence, and making the EU's external border more 'porous' and conducive to cross-border cooperation. These are all mechanisms through which functional integration could be encouraged. If such integration comes about, then the ND could help the EU to devise a strategy for its other neighbouring areas as well. It would not be a strategy in a sense that 'strategy' has been traditionally understood. But then again, the EU is not an actor in the classical sense either.

Notes

1 Hereafter, the Northern Dimension (ND). When written in capital letters the term refers to the specific policy of the Union; if written otherwise, it refers to a more general understanding of the term.

2 Norwegians voted against their membership in a referendum in November 1994.

3 And also Austria. This is not, however, discussed in this context, as it does not pertain to the Northern Dimension.

4 H. Ojanen, 'Introduction: Contested Compatibility', in H. Ojanen, G. Herolf and R. Lindahl, *Non-alignment and European Security Policy: Ambiguity at Work*, Programme on the Northern Dimension of the CFSP, no. 6, Helsinki and Berlin: Finnish Institute of International Affairs and Institut für Europäische Politik, 2000.

5 This kind of analysis is not, of course, without precedents. The best-known example is to be found in D. Allen and M. Smith, 'Western Europe's Presence in the Contemporary International Arena', in M. Holland (ed.), *The Future of European Political Cooperation: Essays on Theory and Practice*, London: Macmillan, 1991, pp. 19–39.

6 H. Ojanen, 'How to Customize Your Union: Finland and the "Northern Dimension of the EU"', in *Northern Dimensions 1999: Yearbook of Finnish Foreign Policy*, Helsinki: Finnish Institute of International Affairs, 1999, pp. 16–17.

7 Paavo Lipponen, 'The European Union Needs a Policy for the Northern Dimension', speech to the 'Barents Region Today' Conference, Rovaniemi, Finland, 15 September 1997.

8 Paavo Lipponen, 'Letter from Paavo Lipponen to the President of the EU

Commission, Jacques Santer', Helsinki, 14 April 1997, Prime Minister's Office, Ref. 97/1510, quoted in Nicola Catellani, 'Short and Long-Term Dynamics in the EU's Northern Dimension', COPRI Working Papers 41, 2001.

9 These challenges have been analysed in detail in C. Pursiainen, 'Soft Security Problems in Northwest Russia', in H. Moroff (ed.), *European Soft Security Policies: The Northern Dimension*, Programme on the Northern Dimension of the CFSP, no. 17, Helsinki and Berlin: Finnish Institute of International Affairs and Institut für Europäische Politik, 2002.

10 See A. Missiroli's contribution in this volume (Chapter 2).

11 *Helsingin Sanomat*, 1 November and 4 November 1997.

12 *A Northern Dimension for the Policies of the European Union*, COM (1998) 589, 25 November 1998. Online. Available http: <http://www.europa.eu.int/comm/external_relations/north_dim/doc/com1998_0589en.pdf> (accessed 24 June 2002).

13 *Vienna European Council, Presidency Conclusions*, 11 and 12 December 1998. Online. Available http:. <http://ue.eu.int/en/Info/eurocouncil/index.htm> (accessed 22 April 2002).

14 See the *Conclusions of the 2186th Council meeting* – General Affairs – Brussels, 31 May 1999, PRES/99/171.

15 *Cologne European Council, Presidency Conclusions*, 3 and 4 June 1999. Online. Available http: <http://ue.eu.int/en/Info/eurocouncil/index.htm> (accessed 22 April 2002).

16 *Foreign Ministers' Conference on the Northern Dimension, Conclusions of the Chair*, 11 and 12 November 1999. Online: Available http: <http://www.europa.eu.int/comm/external_relations/north_dim/conf/formin1/index.htm> (accessed 22 April 2002).

17 *Helsinki European Council, Presidency Conclusions*, 10 and 11 December 1999. Online. Available http: <http://ue.eu.int/en/Info/eurocouncil/index.htm> (accessed 22 April 2002).

18 *Action Plan for the Northern Dimension with External and Cross-border Policies of the European Union 2000–2003*, 9401/00 (14 June 2000), I.1, I.6. Online. Available http: <http://www.europa.eu.int/comm/external_relations/north_dim/ndap/06_00_en.pdf> (accessed 22 April 2002).

19 Ibid., I.5.

20 Ibid., I.22.

21 Ibid., I.22.

22 The sectors found in the action plan are energy, transport, telecommunications/information society, environment and natural resources, nuclear safety, public health, trade, business cooperation and investment promotion, human resources development and research, justice and home affairs, regional and cross-border cooperation, and a special reference made to Kaliningrad.

23 For an account of the earlier development of the EU's presence in the North, see E. Antola, 'The Presence of the European Union in the North', in H. Haukkala (ed.), *Dynamic Aspects of the Northern Dimension*, Jean Monnet Unit Working Paper 4, Turku: University of Turku, 1999, pp. 118–24.

24 Allen and Smith, 'Western Europe's Presence', p. 98.

25 Ibid., pp. 97–8.

26 Antola, 'The Presence of the European Union in the North', p. 118.

27 P. Joenniemi, 'Bridging the Iron Curtain? Co-operation around the Baltic Rim', COPRI Working Papers 22, 1999, p. 3. Joenniemi's observation originally concerned the Baltic Sea region alone, but it is fair to say that the argument can be extended to the whole of Northern Europe.

28 For an in-depth survey of the regional organizations in the North, see Å. Mariussen, H. Aalbu and M. Brandt, *Regional Organisations in the North*, Studies

on Foreign Policy Issues Report 5, Oslo: Royal Norwegian Ministry of Foreign Affairs, 2000.

29 *2002 Annual Progress Report on the Implementation of the Northern Dimension Action Plan*, Commission Staff Working Paper SEC (2002) 1296, 26 November 2002, p. 3. Online. Available http: <http://www.europa.eu.int/comm/external_ relations/north_dim/doc/progrep02.pdf> (accessed 3 February 2003).

30 'Suomen lähialueyhteistyö' (Finnish Neighbouring Areas Cooperation), a draft document of the Finnish Ministry of Foreign Affairs, 21 March 2002.

31 *Finland's Strategy for Cooperation in the Neighbouring Areas.* Online. Available http: <http://www.formin.fi/doc/eng/neighb/strategia/index.html> (accessed 24 June 2002).

32 L. Miles and B. Sundelius, '"EU Icing on a Baltic Cake": Swedish Policy towards the Baltic Sea and EU Northern Dimension', in L. Miles (ed.), *Sweden and the European Union Evaluated*, London: Continuum, 2000, p. 39.

33 Online. Available http: <http://www.utrikes.regeringen.se/inenglish/policy/ balticbillion/billion1.htm> (accessed 24 June 2002).

34 Online. Available http: <http://www.utrikes.regeringen.se/inenglish/policy/ balticbillion/index.htm> (accessed 24 June 2002).

35 *Programme of the Swedish Presidency of the European Union*, p. 23. Online. Available http: <http://eu2001.se/static/pdf/program/ordfprogram_eng.pdf> (accessed 21 April 2002).

36 *One Europe: Programme of the Danish Presidency of the EU*, p. 30. Online. Available http: <http://www.eu2002.dk/ewebeditpro2/upload/OW.Headline/130/EU%20UK.pdf> (accessed July 2002); and *The Danish Presidency in 2002.* Online: Available http: <http://www.um.dk/english/presidency/prec.asp> (accessed 28 April 2002).

37 C. S. Browning, 'A Multi-dimensional Approach to Regional Cooperation: The United States and the Northern European Initiative', *European Security*, 2001, vol. 10, no. 4: 84–108.

38 Ibid., p. 87.

39 Online. Available http: <http://www.state.gov/p/eur/rt/nei/c2214.htm> (accessed April 2002).

40 See Browning, 'A Multi-dimensional Approach'; E. Rhodes, 'The United States and the Northern Dimension: America's Northern Europe Initiative', paper presented to the 'The think-tank seminar on The Future of the Barents Euro-Arctic Co-operation and the Northern Dimension of Europe', Björkliden, Lapland, Sweden, 14–17 June 2001. Online. Available http: <http://www.bd.lst.se/ dimensionen/rapport/rhodes.pdf> (accessed 29 April 2002); and P. van Ham, 'Testing Cooperative Security in Europe's New North: American Perspectives and Policies', in D. Trenin and P. van Ham (eds), *Russia and the United States in Northern European Security*, Programme on the Northern Dimension of the CFSP no. 5, Helsinki and Berlin: Finnish Institute of International Affairs and Institut für Europäische Politik, 2000.

41 See speech by Robert E. Hunter at the Second Annual Conference on Security and Cooperation in the Baltic, Stockholm, December 1997. Online. Available http: <http://www.usis.usemb.se/bsconf/hunter.html> (accessed 24 June 2002). For a lengthier account of the US rhetoric, see Browning, 'A Multi-dimensional Approach', esp. pp. 91 7.

42 See the remarks of Under-Secretary of Political Affairs Marc Grossman to the foreign ministers of Estonia, Latvia and Lithuania in Washington in December 2001. Online. Available http: <http://www.state.gov/p/6918.htm> (accessed 24 June 2002).

43 Online. Available http: Clinton era: <http://www.state.gov/www/regions/eur/ nei/>; Bush era: <http://www.state.gov/p/eur/rt/nei/> (accessed 21 April 2002).

44 Browning, 'A Multi-dimensional Approach', p. 101.
45 D. Arter, 'Small State Influence within the EU: The Case of Finland's "Northern Dimension Initiative"', *Journal of Common Market Studies*, 2000, vol. 38, no. 5: 689.
46 For example, in August 2000 he drew positive links between the ND and the NEI. See P. Lipponen, 'The European Union Policy: The Northern Dimension from an Arctic Angle', Speech to the Fourth Conference of Parliamentarians of the Arctic Region, Rovaniemi, Finland, 28 August 2000. Online: Available http: <http://www.valtioneuvosto.fi/vn/liston/vnk.lsp?r=1996&k=en&old=953> (accessed 24 June 2002).
47 Miles and Sundelius, '"EU Icing on a Baltic Cake"', p. 39.
48 This point has been made in Browning, 'A Multi-dimensional Approach', p.102. For an in-depth analysis of Finnish security strategies, see T. Vaahtoranta and T. Forsberg, 'Finland's Three Security Strategies', in M. Jopp and S. Arnswald (eds), *The European Union and the Baltic States: Visions, Interests and Strategies for the Baltic Sea Region*, Programme on the Northern Dimension of the CFSP no. 2, Helsinki and Bonn: Finnish Institute of International Affairs and Institut für Europäische Politik, 1998.
49 See the contributions of R. Dannreuther and F. Tanner in this volume (Chapters 10 and 9 respectively).
50 See the contribution of A. Zakorski in this volume (Chapter 6).
51 *Financial Times*, 19 February 2002.
52 *Financial Times*, 28 January 2003. See also H. Haukkala, *Towards a Union of Dimensions: The Effects of the Eastern Enlargement on the Northern Dimension*, FIIA Report 2 (Helsinki: Finnish Institute of International Affairs, 2002). Online.   Available   http: <http://www.upi-fiia.fi/english/publications/upi_report/reports/fiia_report22002.pdf> (accessed 3 February 2003).
53 E. Barbé, 'Balancing Europe's Eastern and Southern Dimensions', in J. Zielonka (ed.), *Paradoxes of European Foreign Policy*, The Hague: Kluwer Law International, 1998, p. 126.
54 W. Wessels, *National vs. EU Foreign Policy Interests: Mapping 'Important' National Interests*, Cologne and Brussels: TEPSA, 1998, p. 15.
55 The largest donor was, however, the European Commission with €50 million. Norway and Russia also participated, with €10 million. *Helsingin Sanomat*, 9 July 2002.
56 H. Ojanen, 'Northern Dimension: Fuel for the EU's External Relations?', in H. Ojanen (ed.), *The Northern Dimension: Fuel for the EU?*, Programme on the Northern Dimension of the CFSP no. 12, Helsinki and Berlin: Finnish Institute of International Affairs and Institut für Europäische Politik, 2001, p. 225.
57 Ibid., p. 226.
58 See the speech of the Vice-Prime Minister Viktor Hristenko at the International Forum for the Northern Dimension, Lappeenranta, Finland, 22 October 2001.
59 For more on multi-level implementation of the Northern Dimension, see N. Catellani, 'The Multilevel Implementation of the Northern Dimension', in Ojanen (ed.), *The Northern Dimension*.
60 As Hanna Ojanen has put it, 'its [ND's] instruments stem from the first, its objectives from the second, and its problems from the third'. H. Ojanen, 'The EU and Its "Northern Dimension": An Actor in Search of a Policy, or a Policy in Search of an Actor?', *European Foreign Affairs Review*, 2000, vol. 5, no. 3: 374.
61 *A Northern Dimension for the Policies of the Union: An Inventory of Current Activities*, April 2001. Online. Available http: <http://www.europa.eu.int/comm/external_relations/north_dim/conf/formin2/invent_01.pdf>: and *A Northern*

Dimension for the Policies of the Union: An Inventory of Current Activities, September 1999. Online: Available http: <http://www.europa.eu.int/comm/external_relations/north_dim/doc/inventory.pdf> (both accessed on 28 April 2002).

62 *A Guide to Bringing INTERREG and Tacis Funding Together*, Luxembourg: Office for Official Publications of the European Communities, 2001. Online. Available http: <http://www.europa.eu.int/comm/external_relations/north_dim/conf/formin2/intreg_tac_en.pdf> (accessed 28 April 2002).

63 The external relations commissioner, Chris Patten, and the foreign minister of Sweden, Anna Lindh, acknowledged this in a joint article published on the eve of the Swedish EU presidency when they wrote that 'it has been absurdly difficult to link money from [these] different sources'. C. Patten and A. Lindh, 'The Northern Dimension of EU Foreign Policy: From Words to Action', *Financial Times*, 20 December 2000.

64 C. Hill, 'The Capabilities–Expectations Gap, or Conceptualizing Europe's International Role', *Journal of Common Market Studies*, 1993, vol. 31, no. 3: 305–28.

65 The debate on the possible Icelandic and Norwegian EU memberships has been picking up in recent months. Although the debates are still at their early stages, they might result in a situation where Russia will be the only 'partner country' in the Northern Dimension that remains external to the EU.

8　The Caucasus and Central Asia

Towards a non-strategy

S. Neil MacFarlane

Georgia will easily overcome the economic problems stemming from its withdrawal from the USSR. We will join the EEC.[1]

Introduction

This chapter has five components. The first addresses the regional context(s) of the Caucasus and Central Asia. What challenges do these areas pose for the European Union (EU) in its approach towards the 'wider Europe'? The second discusses EU interests in the region. The third examines how these interests are translated into policy and Commission activities and programmes. The fourth section looks at how effective EU activities have been. The final section looks at the implications of the analysis for future development of the EU's role in the Caucasus and Central Asia.

I take Central Asia to include the five former Soviet republics of Kazakhstan, Kyrgyzstan, Tajikistan, Turkmenistan and Uzbekistan. I take the Caucasus to mean the southern Caucasus (Armenia, Azerbaijan and Georgia). I realize that the EU has attempted to weigh in on northern Caucasian issues (notably the conflict in Chechnya), and that developments in the northern Caucasus do have significant effects for Russia's southern neighbours. However, it is impossible to separate out EU perspectives on the northern Caucasus from their broader approach to Russia.

In examining EU perspectives and approaches to these two regions, it is important to recognize that – unlike in the case of many of the other regions considered here – there is no real history of interaction between the Union and its member states on the one hand and the states of the southern Caucasus and Central Asia on the other. There were moments when these regions were important to West European Great Powers. Central Asia played a key role in the 'Great Game' between Russia and Britain in the last half of the nineteenth century. Azerbaijan's oil resources were a major focus of the emergent petroleum industry in Europe and the United States. During the period immediately after the Bolshevik revolution, Germany and then Britain intervened on a small scale in the southern Caucasus, while small elements of the British Army in India raided into Central Asia. But this was all a long way from the kind of systematic interaction that characterized the West's interactions with Poland, Hungary, Czechoslovakia and the Balkans. And it evaporated with the consolidation of Soviet power along the former Russian Empire's southern periphery. Consequently, there was no significant legacy or track record of European relations with the regions that are the focus of this chapter when the southern union republics of the Soviet Union emerged into independence in 1991.

It is important, finally, to stress that these two sub-regions are a key example of a broader developing challenge for the EU. The Union appears to have decided that the best way to deal with proximate states is to absorb them. Accession negotiations are well advanced in the Baltic Republics, Poland, the Czech Republic, Slovakia, Hungary and Slovenia. They may be moving more slowly in Romania and Bulgaria, as well as Croatia, and Cyprus, but the direction towards accession is reasonably clear. The logic of geography would suggest that, eventually, Albania, Macedonia and the Federal Republic of Yugoslavia or its successor states will find their way into the Union. Even Turkey now appears to be making the political and economic adjustments necessary for serious candidacy. I do not underestimate the difficulties of accession, particularly for the latter six states in this list. But the Union clearly sees these states as potential members.

The Caucasian and Central Asian states, like Russia and Ukraine, are equally clearly perceived not to be potential member states. They are, however, states whose fates are directly linked to the Union and in the stability and prosperity of which the Union has a strong interest. It therefore behooves the Union to have a 'strategy' towards these states. If their problems are not going to be subsumed within the framework of membership, what can the Union do to ensure that the problems they pose for the EU can be minimized and controlled?

The regional context

As regards the first issue, in many respects the states of the region are quite dissimilar. One should, therefore, take care in making generalizations. In territory, Armenia at the small end is 29.8 thousand square kilometres (Table 8.1). At the high end, Kazakhstan is 2.7 million square kilometres. In population, Armenia (again in the low position) is estimated by the World Bank to have a population of 3.8 million, while at the high end, Uzbekistan comes in at 25 million.[2] Some states in the region are almost completely homogeneous in ethnic terms (Armenia post-1988); some are highly diverse (Georgia and Kazakhstan). In economic terms, Tajikistan's gross national income (GNI) per capita is $180; Kazakhstan's is $1,350. In short, they vary substantially in power potential, in the depth of their economic and other difficulties, and in their potential for civil conflict.

Nonetheless, there are a number of general points that serve to distinguish this region usefully from a number of the others covered in this volume. One obvious point is the depth of the economic collapse affecting Central Asia and the Caucasus since 1991. The decline also lasted longer than that of, say, Central Europe. The recovery has generally been slower, not least because of the weakness of foreign investment outside the natural resources sector. A comparative examination of recorded trade flows suggests that the opening of these economies to the international economy has had little impact (again with the exception of energy producers), although the direction of trade statistics indicates greater diversification.

Although time series data for the region's economic performance are hard to come by (see Table 8.1), the figures of GDP shrinkage between 1991 and 2001 for the five countries for which data are available are not out of line with estimates for change in GDP in the official economy elsewhere in the region. In general, production plummeted, unemployment and underemployment rose substantially, and the personal savings of most of the population disappeared in the recurrent inflations of the early and mid-1990s. With the exception of the energy-based economies of Azerbaijan and Turkmenistan, the structure of regional economies shifted from industry towards services (and, in some instances, agriculture) (see Table 8.2). Income differentials rose as state-sector privatization processes favoured those connected to those in charge of the divestiture of state assets.

There was a return to limited growth in 1995 and 1996 throughout much of the region, associated with currency stabilization, and varying degrees

Table 8.1 General data

Country	Territory (square kilometres)	Population (2001 millions)	GDP 1991 (billion US$)	GDP 2001 (billion US$)	GNI/capita (2001 US$)
Armenia	29,800	3.8	3.1	2.1	570
Azerbaijan	90,500	8.1	—	5.7	660
Georgia	69,700	5.0	8.8	3.2	580
Kazakhstan	2,717,300	14.8	31.8	22.4	1,350
Kyrgyzstan	198,500	4.9	—	1.5	280
Tajikistan	143,100	6.2	4.5	1.1	180
Turkmenistan	488,100	5.5	—	7.0	950
Uzbekistan	447,400	25.0	23.7	7.8	550

Source: These figures are taken from the World Bank's Country Briefs and country 'Data at a Glance' for 2001 (published 2002).

Table 8.2 Structure of national economies

Country	Agriculture		Industry		Services	
	1991	2001	1991	2001	1991	2001
Armenia	25.0	27.7	49.2	34.2	25.8	38.1
Azerbaijan	32.8	17.0	31.4	45.2	35.8	37.9
Georgia	28.7	22.3	37.2	21.9	34.1	55.8
Kazakhstan	—	9.0	—	38.8	—	52.3
Kyrgyzstan	37.0	37.9	35.5	27.3	27.6	34.8
Tajikistan	37.9	24.4	37.5	23.6	24.6	52.1
Turkmenistan	32.3	28.8	31.0	50.7	36.7	20.5
Uzbekistan	37.0	34.5	36.6	22.9	26.5	42.6

Source: World Bank country 'Data at a Glance' for 2001 (published 2002).

Table 8.3 Current and projected growth in GDP

Country	2000	2001	2001–5
Armenia	6.0	9.6	—
Azerbaijan	11.1	9.9	7.6
Georgia	1.9	4.5	3.9
Kazakhstan	9.8	13.2	5.8
Kyrgyzstan	5.4	5.3	—
Tajikistan	8.3	10.2	—
Turkmenistan	17.6	20.5	3.8
Uzbekistan	3.8	4.5	2.6

Source: World Bank country 'Data at a Glance' for 2001 (published 2002).

of economic and monetary reform. Some of the rates of growth were impressive. These gains were largely reversed in 1997–8, however, as a result of the Russian currency crisis. Growth resumed for much of the region in 1998–2001 (see Table 8.3). However, the return to growth was from a very low starting point. Moreover, high growth was concentrated for the most part in the region's energy economies (Azerbaijan, Kazakhstan and Turkmenistan).[3] Energy-sector growth is a mixed blessing. In the context of more general economic stagnation, it may widen income differentials within these states. In addition, its foreign exchange effects ('the Dutch disease') may impede the growth of other sectors of the economy by making their products less competitive in international markets and with respect to imports. These effects can be destabilizing, particularly as the widely held popular expectations for general improvement are frustrated.

Turning to Table 8.4, which portrays the region's evolving engagement with the larger international economy, a similar pattern is evident. The majority of states in the region have seen little expansion in total trade,

Table 8.4 Engagement with the international economy (2000) (US$ million)

Country	Exports	Imports	FDI[a]	Debt	Debt service
Armenia[b]	342	877	605	1,001	52
Azerbaijan	2,046	1,465	4,092	1,219	132
Georgia	496	954	747	1,713	77
Kazakhstan	9,101	8,554	10,356	14,373	3,331
Kyrgyzstan	480	472	450	1,681	154
Tajikistan	652	773	191	876	94
Turkmenistan	2,526	2,201	500	1,888	1,072
Uzbekistan	2,740	2,814	1,012	4,626	834

Source: World Bank country 'Data at a Glance' (2001); except for cumulative FDI, which is from European Bank for Reconstruction and Development (EBRD) *Investment Profile 2001* (Armenia, Azerbaijan, Georgia, Kazakhstan, Kyrgyzstan, Tajikistan, Turkmenistan, Uzbekistan), London: EBRD, 2002.

Notes
a Cumulative 1993–2000.
b 2001 data, except FDI.

and, if one factors out the intra-Commonwealth of Independent States (CIS) dimension, largely minuscule trade with the outside world. The exception is again the energy producers. The same is true of investment. In areas other than energy production and transport (and, to a limited extent, the production and export of other resources such as gold in Uzbekistan and Kyrgyzstan), there is almost no foreign direct investment in the region. Even taking the energy sector into account, the total value of FDI in the Caucasus and Central Asia since 1991 is dwarfed by that into either the Czech Republic or Hungary.[4] It is also unsurprising, if depressing, that the countries with the highest debt:public revenue ratios tend to be those with the least capacity to repay (Georgia and Kyrgyzstan). This implies a growing debt service burden for states with minimal tax revenue, and consequent cuts in public services that – in a better world – people could depend on in times of economic crisis and penury.

These data on the regional economy obscure a larger human story. Part of it is told in Table 8.5, which indicates the region's fall from Soviet grace in terms of an aggregated measure of life expectancy at birth, literacy, gross primary, secondary and tertiary enrolment in education, and GDP per capita (US$ ppp). The points of comparison would be the USSR index and ranking of 0.92 and 31, respectively, in 1990. The practical manifestations of this collapse are found in falling educational and literacy standards, egregious public health standards, rising rates of communicable disease, declining life expectancy, rising criminality, growing levels of prostitution and people-trafficking, and massive male emigration.

To turn now to the political context, it is noteworthy that all regimes and political systems in the region have shown remarkable staying power after the dust of the first few years settled. Despite roughly four attempts

Table 8.5 Human Development Index ratings and rankings, 2000

Country	Index	Rank
Armenia	0.754	72
Azerbaijan	0.741	88
Georgia	0.748	81
Kazakhstan	0.750	79
Kyrgyzstan	0.712	102
Tajikistan	0.667	112
Turkmenistan	0.741	87
Uzbekistan	0.727	95

Source: United Nations Development Programme (UNDP) *Human Development Report, 2002* (New York: UNDP, 2002).

against the life of the Azeri president, Geidar Aliev, at least three against the Georgian leader, Eduard Shevardnadze, the assassination in the Armenian parliament chamber of the majority of the sitting government in 1999, one major attempt against Uzbekistan's president, Islam Karimov, and several attempts against Tajikistan's Emomali Rahmonov, these people appear to be survivors. Most led their republican communist parties prior to independence; at least two led republican KGBs before they became party secretaries. They benefit from a substantial residuum of authority from those days, and appointed many of the current officials in their countries earlier in their careers. That is to say, they not only know how to coerce, but have substantial patronage networks and ties of loyalty. Opposition parties and figures are, by contrast, weak.[5] The real business of government occurs outside the official channels in which the opposition is represented. Decisions are, therefore, non-transparent, and official politics is discredited, not least since this real business is massively corrupt.

One problem of this model of governance is that it fails to lay the basis for constitutional succession. The presidents of the region have expended considerable effort in controlling or removing serious challenges to their rule. The result is chronically poor governance, and the delegitimation of the regimes and the political and economic system that they have generated. All this raises real questions about what happens when the intimidating presence of the *vozhd'* (leader) disappears.

Underlying political structure and process, and aspects of political culture, mitigate against long-term, stable and successful processes of political change. The citizens of the region's states have little experience of meaningful participation in government. Given the approach and performance of successor regimes, they have little incentive to learn what democratic participation means, and good reason to avoid trying it. Citizens have little experience of forming parties and fighting elections; most opposition parties within the system tend, therefore, to be shallow and personality based. Finally, for many the idea of association of one's loyalty with a sovereign state and its collective purpose is weak, both for the reasons just discussed, and also because of the significant fragmentation of political society into ethnic and religious groups and family, clan and regional associations.

All this said, it is worth noting that in some of the states of the region (e.g. Georgia, Kyrgyzstan, Kazakhstan, Armenia), there is evidence of the emergence of viable organizations within civil society. The resignation of the cabinet in Georgia in 2001 as a result of massive demonstrations in Tbilisi suggested that, on occasion, civil society organizations can have a significant positive impact. However, it is worth noting that some of the most powerful civil society organizations actually make the government look pretty good. For example, the Abkhaz 'parliament in exile' in Georgia is quite deliberately attempting to undermine the ceasefire in that conflict while advocating the complete suppression of any Abkhaz governmental structures, if not the complete removal of this 'foreign' people. The Islamic Movement of Uzbekistan (IMU) is a civil society organization; it is also a terrorist organization dedicated to the creation of radical Islamic states throughout the region.

Moreover, there is hardly a trend in the region as a whole towards the emergence of a civil society that might constrain those who govern, and hold them accountable for their actions. The pattern appears to be not so much of civil society reaching up to constrain the state, but of the state, or powerful elements within it, reaching down into civil society to remove people who become excessively annoying. Examples, in the most 'liberal' country of the region – Georgia – include the effort by ex-Interior Minister Targamadze to shut the television channel Rustavi 2, the assassination of the Megrel military leader Akaki Eliava, allegedly by agents of the National Security Ministry, and the 'suicide' and subsequent smearing of Rustavi 2's popular news anchor in 2000.

Social fragmentation brings us to civil and interstate conflict. Two states in the Caucasus have frozen conflicts. Prospects for moving beyond cease-fires to political settlements both in Georgia (Abkhazia) and in Azerbaijan (Nagorno-Karabakh) remain poor. Leaders in both countries fear that significant concessions might undermine their hold on power. Substantial economic interests have evolved around the conflicts (e.g. the smuggling of alcohol and drugs through South Ossetia, kidnapping and timber trade in Abkhazia, and illicit petroleum trade from Azerbaijan to Armenia). It is not entirely clear, given the slow erosion of leaders' power in both Georgia and Azerbaijan, that they could impose settlements on those who are already looking beyond their era. The conflict in Chechnya continues, although at a lower level, with the potential for spillover into the southern Caucasus evident, for example, in Russian air raids against Chechen militants trying to cross into Chechnya from Georgia's Pankisi region in July and August 2002, and in the attack on Abkhazia by Chechen militants later in the year. Tajikistan has the distinction of being the one country in the region to have resolved a civil conflict, but the settlement is fragile and the government does not control a considerable portion of its territory.

These various facets of the regional context are interrelated. The region's politics are a significant impediment to economic recovery: corruption and arbitrariness in economic regulation pose significant barriers to indigenous entrepreneurship, while inhibiting foreign investment (outside the energy sector[6]). Economic stagnation reduces revenues available to the state while contributing to the legitimacy crisis of the region's governments. The combination of factors puts the region into the running for the award of the EU's 'most problematic periphery'.

EU interests in the Caucasus and Central Asia

One should perhaps begin by noting that the EU is not very interested in the region, by comparison with North Africa, the Baltics, Russia or the Balkans. North Africa has a strong and vocal lobby within the Union (the Mediterranean littoral EU members), as do the Baltic States (the Scandinavian members) and Russia (Germany and Finland). Instability in the Balkans poses direct perceived threats to the EU's security. The Caucasus and Central Asia do not.

That said, the region does have importance to the EU for three reasons: 'weak state spillovers', the potential of the region as an exporter of energy to Europe,[7] and 'European values'. In the first category, the region's economic torpor has generated substantial flows of economic migrants, mainly to the Russian Federation. The incapacity or lack of will of states to control their territories and enforce their laws – coupled with the overall economic situation – has made the region an ideal venue for the emergence and flourishing of transnational criminal activity. Again, the principal victim here may be the Russian Federation. However, Central Asia in particular is a major trans-shipment area for drugs destined for Europe, giving the EU a stake in strengthening law enforcement capacities there. Limited state capacity to regulate the banking sector makes the region a potentially attractive venue for money-laundering activity. The activities of the IMU in Uzbekistan, Tajikistan and Kyrgyzstan in 1999–2001, the involvement of Islamic militants in Chechnya (and in Georgia), and the close connections between these groups and al-Qaida highlight the significance of the region in the 'war against terror'. Arguably, the EU has an interest in addressing the economic and political problems there that foster such activity. The region's conflicts draw humanitarian resources that might otherwise be used elsewhere. For all these reasons, there is a fairly strong case for EU engagement in the Caucasus and Central Asia.

As for energy, John Gault in Chapter 11 makes a persuasive case for the deepening dependence of the EU on imports of oil and gas. As he points out, there are four significant energy provinces that may meet this growing demand: the Russian Federation, the Middle East, North Africa and the Caspian Basin. European Commission officials are wary of increasing dependence on the Middle East and North Africa, given the uncertainties of these regions' politics. They are concerned over deepening dependence on Russia for supplies of natural gas, since they fear that such dependence may give Russia an uncomfortable degree of leverage in its relations with the Union. In short, the watchword is diversification of supply. The Caspian Basin may play a significant role in this diversification.

One challenge here is to develop the infrastructure to export energy product from the region. In this area, substantial progress has been made. The Caspian Pipeline Consortium (CPC) pipeline from Kazakhstan to the Middle East opened in 2001, resulting in a substantial increase in Europe's capacity to tap Kazakhstan's considerable petroleum reserves. Ground has now been broken for the large-diameter Baku–Tbilisi–Ceyhan oil pipeline from Azerbaijan to the Mediterranean coast of Turkey. Plans are well advanced to couple the oil pipeline with a natural gas line from Baku to Erzurum. Another challenge is to ensure that the product flows west. Europe is only one potential market for this product; others include Turkey and Asia. The existence of such competition creates a second incentive for an active EU engagement in the region's deliberations on energy development.

The energy issue is part of a larger trade dimension to potential EU interest in the region. Table 8.6 outlines the evolution of the Union's trading relationship with the Caucasus and Central Asia. The trade figures are hardly overwhelming, but if one takes into account the probability of significant increases of energy exports from the region, and associated increase in the demand for, and the capacity to pay for, imports, then there is sizeable market potential for European exports to the region.

The final reason for EU engagement is normative. The EU apparently conceives itself to be wedded to the promotion of liberal values (democracy, the liberal economy, the rule of law, human rights) in international

Table 8.6 EU trade with key partners in the Caucasus and Central Asia (in millions of euros)

Country	1995		1997		1999	
	EU X	*EU M*	*EU X*	*EU M*	*EU X*	*EU M*
Azerbaijan	120.3	48.1	253.9	67.9	213.7	444.4
Kazakhstan	447.3	359.4	1,394.1	1,442.3	972.9	1,763.4
Turkmenistan	79	152.9	142	62	206.6	247.9
Uzbekistan	409	500	762	541	496	392

Source: Department of External Relations, European Commission.

Note
EU X refers to exports from the EU, EU M to imports into the EU.

relations. This reflects the judgement that an international system of states embracing these values will be one in which it is easier to pursue the Union's external objectives. However, these norms are also considered to have intrinsic as well as instrumental significance. They are judged to be right. This commitment is not merely a product of elite calculation. The commitment to such values (and particularly those related to human rights and the rule of law) also has roots in the presence of large, and frequently vocal, civil society organizations that promote them in the domestic arenas of member states.

EU policies and instruments

The abstract objectives of EU policy in the region are quite transparently stated in EU official documentation. EU cooperation objectives in Armenia, for example, are 'to build a relationship with Armenia in which the respect of democratic principles, the rule of law and human rights, as well as the consolidation of a market economy are fostered and supported'.[8] This formulation is repeated more or less verbatim in the equivalent document for Georgia. Interestingly, the other six country documents do not include initial statements of EU policy objectives, reflecting perhaps a degree of realism as to how long it would take them to reach liberal democratic modernity. However, similar normative commitments are evident in the comments on elections, economic difficulties and rights issues in all the others.[9] Four additional general policy objectives are evident in EU documents: political stability; conflict resolution and conflict prevention; the consolidation of the independence of these states; and fostering a westward orientation in their engagement with the international economy.

The EU deploys a range of instruments in pursuit of these objectives. In the first years after independence, humanitarian assistance held pride of place. As things settled down, other instruments have gradually eclipsed the role of the European Commission Humanitarian Office (ECHO).[10] The major instruments of the EU in the region include one major technical assistance programme to CIS states (TACIS) and several programmes intended to foster regional development and cooperation or to deal with cross-border problems. In addition, the EU has sought both to regulate its bilateral relations with states in the region and to foster reform through Partnership and Cooperation Agreements (PCAs). At various times and in various circumstances, partners in the region receive allocations from other EU sources on an ad hoc basis (e.g. exceptional financial assistance, the food security programme, the food aid programme).

Total EU assistance to the countries of the region is listed in Table 8.7. TACIS funding by country is shown in Table 8.8. As for regional cooperation programmes in the current period, three are of specific relevance to the Caucasus and Central Asia: Transport Corridor Europe–Caucasus–Asia (TRACECA), the regional seas component of the environment

Table 8.7 Total EU assistance by country, 1991–2001

Country	Amount (million ecus/euros)
Armenia	286.13
Azerbaijan	333.9
Georgia	342.88
Kazakhstan	116.9
Kyrgyzstan	144
Tajikistan	78
Turkmenistan	44
Uzbekistan	111

Source: Department of External Relations, European Commission.

Table 8.8 TACIS allocations by country, 1991–9 and 2002–3

Country	Cumulative 1991–9	2000
Armenia	58.9	10
Azerbaijan	58.5	7
Georgia	55.0	15
Kazakhstan	119.6	10 (2001)
Kyrgyzstan	53.2	10 (2001)
Tajikistan	8[a]	0
Turkmenistan	42.3	0
Uzbekistan	102.8	15.4

Source: European Commission Department of External Relations, *Overview* (by country) and *Strategy Paper 2002–2006 and Indicative Programme 2002–2004 for Central Asia* (Brussels: European Commission, 2002).

Note
a A relatively small amount of this allocation was actually dispersed, given difficulties with the security situation in 1997–8.

programme, and the drug trafficking element of the justice and home affairs programme. The total envelope for these programmes is €24 million from 2002 to 2004.

TACIS programming has largely focused on capacity-building in state institutions. At the national level it proceeds on the basis of a bilateral process whereby the recipient state identifies priorities and projects and the EC then chooses those which it wishes to support. Generally speaking, EU preferences in the national programmes are support for institutional, administrative and legal reform; support for private-sector development; assistance in the development of infrastructure; and support for the development of the rural economy. With the coming into force of PCAs (see p. 129), TACIS programming has focused increasingly on technical assistance in the implementation of these agreements, while also targeting the social consequences of economic transition. In certain instances (e.g. Azerbaijan and Georgia), limited amounts of TACIS monies are used to promote post-conflict rehabilitation. This assistance may be made conditional, to a degree, on progress in conflict resolution.

The principal activity of the TRACECA programme is technical assistance in planning for infrastructural development in transport (pipelines, roads, railways, ports, border crossing facilities) and communications, linking the states of the region on an east–west axis from Central Asia to the Black Sea. As of 2000, the programme had disbursed some €35 million in this area. By and large, this assistance (feasibility studies, route surveys, etc.) is seen as a means of assisting states in the region to access multilateral lenders (the European Bank for Reconstruction and Development, the World Bank and the Asian Development Bank), as well as private financial markets. In addition, the programme does make small investments in specific rehabilitation projects intended to remove bottlenecks in the developing transport corridor (e.g. the optical cable project to render signalling on Caucasian railways more effective and safe, and partial funding of the rehabilitation of the Red Bridge linking Georgia and Azerbaijan). Some €42 million has been disbursed under this element of the programme. The 2002–3 funding envelope is €10 million.

The final instruments under consideration here are the PCAs. All the states on the southern tier of the former Soviet Union signed PCAs in 1999, with the exceptions of Tajikistan and Turkmenistan. Each agreement provides for a framework of political dialogue, EU support of democratic and economic transition, the promotion of trade and investment, and the establishment of frameworks for legislative, economic, social, financial, scientific, technological and cultural cooperation. The documents are interesting in that, although they generally run to 70 pages, the great bulk is devoted to technical measures to be taken by EU partner states to facilitate economic exchange. In contrast, discussion of the political and other objectives of the agreements is minimal. They are also interesting in that while they provide for most-favoured-nation status in trade, they contain reservations allowing either partner to restrict trade where unanticipated damage to importing economies and societies is experienced. In some instances, negotiation of the PCAs was accompanied by side deals in which the partner country agreed to restrictions on particular categories of export to the EU.[11]

The EU's impact in the Caucasus and Central Asia

A comparison between the objectives of the EU and the situation in the region 12 years after the EC began to engage there would suggest that the Union has encountered significant difficulties in the pursuit of its agenda. There has been substantial privatization of economies. This has been accompanied by a significant return to growth in most of the states of the region (see Table 8.3, p. 121). In many instances a degree of monetary stabilization has occurred. On the other hand, there has been little movement on the rule of law, rights and democratization fronts; indeed, there may be evidence of slippage. Outside the energy sector, there has been little progress in integrating the economies of this region into broader European markets, despite the PCAs, and not least because the European Commission has chosen to limit regional exports to the EU in key sectors (e.g. metals).[12] The privatization process has been deeply corrupt. The growth that is occurring is from very low baselines of income per capita, is often highly concentrated in particular sectors, and is extremely uneven in its effects on national economies and societies. Monetary stabilization has been accompanied by significant shrinkage in public services and in social safety nets.

Moreover, it is unclear to what extent the limited positive result has anything in particular to do with the EU itself. Other international institutions operating in the region pursue similar objectives, and the EU has a far lower profile in the region than they do. The European Bank for Reconstruction and Development (EBRD) and the World Bank have real money; the International Monetary Fund (IMF) can inflict real pain. In addition, comparing the figures in Table 8.4 (p. 122) to those in Table 8.7, one immediately discovers that EU resources committed to the region are dwarfed by those of the private sector in areas of the regional economy that they are interested in. For example, cumulative EU assistance to the region as a whole to 1999 amounted to approximately one-fortieth of Chevron's investment in Kazakhstan (largely in one oilfield), or one-twenty-fifth of the investment of British Gas in the same country. At the level of the region as a whole, Official Development Assistance (ODA) is not the story in terms of external economic impacts.

As regards conflict resolution, the EU has avoided the diplomatic limelight in these areas; its limited programmes supporting processes led by other organizations – the UN in Abkhazia, the Organization for Security and Cooperation in Europe (OSCE) in South Ossetia and Nagorno-Karabakh – have had no identifiable impact. For all these reasons, it is fair to say that the EU is a bit player in the Caucasus and Central Asia compared to Russia, other major powers such as the United States, other international organizations, EU member states, and the private sector.

How do we explain the EU's limited impact? One initial point is technical. The TACIS programme has extremely rigid and opaque decision-making and implementation criteria. The money is very hard to get, takes a very long time to disburse, and is largely consumed by the salaries of those EU citizens doing the implementing. The latter often have little knowledge of the countries they are dealing with and (frequently) a remarkably dismissive attitude towards local capacity. Second is the resources gap. Even if implementation were effective, the EU has not been willing or able to commit resources at a level that might make a significant difference by encouraging policymakers to change their behaviour on issues that matter to them. One particularly poignant example was the European Commission's declaration that levels of TACIS assistance to Azerbaijan would be linked to progress in conflict resolution. The relevant budget envelope is in the tens of millions of euros, which is dwarfed by Azerbaijan's income from oil revenue.

A third problem, linked to the second, is the gap between the demands of the situation and the EU's will to address it. EU member states and the Commission do not want a significant engagement in the region, given their preoccupation not only with peripheral areas of greater importance to Europe, but also with the impending enlargement, and the dilemmas of reform in structural programmes, agricultural policy, and decision-making that is long overdue. In the meantime, to the extent that member states have agendas in the two regions, there is little evidence of any willingness on their part to subordinate national prerogative to community solidarity.

The result is another gap: that between rhetoric and reality. The EU's rhetorical reach exceeds its grasp. Regional leaders find the moral posturing of outsiders on things that matter to be tedious and occasionally infuriating. When the organization is unwilling or unable to apply meaningful pressure where its preferences are ignored (as in Azerbaijan) or derided (as in Turkmenistan), and when it is not willing to put in significant resources to implement its preferences, it is viewed at best as irrelevant.

A fourth problem is the inherent conflict within the EU's suite of interests. If the real point of EU engagement is access to the region's energy resources, and these resources lie in the hands of people who fall rather short of Western liberal principles of democracy, the rule of law and human rights, then the democratizing agenda complicates the pursuit of the energy one. If the real point in the current framework is addressing the threat of terrorism, then one might be willing to trade democratic principle for strong leadership *à la* Karimov or Aliev. It is not surprising in this context that the EU appears content to ignore the transgressions of leaders of countries who play significant roles in the energy sector (Kazakhstan and Azerbaijan) or putatively in the struggle against terrorism and drugs (Uzbekistan). The message here is not lost in the region.

Finally, even if it were possible to get the EU end right, one should not forget the local political and cultural context of the region. Reforming states is not only expensive; it is an extraordinarily complex endeavour. The pursuit of the liberal agenda is limited not only by the resources gap and the effectiveness of the institutions pursuing it, but also by the absorptive capacity of the states and societies that are the targets of the programmes. Weak, under-institutionalized and corrupt states generally have poor records in using resources effectively. Many members of the state apparatus benefit from the irregularities of transitional administration. They can be expected to oppose the imposition of transparency and accountability in governance.

Beyond the state, the important relations among the region's peoples are patrimonial, founded on kinship, and ethnically and regionally based.

What appears to be corruption to us may appear to those engaged in the practice as serving the needs of their community.[13] This impedes the development of the civic nation and civil society that the EU purports to seek. Moreover, the experience of the region with politics is not such as to facilitate the absorption of Western normative agendas. People have little experience of political competition between parties. The law has historically been owned by those in charge. Post-Soviet states have combined the unrepresentativeness and opacity characteristic of the Soviet era with the collapse of services that the Soviet state did provide to most people most of the time. The experience of the past decade suggests that Western institutions do not know how to implement their liberal agendas in this environment. It highlights both the resilience of local social, cultural and political centres of power as they deal with the assault from the West, and the naivety of Western institutions in addressing these structures.

Towards an EU strategy?

To sum up, if by strategy we mean a coherent relationship between ends and means, there is no EU strategy in the Caucasus and Central Asia. Nor, for the foreseeable future, is one likely to appear. Enlargement, constitutional reform and reform of structural programmes and agricultural policy are likely to absorb the energies of the Commission and the Councils for the foreseeable future. The limited budgetary envelope for 'stabilization' is likely to be monopolized for the foreseeable future by the Balkans. Member states show little interest in policy coordination in the two regions. There does not appear to be any strong member-based lobby for the activation of EU policy there. 'Strategic' initiatives in the CIS focus now, and are likely to continue to focus, on the Russian Federation and Ukraine.

By way of conclusion, it is worth noting that EU diffidence and lack of commitment with respect to the southern Caucasus and Central Asia is not necessarily bad policy. Strategic choice is about the optimal employment of limited resources in pursuit of identified interests. The resource endowment of the EU is not infinite, and there are multiple demands upon it. The southern tier of the former Soviet Union does not rank highly in the EU calculus of interest. One could, therefore, question whether the devotion of substantial strategic effort and resources to the region would be rational. It is sensible for lesser interests to give way to larger ones.

This is not to say that the EU's engagement has been pointless or worthless. It is probable, for example, that TRACECA has been instrumental in enhancing access to multilateral financial assistance in the energy and transport sectors. EU initiatives in the justice and home affairs area may make a difference in the struggle against drug trafficking in Central Asia. The promise of access to EU markets may well have had an effect in accelerating economic reform in partner countries despite the problems that remain in the transition process. In other words, although the EU lacks a credible overarching strategy and is reluctant to commit the resources to undergird such a strategy, this does not mean that it does not or cannot play a useful role.

However, one should recognize the implications for the EU's profile in the region. In the roster of external engagement, it has been a bit player. It is recognized as such by regional actors. It will continue to be so seen. And, correspondingly, its leverage (beyond trade issues) is, and will continue to be, limited. This was true before 11 September 2001. It is all the more true after the events of that day, given the deepening of US engagement in the region and the emergence of apparently robust Russo-American cooperation in addressing the security challenges of the former Soviet Union's southern tier.

Notes

1 From an interview with the chairman of the Economic Reform Committee of the Georgian Parliament, January 1990.
2 These figures are from the World Bank. They apparently do not take into account the substantial emigration of unemployed young people (mainly male, and particularly, although not exclusively, from the Caucasus).
3 Armenia and Tajikistan being exceptions to this generalization. In both instances, the countries were recovering from war and coming up from a very low base.
4 It is striking that the inward investment to either the Czech Republic ($19,424 million) or Hungary ($19,420 million) exceeds the total for the eight states of the Caucasus and Central Asia over the time period covered by the FDI data in Table 8.4. If one removed FDI in natural resources and associated activities from the regional FDI figures, the regional figures would be truly negligible.
5 The one major exception here is Tajikistan's democratic and Islamic oppositions. Subsequent to the creation of a coalition in this case, the circle around the president set about dismantling their partners by co-opting their leaders into the system. The consequent fragmentation of the Islamic Republican Party has left a vacuum on the religious end of politics that may be being filled by more radical Islamic organizations. See A. Rashid, *Jihad: The Rise of Militant Islam in Central Asia*, New Haven, Conn.: Yale University Press, 2002.
6 Regarding the energy sector, leaders see a substantial interest in creating conditions of predictability for foreign concerns, and have had considerable success in insulating the sector from the broader failure of economic governance. Interviews with IFI officials in Baku, 1998 and 2000.
7 The Commission has identified access to Caspian Basin energy reserves as a strategic interest of the EU. See European Commission, *TACIS Regional Cooperation Indicative Programme, 2000–2003*, Brussels: EU, 2000, p. 4.
8 EU Department of External Relations, 'The EU's Relations with Armenia', p. 1. Online. Available http: <http:/www.europa.eu.int/comm/external_relations/armenia/intro/index.htm> (accessed 10 January 2003).
9 Moreover, the 2001 version of *TACIS Regional Cooperation: Strategic Considerations 2002–2006 and Indicative Programme 2002–2003*, Brussels: European Commission, 2001, which covers the CIS region as a whole, identifies EU cooperation objectives as the support of 'democratic principles and human rights and the transition towards market economy'.

10 ECHO began to draw down its emergency programmes in 1996 in the southern Caucasus (its major focus), and wound them up in 2000.
11 For example, Kazakhstan and the European Coal and Steel Community (ECSC) agreed to limitations on Kazakhstan's steel exports to the EU in July 1999, simultaneously with the coming into effect of the PCA.
12 In 1993 the EC applied anti-dumping provisions to Kazakhstan's exports of ferro-silicon products to Europe. These restrictions are currently under review.
13 In Azerbaijan it is reported that it costs some $20,000 to obtain a job as a customs inspector. This sum is generally borrowed through extended family and or other personal networks. The money is loaned in the expectation of return to the group. There is no way that the sum could be recouped through salary. The individual concerned consequently fulfils the obligations he cares about through corruption.

9 North Africa

Partnership, exceptionalism and neglect

Fred Tanner

Introduction

There is not just a geographical proximity between Europe and North Africa but also a long common history of conquest and cooperation. With the advance of globalization and the diffusion of risks and threats, the forthcoming European Union (EU) enlargement eastwards and southwards, and the apparent paradigm shift after 11 September 2001, what are Europe's current security interests in its southern neighbourhood? The EU – as a 'civilian power' – is obliged to consider its security interests in the region in terms of challenges and partnerships. Challenges include not only the root causes of conflict, such as poverty, underdevelopment and socio-economic unrest, but also cross-cutting issues such as international terrorism, narcotics trafficking, illegal migration and energy dependence. Europe's stake in the Mediterranean region goes well beyond the risk of potential spillovers: it is anchored deeply in a colonial legacy and an increasingly troublesome presence of North Africa inside Europe. The al-Qaida attacks on New York, and also the killing of German tourists in Djerba in Tunisia in April 2002, demonstrated a dangerous connection between Europe's North African diaspora and international terrorism. The danger lies also with xenophobic over-reactions by European politicians that could lead to a strengthening of 'Fortress Europe' – a development that would invalidate the EU's efforts to engage in political, economic and civil society partnerships in the Euro-Mediterranean region.

To respond to these challenges, Europe is struggling to develop a coherent strategy for the Mediterranean. To achieve this strategy, the EU needs internal cohesion and an external identity. This chapter argues that these requirements are currently not present: the EU's internal cohesion is challenged by national exceptionalisms and the inadequate use of multi-layered policymaking instruments, such as the intergovernmental Common Foreign and Security Policy (CFSP), the European Security and Defence Policy (ESDP) as well as the Common Mediterranean Strategy (CMS), and the Euro-Mediterranean Partnership (EMP) with its MEDA programme.[1] The EU's external identity is largely absent because the EU has thus far not been able to define its interests as a security actor. With regard to North Africa, the foreign policy issue is even more complex, owing to the blurring between internal and external security agendas that are linked to the colonial legacy, migration and Islamist terrorism.

From protector to partner?

The EU's relations with North Africa are profoundly marked by the colonial legacy of the European countries such as France, Italy, Spain and the United Kingdom. Algeria – by far the most populous country of the Maghreb – was until 1962 an integral part of France. Tunisia was a French protectorate from 1881 until 1956, Morocco from 1912 to 1956, and the Western Sahara was a Spanish protectorate from 1884 to 1976. Spain still controls the last remnants of colonial history with Ceuta, Melilla, the Chafarinas Islands, the Rock of Alhucemas and the Rock of Vélez de la Gomera. Italy invaded Libya in 1911 and imposed colonial rule until World War II. The colonial period established the 'hub–spoke' dependency that continues to mark relations between Europe and North Africa. For the Maghreb countries the EU is by far the largest trading partner both in terms of imports (Tunisia 71.6 per cent, Algeria 58 per cent, Morocco 57.7 per cent) and even more in terms of exports (Tunisia 80 per cent, Algeria 62.7 per cent, Morocco 74.3 per cent).[2] The South–South or 'horizontal' relations are almost non-existent, despite certain recent initiatives such as the Agadir Process, the Eisenstadt Initiative and the regional and sub-regional programmes under the Barcelona Process. These colonial ties, combined with geographical proximity, have also led to a strong influx of North Africans to Europe, including nearly 1 million of French descent and other Europeans who fled Algeria during its war of liberation in the mid-1960s.

The European Community (EC) developed its first Mediterranean policy in 1972 with the conclusion of several commercial agreements under the overarching heading of European Political Cooperation (EPC). The Arab oil embargo of 1973 and the ensuing energy crisis for the first time highlighted Europe's energy vulnerability towards the Mediterranean and the Middle East. As a consequence, the EC sought to engage in a political dialogue with Arab states. The resultant Euro–Arab dialogue represented the first attempt by the EC to institutionalize a politically structured exchange with its southern Arab neighbours. Even though this rapprochement did not last, it accelerated the economic multilateralization of the EC with the Mediterranean region. Under the label of the Global Mediterranean Policy, the EC concluded from 1973 until 1980 numerous 'first-generation association agreements' with Arab states and Israel. In addition, the accession to the EC of the northern Mediterranean states of Greece (1981) and Spain and Portugal (1986) significantly reinforced EC policy towards the Mediterranean. These countries, together with France and Italy, henceforth constituted a southern club within the EU that has acted as a lobby in favour of the Mediterranean in terms of policy initiatives and resource allocations.

With the end of the Cold War, the EU was able to reach out politically to the whole Mediterranean region, which had previously been divided on East–West ideological lines. At the Lisbon European Council in 1992, the EU declared the Mediterranean region a 'zone of interest' for the Joint Actions of the newly created CFSP.[3] The determining criteria for such a declaration were geographical proximity, interests in the political and economic stability of the region, and the existence of possible threats that could directly affect the EU.[4] The idea of a Euro-Mediterranean Partnership (EMP) was originally proposed by Italy and Spain in 1992 but was blocked at that time by the other EU states. The breakthrough to a pan-Mediterranean strategy resulted from the concerns of France and the other southern states of increased EU orientation eastwards under the pressure of a unified Germany. Indeed, as Jürg Monar argues, the EMP was accepted by the EU once 'France started to present a reinforced policy in the Mediterranean as a strategic counterpart to the pre-accession strategy towards the East Central European countries'.[5]

With the launching of the EMP or 'Barcelona Process' in 1995, the EU increased its strategic orientation towards the South. It provided a normative framework for a holistic policy that covered the entire pan-Mediterranean region stretching from the Atlantic (Morocco) to the eastern Mediterranean and the Near East.[6] The Barcelona Process was not itself an instrument for EU foreign policy but rather served as the foundations for a long-term exercise in soft power projection. The formal objective of the EMP was to create a 'zone of peace, stability and shared prosperity'. The unofficial purpose was to defuse migratory pressures from the South by creating stability and supporting economic development. Like the framework of the Organization for Security and Cooperation in Europe (OSCE), Europe's launching of a comprehensive security area included security, economic and cultural/human chapters. This policy was driven by the European Commission, which linked its programmatic and financial EMP commitment to the promotion of democracy, human rights, good governance, the rule of law and a free-market economy. This liberal set of values found its way into the Barcelona Declaration itself and was also enshrined in each Association Agreement that the EU signed with individual Barcelona partner states.[7] It was supported by democracy assistance programmes, human rights projects and civil society promotions.

However, the political and security dimension of the Barcelona Process has been in trouble from the very outset. The Israeli–Palestinian breakthrough in Oslo in 1993 allowed the EU to design a political forum that would include Israel and Arab states, including the Palestinian Authority. But while Israel remained militarily present in southern Lebanon, Syria and Lebanon objected to any kind of military–political arrangements, including confidence-building measures that included a military component. With the arrival of the hardline government of Binyamin Netanyahu in mid-1996, Arab states shied away from security and defence matters in the Barcelona context. These developments fuelled Arab scepticism about the European proposal for a Stability Pact for the region (similar in conception to the pact for South-Eastern Europe), which was renamed the Charter for Peace and Stability in the Mediterranean. This Charter was to provide the EMP with a normative base in the broad field of security cooperation. However, with the worsening of Israeli–Palestinian relations in 2000, the Charter was delinked from EMP meetings and was formally frozen at the Marseilles ministerial summit in November 2000.

The Valencia ministerial summit of 2002, in contrast, adopted an action plan that for the first time also included the ESDP in the pan-Mediterranean security discourse. This action plan primarily addresses the need to increase information exchange and reduce transaction costs across the EMP area through an institutionalized political dialogue. The impact of 11 September 2001 also forged the determination of the Barcelona partners to pursue the mandate for an ad hoc Group on Terrorism. Related to this, the Valencia meeting also reached agreement on a programme of cooperation in the field of justice and home affairs, in combating drugs, organized crime and terrorism as well as in promoting cooperation relating to migration and the movement of people.

The strategic inadequacies of EU instruments

The EU is one of the few international actors that commands a wide variety of policy instruments to foster security, development and governance. The problem with European policy towards North Africa is that the unanimity requirement in decision-making relating to the CFSP impedes the formulation of a European policy and, instead, external trade relations and financial assistance act as substitutes for such a policy. This reveals the 'consistency of inconsistency' between the EU's external relations and the CFSP, national foreign policies and EU policy, and the rhetoric and reality of EU declarations and policy.[8] As this section shows, EU policy instruments such as the CMS, the Association Agreements, the Barcelona Process and the MEDA programme have been only partially implemented and are not fully supported by the CFSP, because member states try to instrumentalize these programmes or do not prioritize their national agendas to an EU-wide foreign policy approach. Furthermore, the emerging security and defence dimension of the EU needs to be positioned within a comprehensive EU strategy towards the region.

The Common Mediterranean Strategy of the EU

The making of a common strategy should include, prima facie, a strategic and holistic commitment of Europe towards the Mediterranean. It should provide clear mandates regulating the competencies and division of labour between CFSP and the High Representative for the CFSP, the Special Envoy for the Middle East and the Commission. Instead, owing to its limited scope and abstract nature, the CMS agreed at the Feira Council in June 2000 has proved unable to produce anything close to a European grand strategy for the Mediterranean. There are several explanations for this deficiency and the large number of issues which have failed to be clarified.[9] First, the CMS document is not much more than a combination of the Barcelona principles, the Berlin Declaration on the Middle East of March 1999 and the Tampere European Council Conclusions of 1999 concerning justice and home affairs. In other words, the 'strategy' amounts to not much more than reiteration of existing EU commitments. Second, the French, considering themselves the guardians of the Charter for Peace and Stability in the Mediterranean, insisted on making the Charter a core element of the CMS, to the detriment of other substantial elements. Thus, the CMS accords to the Charter a key role for stability-building in the Mediterranean, including the EU's role in a 'post-peace era' in the Middle East.[10] The CMS assumes that the Charter – which is in fact still a work-in-progress – will sooner rather than later be an integral part of the EMP. Finally, the CMS was not able to position the ESDP in an overall approach to the Mediterranean.

On the positive side, the CMS does provide a more explicit basis for the EU to strengthen the Barcelona Process in areas going beyond the Barcelona Declaration. This is particularly relevant with regard to the involvement of the EU and the Euro-Med Partnership in peacebuilding efforts in the Middle East in the eventuality of an Israeli–Palestinian settlement. The CMS also requires the EU presidency to evaluate the EU's progress in the Mediterranean region on a regular, 'not less than annual', basis (article 33). Finally, the existence of a Common Strategy, even if it is not as effective as anticipated, can serve as a safeguard against the bilateralism or exceptionalism of the policies of individual EU states towards North Africa.

Problems with the Barcelona Process

The Barcelona Process is driven primarily by the Commission and the MEDA programmes. By 2003, eight years after the initiation of the process, the lack of visible results has given way to considerable criticism, by both government officials and policy analysts. The problem is that the long-term structural approach of the process cannot in itself enable the EU to act as a strategic actor in the Mediterranean region. Symptomatic of this is the fact that the formal parameters of the Barcelona Process do not permit the EU to tackle individual conflicts. For instance, conflict resolution for Cyprus and the Western Sahara are under UN auspices, and the Middle East peace process remains under US patronage. The Arab–Israeli conflict has been a paramount obstacle to EMP cooperation in the politico-security areas. Syria and Lebanon have consistently refused to participate in EMP activities that involve extensive political discourse or developing confidence-building measures because of the presence of Israel. This is why several initiatives to promote cooperation among defence academies in the EMP area have been stalled. This initiative has now been taken up by NATO, with a diplomatic initiative to promote seminars with Mediterranean Dialogue states.

The real problem with the Barcelona Process is the implementation gap between rhetoric and policy and the contradictions with the liberal philosophy behind the projection of soft security. The EU, internally constrained by the Common Agricultural Policy (CAP) and farmer lobbies from South European states, restricts the import of agricultural products from the South and applies free trade only to oil, gas and industrial products. Even in the textile sector, the South has been pressurized to accept 'voluntary restraint agreements', while exposing previously protected domestic sectors 'to the full force of European competition'.[11] Béchir Chourou argues that the EU's policy of conditionalities and half-measures towards North Africa actually worsened domestic socio-economic conditions, which in turn 'led to mounting social unrest, and where organised opposition existed, it was led by the fundamentalists'.[12] Chourou's warning clearly points to the lack of EU leadership and decisiveness with regard to its southern periphery.

The future of the Barcelona Process is not just affected by its slow progress on the political and economic fields. It also risks changing its character with the impending enlargement of the EU towards the South: Malta and Cyprus are expected to join the EU as of 2004, and Turkey will take longer but, as a candidate state, it already has privileged access to EU funds and policymaking mechanisms that are not open to the southern Mediterranean states. Thus, the EU enlargement will leave the EU in a partnership that essentially reverts back to a Euro–Arab dialogue plus Israel. This anticipated development highlights even more the salience of Israeli–Arab relations for the EMP and adds therefore yet another reason why Europe should be more involved in peacemaking in the Near East.

MEDA and democracy promotion

North Africa is an important testing ground for the promotion of democracy by the EU to its immediate neighbourhood. MEDA, a sister programme to TACIS and PHARE, was created to support the liberalization and economic development efforts of the southern partner states. Chris Patten, Commissioner for External Relations, has repeatedly made the point that the EU financial commitments are 'dependent on adequate progress'.[13] But the North African states have generally refused in their reform plans to go beyond a declaratory acceptance of EU conditionalities

that have been focused towards good governance and market liberalization. Governing elites have succeeded in resisting legal harmonization,
deregulation, privatization and institution-building under MEDA or IMF
auspices. Thus, beyond the strictly economic difficulties, one of the main
obstacles to liberalization is the authoritarian regimes reigning in most
southern Mediterranean countries.

However, the EU has not taken any clear stance against, for instance, the
military-dominated government in Algeria, or the increasingly authoritarian
regime of Zine el-Abidine Ben Ali in Tunisia. Thus far, even faced with
clear reversals of political reforms in countries such as Tunisia, the EU has
not taken any concrete measures, not even through the new Association
Agreements, which include a suspension clause for democracy-related projects. In this context, Richard Youngs rightly observes that the EU conditionality towards North Africa is 'oriented overwhelmingly to economic and
not political criteria'.[14] In the aftermath of 11 September, the EU has further
lost the moral high ground from which to criticize Arab states for their
crackdowns carried out in the name of global anti-terrorist campaigns.
Tunisia, and also Morocco, reversed the political liberalization of the 1980s
'in the face of Islamist challenges'.[15] Furthermore, any European criticisms
of human rights violations by Israel in the occupied territories have led to
Israeli and US allegations of anti-Semitism in Europe.[16]

The MEDA programme as the main vehicle for EU democracy promotion must be considered a failure for the 1995–9 period, as disbursements
have reached only 26 per cent of the total amount committed (€4.685
billion). The pledged amount represented about 11 per cent of the total
annual EU budget for external action. The more general reasons for this
failure are the disconnection between the EU's overall stated objectives
towards the South and its actual policies on trade, development assistance
and democracy promotion. Furthermore, the asymmetrical North–South
relationship puts the South clearly at a disadvantage: the EU, as a single
representative of the North, negotiates with each North African country
on an individual basis, therefore ignoring their common concerns. In addition, southern states are very reluctant to engage in MEDA economic projects that are linked to political reform. Other, more specific reasons for
the underperformance of MEDA include a lack of sufficient numbers of
Commission personnel dedicated to the Mediterranean, the complicated
bureaucratic procedures in Brussels and delayed disbursements of funds.
Chris Patten did acknowledge the shortcomings, and he initiated 'a comprehensive review of the Barcelona Process with the aim of reinvigorating
the Process and making it more action-oriented and results-driven'.[17]

As a consequence of this review, the MEDA programme for 2002–6
was redesigned to produce faster pay-offs with the help of 'short and
medium-term goals'. They include more Commission staff for the MEDA
programmes; devolution of the implementation of the programme to
the Commission's delegations in the partner countries; faster delivery of

financial assistance; and fewer projects but more generously financed. The amount available for MEDA is €5.35 billion for 2002–6, which should allow the EU to sustain current efforts but will preclude expansion with major new projects. It is clear that commitments to the Balkans and the EU enlargements towards the North and the East will prevent a further increase of EU resource allocations to the South.

The Common Foreign and Security Policy, European Security and Defence Policy and national 'exceptionalisms'

The notorious dichotomy between EU policies and the national agendas of member states is particularly acute in the North African context. Recent French–Algerian and Spanish–Moroccan relations demonstrate that a credible CSFP requires more constraints on member states and more coordination between the Union and its member states.

As regards French–Algerian relations, France became at times directly involved in the Algerian civil war of the 1990s by providing political and military support, especially under the reign of French interior minister Charles Pasqua, who largely accepted the thesis that Europe must join in a war against 'international Islamic terrorism'. The French exceptionalism on Algeria blocked the EU from embracing a clear policy against the Algerian military authorities. The EU did not attach any conditionality to the existing assistance programmes and the substantial trade relations with Algeria. Youngs argues that the European Commission's political aid towards Algeria has become an extension of French policy and that – as a result – other EU states felt 'their work became more associated with French policy and consequently more politicised'.[18] Stavridis and Hutchence also argue that Europe's energy import dependence on Algeria played a role in the EU's reluctance 'to use civilian means to pressure the Algerian government to protect its own citizens'.[19]

Another example where parochialism prevails over the CFSP is the Spanish–Moroccan feud that has simmered over fishery rights, migrant workers and the cities of Ceuta and Melilla. Morocco has repeatedly accused Spain of double standards for demanding free passage of goods while denying free passage of labour migrants. Spain, in turn, has accused Morocco of being lenient on illegal migration and ineffective in dealing with transit migrants from black Africa and beyond. The dispute escalated when Morocco withdrew its ambassador from Madrid in October 2001 amid allegations of Spanish interference in the Western Sahara issue. This decision to withdraw the ambassador was also taken one day after a Euro-Mediterranean ministerial meeting in Agadir when Spain could have submitted the issue to the multilateral forum through the CFSP. The dispute further escalated in July 2002 over the forceful removal of Moroccan interior forces from Perejil, an uninhabited islet off Morocco, by a Spanish rapid reaction force. This time the EU did get involved, but in most lamentable terms. The European Commission, under pressure from various member states and the EU presidency, had several times to change and revise its offer to 'mediate' in the dispute.[20] Furthermore, France vetoed an ESDP statement of solidarity with Spain in order to punish the latter for not informing the ESDP institutions about plans to retake the islet by force. As the *Financial Times* argued, it was the close personal relations between President Chirac and King Mohamed as well as 'lucrative economic deals that took precedence over EU solidarity'.[21] The irony of the entire episode was that Washington finally had to mediate in the dispute. The case also showed that the European Commission could in general play only a limited role in CFSP matters. In this instance, the Commission was even more constrained as Spain was holding the presidency.

The EU has to date only a very limited possibility of supporting its approach to the South with a combination of soft and hard power projection. Indeed, the EU has no strategic or security concept towards the South, even though the EU Headline Force has been declared operational at the Laeken summit in November 2001. NATO, in contrast, did not – with its strategic concept of 1999 – rule out operations in the Middle East, and it is currently deployed in the eastern Mediterranean in support of the Afghanistan campaign.[22] But NATO has no strategy towards North Africa or the Mediterranean region, primarily because such a regional template would not fit into the global security assessment of the United States. Especially in view of the 'exceptionalisms' of various EU member states with regard to North Africa, it is important for the EU to engage in a transparent strategic review process in order, as François Heisbourg has argued, 'to determine what is the full range of Petersberg tasks and the strategic framework in which they should fit'.[23] There is a distinct need to associate the southern partner states with ESDP, not just because the Mediterranean would be – together with the Balkans – one of the most likely 'theatres' of Petersberg operations.

There are, however, a number of obstacles to such an engagement with ESDP. Given the colonial legacy, many observers from the Maghreb perceived the launching of the European Maritime Force (EUROMARFOR) in 1997 as yet another tool of Western interventionism in the Mediterranean, and similar perceptions pervade southern assessments of ESDP. There exists a clear information deficit in the South on European forces and ESDP. In this context, recommendations have been made for a number of confidence-building measures such as the accreditation of southern military liaison officers to the military cell in Brussels and the sending of military observers to ESDP military exercises.[24] A possible association of Barcelona partners to EU military crisis management could be envisaged through extending the 'third states concerned' category, as defined at the 2000 Feira European Council summit, to Barcelona states. The Feira statement concentrated on Russia, Ukraine and Canada, but it left the door also open to 'other interested States'.[25] Such an involvement would go in parallel with a stronger involvement in Partnership for Peace (PfP) activities, in which all the North African states except Libya already participate *à la carte*, through NATO's Mediterranean Dialogue Process.[26] The 2002 NATO summit in Prague reaffirmed the security commitments to the Mediterranean and promised 'to upgrade substantially the political and practical dimensions of our Mediterranean Dialogue as an integral part of the Alliance's cooperative approach to security'.[27]

It remains unclear to what extent the ESDP will in the future be able to take over part of NATO's security cooperation with the Mediterranean states. The envisaged European Defence College could become a contact point and interlocutor for defence academies in the Barcelona area. This may or may not be linked to the promotion of pan-regional interoperability for civilian and military crisis response. Whether the EU and its ESDP will use NATO's PfP network will depend on the future relevance of PfP for Petersberg tasks as well as on the attitude of some European states, such as France, towards future transatlantic security cooperation. The NATO summit in Prague in 2002 left this question deliberately open and only stressed that the NATO Mediterranean Dialogue Process and the EU Barcelona Process remain 'complementary and mutually reinforcing'.

Euro-Med cooperation under ESDP auspices could also include the training of police forces. Here the EU already has a track record, with the extensive training programme of Palestinian police officers and security forces. Equally, under the MEDA 2000 programme, the EU is financing a police modernization project in Algeria to the amount of €8.2 million. The EU has itself taken up policing under the first official ESDP field mission: the EU police mission replaced the UN International Police Task Force (IPTF) in Bosnia and Herzegovina in January 2003.

However, the transatlantic crisis over Iraq in 2002–3 represents a serious challenge for ESDP and NATO. In February 2003, NATO was struck a serious blow by the vetoes of Germany, France and Belgium over the Turkish request for assistance in anticipation of the US-led preparations for a military campaign against Iraq. As of spring 2003, Europe was profoundly divided over the role of NATO as concerns intervention in the Mediterranean region. Beyond the spectre of Iraq, it remains unclear to what extent European states are committed to joint operations against terrorism in the greater Mediterranean. NATO, or a 'coalition of the willing' drawing on NATO assets, could be a potential vehicle for such Western interventionism, which would take the form of coercive counter-proliferation policy in the Mediterranean under the guise of the global US-led anti-terrorist campaign. This scenario has gained more currency with the extension of President Bush's 'axis of evil' to include Libya and Syria.

The blurring between internal and external security agendas

The links between European and Mediterranean security have become more visible since the end of the Cold War. In terms of security, a number of recent crises support this observation. These include the Algerian civil war and the bombing campaign of Algerian Islamists in France in the mid-1990s; the al-Qaida attacks on New York and Washington, which displayed strong North African–European connections; and the general regional repercussions of the bloody escalation of violence in the Israeli–Palestinian conflict. All these events have posed a policy challenge to the EU and have demonstrated that proximity matters in the North African–European nexus. The terrorist attacks of 11 September not only triggered a global response against terrorism, but also gave rise to a renewed civilizational debate on 'Islam and the West' – a highly controversial and potentially combustible issue for Europe's relations with the Maghreb. There are approximately 10 million Muslims in Western Europe, many of whom are second- or third-generation Muslims of North African descent. In France alone, there are about 5 million Muslims, and in Germany about 3.5 million.

It has become increasingly evident that many al-Qaida terrorists are North Africans living in European countries and that Islamists have maintained terrorist cells all across Europe, benefiting from disaffected Muslims in Europe.[28] According to Sami Zubaida, many Muslims in the West, especially the younger generation, may have shared in the enthusiastic adulation of Osama bin Laden and his organization, and the fact that

> some British, American and European young Muslims were found in the ranks of al Qaida shows that there are organisations and networks active in these countries, recruiting young Muslims for militant action in other parts of the world, even for violent intervention in their countries of residence.[29]

Since the attack of 11 September, a European-associated al-Qaida terrorist from Tunisia was involved in the killing of 15 German tourists in Djerba on 11 April 2002.[30] According to Magnus Ranstorp, about 200 terrorist-related arrests were made in Europe up to the end of 2002. Most of the suspects 'have been from North Africa ... and a significant portion have been Algerian'.[31] The North African connection has been further compounded by the arrest in January 2003 of North African men in London who were in possession of the poison ricin, and by the arrest in Morocco of al-Qaida operatives who planned attacks on US and British ships in the Strait of Gibraltar in May 2002.

The terrorist attacks of 11 September, the Djerba tragedy and the numerous arrests all over Europe have triggered an intense debate in Europe about internal and external security measures in the fight against terrorism. The Mediterranean dimension of the international fight against terrorism was also highlighted by the unexpected Israeli accusations that the EU finances terrorist activities in the Middle East.[32] The anti-terrorist debate has led to anti-Arab sentiments within European societies, which were cleverly exploited by rightist populists such as Jean-Marie Le Pen in France. The general move to the political right, driven by anti-migratory sentiments, has therefore had an impact upon EU policies, even if these extreme right groups have not gained power. In particular, national governments, and the EU more generally, are under pressure from the general public to act more forcibly against illegal migration.

As a response to the right-wing vote in France in early May 2002, the European Commission proposed that the EU set up a multinational EU border guard that would work with Europol to help safeguard the EU's external borders from illegal immigration and terrorism. In the Mediterranean, a first concrete result of these pressures was the launching of Operation Ulysses in January 2003 by five European states: France, the United Kingdom, Spain, Portugal and Italy. This operation was closely associated with the already operational EUROMARFOR and currently consists of several vessels patrolling the Mediterranean coast. The purpose is primarily 'observation and reporting' with regard to illegal immigration and mafia-operated networks in the Mediterranean. However, these European border guards were also given the authority to make arrests, even though the harmonization of the EU common arrest warrant had not yet been fully implemented.

The fight against international terrorism raises calls for better coherence and coordination between the EU's internal and external security concerns. It basically implies that a future strategy towards the Mediterranean would have to rely on all three pillars. This represents a great challenge to EU policymakers as each pillar has different modes of decision-making and, as a consequence, numerous EU–North African issues, such as immigration, terrorism and development assistance, need coordination between the pillars. But in spite of these apparent difficulties, European states have been able to work together effectively against terrorism in the past. Under the heading of Terrorism, Radicalism, Extremism and International Violence (TREVI), EU governments coordinated their response against international terrorism in the 1980s, which led to the dismantling of the Hizbullah's West European network in 1987.[33] Since 11 September the EU has taken several steps in the fight against terrorism which include measures against the financing of terrorist organizations and activities, a common EU arrest warrant and a common definition of terrorist acts. The EU response to terrorism and migration will also have an impact on visa and immigration policies that will also apply to new member states, including the new Mediterranean states of Malta and Cyprus.[34] Furthermore, the EU will have to enforce more consistently the provisions in its Association Agreements that require the North African states to cooperate closely together in the fight against illegal migration and, in particular, against transit migration from sub-Saharan states.

However, the 'Fortress Europe' approach does clash with the Barcelona ideal of creating an all-inclusive Euro-Med zone of peace and prosperity. According to Claire Spencer, many of the Euro-Med co-operative programmes would be jeopardized by an increasing anti-immigrant stance on the part of the EU:

> In the socio-cultural sphere, the controversies aroused by the visa, asylum and migration questions in both the Justice and Home Affairs arena and more immediately at national European level, have prejudiced the EMP's ambitions towards encouraging greater contacts among civil societies of the Mediterranean and European regions.[35]

Conclusion

The EU cannot be considered to be a strategic actor in North Africa and the Mediterranean, or to have a strategic vision towards the area. This chapter shows that this is largely due to the colonial past and national exceptionalisms that block EU intergovernmental decision-making. Furthermore, the Mediterranean is too large and too diverse for there to be a focused EU policy. It may be time to have a more focused approach on specific regions, such as North Africa, even though this may collide with the pan-Mediterranean templates of the Barcelona framework. This argument increasingly gains currency so long as the unresolved Arab–Israeli conflict threatens to paralyse the EU's multilateralist approach to the region.

More generally, how can the activities of the EU in the Mediterranean be strengthened and be made more coherent? First, the Common Mediterranean Strategy should be reviewed. Such a strategy should go beyond a mere accumulation of various *acquis* and spell out a clear strategic vision. The second requirement is to associate more closely the Common Foreign and Security Policy with the implementation of Association Agreements and the MEDA programmes. Third, the EU enlargement policy, which *ipso facto* is an integrative policy, should avoid the impression that 'Fortress Europe' has simply been moved south. It is an axiomatic truth that North African states cannot join the inner circle of the EU. But this also imposes implicit limits to the EU's policy of conditionality and to the southern regimes' interest in going along with economic and political reform, and their motivation to do so.

The EU remains for the time being a civilian actor that relies on its economic might and liberal vision, both of which are – *faute de mieux* – implemented through programmes rather than through strategy-orientated policies. But the policy of democracy promotion experienced a serious setback with 11 September, which served as a convenient pretext for various partner states to clamp down indiscriminately on non-violent opposition groups. Nevertheless, the EU is building up a toolbox for flexible crisis management with various military and civilian instruments. The strength of the EU is its increased ability to mix the various instruments of soft and hard power. According to Heisbourg, this ability provides Europe with a comparative advantage even over the United States, which tends to 'give pride of place to the military component of policy'.[36] The need for the right combination of ESDP with long-term structural measures requires effective cross-pillar coordination.

This chapter shows that the delicate nexus between international terrorism, Islam and migration can have a serious impact on the EU's relations with North Africa. The intermingling of economic, political and security (both external and internal) issues inevitably tests the EU's capabilities for multi-layered policymaking. This test is difficult to pass, given the various stakes and legacies of South European states in the Mediterranean region. In the final analysis, the EU strategy towards North Africa remains very much a function of where the EU is heading institutionally – towards a federal state or a multi-speed construct. However, the efforts aimed at promoting European integration in the areas of foreign policy, security and defence have received a serious blow with the Iraq crisis. The Middle East crisis has also become a crisis for Europe and its institutions, particularly NATO, but also for the development of a common security and defence policy. Nevertheless, the EU's policy of benign neglect of North Africa might be coming to an end, as the US–Iraqi showdown in the Greater Middle East will inevitably have serious political and socio-economic ripple effects upon the North African region.

Notes

1 The EMP is also called the Barcelona Process; the MEDA programme is the principal financial instrument of the EU for the implementation of the Euro-Mediterranean Partnership.
2 European Commission, *Country Profiles of the 12 Non-EU Mediterranean Partners*, SMAP, 2001.
3 European Council, 92/253, *Conclusions of the European Council Meeting in Lisbon*, held on 26–27 June 1992 (extracts only), in *European Cooperation Documentation Bulletin* Office for Official Publications of the European Communities, Luxembourg, 1995, p. 351.
4 See *Bulletin of the European Communities*, 1992, no. 6: 22.
5 J. Monar, 'Institutional Constraints of the European Union's Mediterranean Policy', *Mediterranean Politics*, 1998, vol. 3, no. 2: 50.
6 The 12 Mediterranean partners are Algeria, Cyprus, Egypt, Israel, Jordan, Lebanon, Malta, Morocco, the Palestinian Authority, Syria, Tunisia and Turkey.
7 Association Agreements with Tunisia, Israel, Morocco, the Palestinian Authority and Jordan have come into force. Those with Egypt, Lebanon and Algeria await ratification as of May 2003. Negotiations are taking place with Syria.
8 S. Stavridis and J. Hutchence, 'Mediterranean Challenges to the EU's Foreign Policy', *European Foreign Affairs Review*, 2000, no. 5: 38.
9 Felix Neugart, 'Europe, the Mediterranean and the Middle East', CAP Discussion Paper, Bertelmann Foundation, January 2002.

10 Javier Solana argued that the 'unspoken competition between the CMS and the ongoing effort to draw up a "Charter for Peace and Stability" in the Barcelona framework' has led to considerable confusion about the CMS. See Report by the Secretary-General/High Representative, *Common Strategies*, Council of the European Union, no. 1487/100, 21 December 2000.

11 G. Joffé, 'European Multilateralism and Soft Power Projection in the Mediterranean', in F. Tanner (ed.), *The European Union as a Security Actor in the Mediterranean*, Zürich: Zürcher Beiträge, 2001, p. 39.

12 Béchir Chourou, 'Security Partnership and Democratisation: Perception of the Activities of Northern Security Institutions in the South', in H. G. Brauch, A. Marquina and A. Biad (eds), *Euro-Mediterranean Partnership for the 21st Century*, New York: Palgrave, 2000, p. 177.

13 Chris Patten, 'Common Strategy for the Mediterranean and Reinvigorating the Barcelona Process', speech to the European Parliament, Brussels, 31 January 2001. Online. Available http: <http://europa.eu.int/comm/external_relations/news/patten/speech_01_49.htm> (accessed 10 May 2003).

14 R. Youngs, 'Democracy Promotion: The Case of European Union Strategy', CEPS Working Document 167, October 2001, p. 35.

15 B. L. Dillman, 'Facing the Market in North Africa', *Middle East Journal*, 2001, vol. 55, no. 2: 198–215.

16 See the notorious opinion piece by George Will, '"Final Solution" Phase 2', *Washington Post*, 2 May 2002; and the reply by Chris Patten, 'Stop Blaming Europe', *Washington Post*, 7 May 2002.

17 Chris Patten, *Reinvigorating the Barcelona Process*, COM (2000) 497 final, 6 September 2000.

18 Youngs, 'Democracy Promotion', p. 18.

19 Stavridis and Hutchence, 'Mediterranean Challenges', p. 51.

20 The president of the Commission was asked by the Spanish government to enter into contact with the prime minister of Morocco in order to express the grave concern of Europe about the further evolution of this issue. The president then backtracked from an offer to 'facilitate dialogue' to a statement that the Commission 'stands ready to facilitate, while not suggesting any mediation'. See *Financial Times*, 19 July 2002.

21 Ibid.

22 For NATO, there are currently five reasons why the Mediterranean matters: instability, terrorism, link to the Middle East and Iraq, WMD proliferation and energy security. See 'NATO and the Mediterranean: Moving from Dialogue towards Partnership', speech by NATO Secretary-General Lord Robertson, Royal United Services Institute, London, 29 April 2002.

23 F. Heisbourg, 'Introduction', in Tanner (ed.), *The European Union as a Security Actor in the Mediterranean*, p. 7.

24 Euro-Mediterranean Study Group Commission (EuroMeSCo), Working Group III, *First Year Report: European Defence: Perceptions and Realities*, EuroMeSCo Paper 16, June 2002.

25 Santa Maria de Feira European Council, 19/20 June 2000, *Conclusions of the Presidency*, Annex 1: Strengthening the Common European Policy on Security and Defence.

26 See, for instance, the 2002 Mediterranean Dialogue Work Programme. Online. Available http: < http://www.nato.int/med-dial/2002/mdwp-2002.pdf> (accessed 12 Januray 2003)

27 North Atlantic Council, *Prague Summit Declaration*, 21 November 2002.

28 J. Bruke, 'Al-Qaeda trained hundreds from UK', *Observer* (London), 24 February 2002.

29 S. Zubaida, 'Islam in Europe', paper presented at a GCSP Seminar on Islam and the West, 2–3 May 2002.
30 German Minister of the Interior Otto Schily argued that the attack was linked to the al-Qaida network: *Djerba: Schily sieht Verbindung zu El Kaida*, BBV Online-Dienst, 11 May 2002.
31 Quoted in 'North Africa a New Haven for Europe Terror', *CNN Report*, 11 January 2003.
32 'EU soll palästinenische Terroristen finanziert haben', *Spiegel on-line*, 12 January 2002.
33 J. Stevenson, 'Countering Terrorism at Home: US and European Experiences', paper presented at IISS/DCAF Conference on Implications of 11 September for the Security Sector: A Year On, 11–13 July 2002, p. 9.
34 S. Everts, 'Shaping a Credible EU Foreign Policy', *Centre for European Reform*, 2002, p. 6.
35 C. Spencer, 'The EU as Security Actor in the Mediterranean: Problems and Prospects', in Tanner (ed.), *The European Union as a Security Actor in the Mediterranean*, p. 15.
36 Heisbourg, 'Introduction', p. 6.

10 The Middle East

Towards a substantive European role in the peace process?

Roland Dannreuther

As with the Maghreb region, Europe has a complex set of historical legacies, close economic, social and political ties, and deeply embedded fears
and security concerns that define and characterize its overarching relationship with the 'classical' Middle East, meaning the countries of the Levant
or Mashreq and the Gulf region.[1] Although the European colonial penetration of the region was less intensive or drawn out than in the Maghreb,
European states, in particular the United Kingdom and France, became
the undisputed external actors after World War I and in large part created
the modern Middle Eastern state system, including its most acute and
enduring conflict over Palestine/Israel.[2] European domination was only
finally displaced in the mid-1950s when the Middle East was incorporated
into the structure of the Cold War, with the countries of the region being
aligned with their respective superpower patrons. In this more rigid
bipolar structure, an independent European strategic role either was made
redundant or became, as with the continuing presence of the British in the
Persian Gulf, economically unsustainable.

Despite the loss of Great Power status, Europe's social, economic and
political stakes in the region have only grown in magnitude along with the
sense of vulnerability to the various developments and conflicts in the
region. In the 1970s the OPEC embargo and the oil price rises appeared to
threaten the economic lifeblood of the European economies, and Palestinian international terrorism presented a complex challenge to European
internal security. The Iranian Revolution in 1979 raised the spectre of
Islamic fundamentalism and the perceived threats not only to international and regional security but also to European and Western values of
secularism and humanism. The potential appeal of this ideology to the disaffected among the 10 million Muslims in Europe created a new internal
security challenge for European governments. The end of the Cold War,
which eliminated or at least greatly reduced the perceived threat from the
East, only accentuated the sense of 'otherness' of the Arab and Muslim
Middle East, and, with the exclusion of most of these states from the
enlargement process, appeared to confirm their non-European status, with
all its cultural and value-laden connotations, despite their geographical

propinquity and the cultural and historical ties.[3] The terrorist attacks of 11 September 2001, with the evidence of close involvement of Muslim and Arab networks based in Europe, added to the sense of a threat that directly links the problems of the Middle East with the very heart of Europe.

European leaders have been fully conscious of this mutual vulnerability, with the former French foreign minister, Hervé de Charette, noting that 'when violence returns to the Middle East, sooner or later it will show up in Paris'.[4] For many in Europe, the fears of terrorism, religiously sanctioned violence and unwanted immigration are intimately, or even exclusively, tied up with the Middle East. As a consequence, European governments have consistently argued that such dependencies provide a compelling justification for a more prominent and expanded role for European diplomatic action in the Middle East, particularly with the withdrawal of the Soviet Union/Russia after the end of the Cold War. They point to the region's geographical proximity, the economic penetration by European business, and the degree of dependence and vulnerability, not only in terms of oil imports but also for domestic order and stability. There also remains the conviction, however justified in practice, that Europe's historical associations and knowledge grant it a more nuanced understanding and sensitivity to regional and local dynamics, and that Europe can play an essential and constructive role complementing and, if necessary, balancing the US predominance in the region.[5]

However, the reality has been that the Middle East, instead of being a source of unity and common purpose for Europe, has consistently been a source of disunity and loss of purpose, threatening at times to damage or even undermine the European project. There has been the problem of defining common positions where individual European states have their own diverging national priorities and interests, related to complex historical, economic, social and political ties and legacies. These national exceptionalisms have added to the difficulty for the European Union (EU) to develop a strategic approach and sense of priority consonant with the magnitude of the security challenges emanating from the region. Other priorities, such as eastwards enlargement, the Balkans, monetary union and internal institutional reforms continually distract the strategic focus from the Middle East. In addition, the Middle East remains the region in Europe's immediate neighbourhood where the United States has the most significant strategic interests and distinctive policy objectives, and where it has been willing, if necessary, to play on and accentuate European divisions in the pursuit of these policies. This was at no time more apparent than during the build-up to the military intervention in Iraq in March 2003, when European divisions, partly promoted by US encouragement of a schism between the so-called new and old Europe, reached an intensity that potentially threatened to weaken not only NATO and the transatlantic relationship but also the further promotion of European integration.

This broader context of Europe's complex relationship with the Middle East provides the background for the analysis in this chapter on the evolution and prospects for a distinctive and substantive European/EU role in the Middle East peace process (MEPP). The specific focus on the MEPP, rather than on the Middle East more generally, is partly driven by limitations of space but also reflects the fact that it is this policy area where Europe as a collectivity, institutionalized through the EU, has most consistently sought to define a distinctive role and function. Certainly, in the Gulf region, individual European states, such as the United Kingdom, France and Germany, have played and continue to play distinctive roles. But the EU as a body is much less present or engaged: it either lacks completely a policy, such as over Iraq, owing to internal European divisions, or has only a very limited economic engagement, as with the Gulf Cooperation Council (GCC) states, or has sought to define a policy, such as the 'critical dialogue' with Iran, but has barely moved from policy formation to implementation.[6] In contrast, in relation to the MEPP, the EC/EU's attempts to gain a substantive role go back to the 1970s and there has since then been a consistent resolve and determination for Europe's distinctive voice and policy preferences to be included in any process towards a peace settlement.

The central argument of this chapter is that, particularly since the mid-1990s, Europe has emerged as a more coherent and strategic actor towards the MEPP, which has ensured its direct involvement in a process from which it had earlier been excluded. It is argued that this role has been strengthened by the adoption of a comprehensive regional strategy, as outlined in the Euro-Mediterranean Partnership (EMP) or 'Barcelona Process'. This more substantive role is certainly constrained by the strategic deficiencies, the lack of a compelling vision for the region, the political disunity and institutional weaknesses of the EU which have been noted above. As a consequence, Europe cannot realistically be expected to supplant the role of the United States, which has the political and military capabilities that Europe lacks. However, conversely, the strengths that Europe possesses, such as its greater economic penetration and its more intensive relations with some of the Arab parties to the dispute, make it a partner that the United States has increasingly come to realize it cannot ignore and marginalize as it did during the Cold War.

There are two main sections to this chapter. First, there is an analysis of the historical evolution and progress in Europe's engagement and involvement in the MEPP from the 1970s to the present day. Second, there is a more general assessment of the strengths and weaknesses of Europe's role and the degree to which Europe has managed to be taken as a more serious actor in the resolution of the central conflict in the Middle East. The conclusions will address the implications of this enhanced role in the MEPP for Europe's strategic engagement with the Middle East more generally.

Europe and the MEPP

The attempts by the member states of the European Community (EC) to play a collective role, independent of the superpowers, in the Arab–Israeli peace process can be traced back to the 1970s.[7] The 1973 war and the subsequent Arab use of the oil weapon had heightened a deep sense of vulnerability, particularly as Europe depended for 80 per cent of its energy supplies on the region as compared to only 12 per cent for the United States. In its subsequent efforts to play a mediatory role in the Arab–Israeli conflict, European diplomacy appeared, at least from an Israeli and US perspective, to place its interests in energy security before those of impartial peacemaking. Significant European statements, such as the Brussels Declaration of November 1973, were to entrench a distinctly pro-Arab orientation. The subsequent Euro-Arab dialogue that followed was left unmatched by any parallel mechanism for ensuring a high-level interaction with the Israelis. During the proclaimed 'year of Europe' in 1973, the United States became disillusioned by Europe's failure to adopt a common Western stance and its willingness to submit to Arab demands to escape the oil embargo.[8]

The Venice Declaration of June 1980, issued one year after the signing of the peace treaty between Israel and Egypt, was to represent the high point in European attempts to promote a distinct and common European stance towards the Arab–Israeli conflict. The Declaration asserted that the Palestinian problem was not 'simply a refugee issue', that the Palestinian people should be allowed to 'exercise fully its right to self-determination', and that the Palestine Liberation Organization (PLO) should be included in any negotiations for a settlement. The Declaration also included unambiguous statements on the illegality of Israeli settlements, the need for an end to the Israeli occupation, and the inadmissibility of any unilateral initiative designed to change the status of Jerusalem.[9]

Twenty years later, the Venice Declaration still constitutes the basic principles of European policy towards the peace process. European leaders regularly highlight the historical prescience of the Declaration and how many of its key demands have been accepted and legitimated over time, most notably the need to include the PLO in the negotiating process and to accept the Palestinian right to self-determination. However, in terms of providing an immediate opening for a more assertive European role in the peace process, the Declaration was to prove a failure. For Israel, the Declaration only appeared to confirm Europe's anti-Israeli bias, as was revealed in the furious denunciation issued by the Israeli cabinet a couple of days afterwards: 'Nothing will remain of the Venice decision but a bitter memory. All men of good-will in Europe, all men who revere liberty, will see this document as another Munich-like capitulation to totalitarian blackmail.'[10]

The Venice Declaration represented a low point in Israel's relationship with the EC. Relations were not to improve during the 1980s, as a series of European statements and declarations, following the Israeli invasion of Lebanon in 1982 and the start of the Intifada in December 1987, became increasingly critical of Israeli policies and more open in their support of the PLO and the right of Palestinian self-determination. A consistent Israeli stance emerged, which gained support from across the political spectrum, that the EC had no legitimate role to play in the peace process. The United States, for its part, felt under no obligation to pressure Israel to accept a more prominent European role, given that European conceptions of the modalities of the peace process differed substantially from those held by successive US administrations. The Arab states were, naturally, gratified by the support given to them by the Europeans and were keen to have a counterweight to the United States' perceived uncritical support of Israel. But they were conscious of the inability of the Europeans to exert leverage on Israel, and more radical Arab states could rely on the Soviet Union to play a more consistent and practical role in balancing the US–Israeli alliance, most notably by providing the arms and weapons needed to gain a strategic counterweight to Israel's military dominance. Symptomatic of Europe's marginalization in the peace process was that the Venice Declaration was quickly eclipsed by an Arab peace plan, the Fahd Plan of 1981, which was itself overtaken by the Reagan Plan of the same year.[11]

The end of the Cold War, the decline of the Soviet Union/Russia as a regional actor in the Middle East, and the successful UN coalition formed to expel Iraq from Kuwait appeared to offer the EC a new opportunity to become more substantively involved in the peace process. In European capitals there was an expectation that an international conference, under the auspices of the United Nations, would be convened, where the EC/EU would play a major role.[12] These hopes were not, however, to be realized. The United States took it upon itself to set up the institutional framework for developing the peace process, which, even though the conference was held in Madrid, offered only a minor role for the EC/EU. Responding to the changed international conditions, the US administration decided to accede to the long-standing Soviet demand to be treated as a co-equal in the peace process, granting the now exhausted and disintegrating Soviet Union the formal role as co-chair of the conference. The Europeans were excluded from any role in the principal bilateral negotiations between Israel and the respective Arab parties to the dispute. Instead, they were invited to participate in the multilateral talks that were set up to deal with the more regional and functional issues related to the peace process.

The end of the Cold War and the successful prosecution of the Gulf War did not, therefore, immediately advance the EU's ambitions to secure a more prominent role in the Arab–Israeli peace process. As before, Europe's credentials for such a role were undermined by a combination of Israeli–US distrust and an incapacity to back the rhetorical support it provided for the Arab and Palestinian cause with any effective tools of leverage. The breakthrough in Oslo in 1993, when Israel acquiesced to the principle of direct negotiations with the PLO, did not immediately improve this situation. Despite the seeming confirmation of the long-held European principle of the need for direct Israeli–PLO negotiations, the EU had no role in promoting the agreement. Instead that role was taken by Norway, a non-EU country, which had managed to foster good relations with both parties to the dispute and had acted as the impartial mediator. Both Israel and the PLO also sought to legitimize and crown this breakthrough by obtaining a US blessing through a ceremonial signing of the Oslo Accords on the lawn of the White House.[13]

Towards a European role

With the signing of the Declaration of Principles, the EU's fortunes did, however, begin to improve. In fairly swift succession there were three significant developments that provided an impetus to the enhancement of the EU's presence and engagement in the peace process. First, the EU capitalized on the role that it was given in the multilateral track of the Madrid process to promote a constructive image of its activity and to emphasize the substantive contribution it was playing in promotion of the peace process. The EU was entrusted with the running of the Regional Economic Development Working Group (REDWG), which was the largest of the five working groups and whose objectives were to facilitate the emergence of a more economically interdependent and pluralistic regional environment. The EU was naturally suited to this economic-driven multilateralist agenda and set about its responsibilities as 'gavel-holder' for the working group with some energy and direction. A number of projects were identified which focused primarily on infrastructural development or on exploring areas of sectoral development. These projects were coordinated into the so-called Copenhagen Action Plan, and the EU provided a significant proportion of the financial resources for their implementation. The EU also sought to institutionalize this emerging multilateral cooperation through establishing in 1994 a monitoring committee of the core regional parties – Egypt, Israel, Jordan and the Palestinians – which would oversee the implementation of the Copenhagen Action Plan. In 1995 a secretariat was established in Amman where, under EU tutelage, officials of these countries cooperated and worked together.[14]

These admittedly relatively modest successes did nevertheless cause some tensions with Washington, which sought to re-establish greater political control over the process of economic integration. The EU was angered by the unilateral US decision to host the donor's pledging conference for the Palestinians in Washington in October 1994 and its insistence that the World Bank rather than the REDWG should be responsible for overseeing the dispersal of the aid.[15] Despite this setback, the Europeans continued to seek to nurture their image of disinterested economic support for the peace process through commitments of substantial financial assistance. The EU established itself as the most substantial non-military financial supporter of the peace process.[16] In particular, the EU took on the main financial burden of supporting the Palestinian Authority. Over the period from 1994 to 1999, the EU provided over US$2 billion of support to the Palestinians and became the economic lifeline for the administrative operations of the Palestinian Authority.[17] Indeed, it is questionable whether the Palestinian Authority could have survived over this period without this European financial support. Such European support for the Authority became even more critical with the second, or al-Aqsa, Intifada which broke out in late 2000 and led to a massive decline of economic activity in the West Bank and Gaza Strip.

The second development that projected a more visible European presence in the peace process was the launching of the EMP with 12 Mediterranean countries in November 1995, more commonly known as the 'Barcelona Process' after the city in which it was launched. The Barcelona Process was, from the beginning, self-consciously designed to be independent from, and not to be held hostage to, the MEPP. A strict formal distinction was made between the two processes, with different institutions and actors within the EU holding primary responsibility for these two policy areas. Although Israel and the Arab states represented the majority of the Mediterranean partners, the EU deliberately included a number of non-Arab partners, such as Malta, Cyprus and Turkey, to counterbalance the in-built Arab majority.[18] The promotion of the idea of a Mediterranean region, which many have been regarded as an artificial construct, had a similar underlying rationale.[19] The idea was to encourage a regional process of integration which would break down barriers not only between the rich European countries and the poorer South but also between the southern Mediterranean countries themselves. It was hoped that this vision of regional cooperation would transcend traditional regional configurations, such as the normal distinction between North Africa and the Middle East. In a similarly unconventional manner, security concerns were included in the Barcelona Process but approached through a 'comprehensive' security paradigm which saw the roots of conflict as primarily due to the failure of economic development, regional economic integration and the lack of respect for human rights and democracy. It was these longer-term 'deeper roots' of conflict, rather than the immediate political resolution of current conflicts, that the EMP sought to address.[20]

Even if the vision of the EMP has obtained wide support and even praise, it has been far more difficult to translate into practice, as also highlighted in Chapter 9 in this volume, by Fred Tanner.[21] The economic objectives which are at the heart of the process, and which envision the establishment of a free trade area by 2010, have not developed a significant momentum. In contrast to the advances made by the countries of East-Central Europe

(ECE), the Arab partners have fallen even further behind in terms of economic development and liberalization. The ambition to promote South–South trade, meaning enhanced trade between the Mediterranean partners, has also failed to materialize. The traditional hub–spoke pattern of EU trade with the region remains intact. A key problem has been the absence of an economic elite in the South pushing for the opening up of domestic markets to competition and able to pressure the predominantly introspective and security-obsessed regimes.[22] For the EU's part, its institutional weaknesses and the failure to prioritize the often conflicting objectives of the EMP have also contributed to the slow progress.[23] When one compares the Mediterranean partners with the ECE countries, it is clearly evident that the EU has been less willing to promote political conditionality; the financial support has been less generous, less focused and less readily disbursed; and EU member states have been even less open to providing access to certain sensitive markets, such as agriculture.[24]

Policymakers have also found it almost impossible to promote substantive advances in the EMP without there being a corresponding progress in the MEPP. In practice, it has been difficult to disentangle the two processes. The Barcelona Process was built upon the foundations of the advances made by the peace process during 1993–4, most notably the agreements between Israel and the Palestinians and Jordan. The EMP, to a certain degree, replicated and expanded the model of the multilateral form of the Madrid Process, the so-called Multinationals. This close synergy has meant that whenever the peace process has been in crisis, the EMP has also suffered. During 1996–7, when Netanyahu was in power and there was a breakdown in Arab–Israeli relations, progress on the EMP almost ground to a halt.[25] With the onset of the al-Aqsa Intifada in 2000, the long-awaited Charter for Peace and Security, which was expected to be signed in Marseilles, had to be shelved.

Despite all these problems associated with the Barcelona Process, its overall impact has been to improve Europe's profile in the region generally, and in the MEPP in particular. Three specific factors can be identified in relation to the peace process. First, the EMP provided a multilateral forum in which Israel, the Palestinians and the front-line Arab states have become participants, and which is more inclusive than the narrower focus of a US-dominated peace process. It is notable that Syria and Lebanon agreed to participate within the regional bodies associated to the EMP and not in the Multilaterals. As Volker Perthes has noted, the EMP has a potential, if as yet unrealized, role to play for Syria and Lebanon in providing an institutional framework for their economic and political opening up that is not dominated by Israel's regional economic and political might.[26] Second, the EMP, despite all its faults and failures, remains, in Eberhard Rhein's terms, 'the only game in town'.[27] The key challenge for the Arab partner states is to participate more fully in the global economy and to liberalize their economic and political systems, which, in practice, entails a process of integration with the neighbouring economic giant of the EU. The EMP has provided the institutional mechanism in which this reality of the economic, political and social linkages between the EU and the neighbouring Arab world has been formalized and made transparent. The success or failure of the EMP will, to a significant extent, determine the success or failure of the countries of the Arab Middle East in escaping their current marginalization in the global economy. The third factor is that the EMP has raised considerably Europe's economic and political stakes in overseeing the success of the peace process. Paralysis in the peace process not only represents a threat to the significant European financial commitments to that process (most notably the EU's investments in the Palestinian Authority), but also threatens to undermine the much broader objectives and purposes of the EMP, which seek to deal with the more general problems of regional instability and to stem the migratory flows and the export of terrorism and extremism, especially from North Africa. As a breakdown in the peace process threatens to undermine these broader and more vital European interests, so Europe's need for an enduring Arab–Israeli peace settlement has become more urgent.

It is this increased structural dependence of Europe for progress in the Arab–Israeli conflict which, at least in part, contributed to the third development in the mid-1990s that enhanced the EU's profile. This was the prominent and activist role taken by EU states and by the EU when Arab–Israeli relations deteriorated in late 1995 and in 1996. A succession of events contributed to this breakdown: the Israeli 'Grapes of Wrath' intervention in Lebanon; the election of the Netanyahu government in March 1996; the provocative opening of a tunnel near Arab holy places in Jerusalem in November; and the decision to construct a new Israeli settlement in East Jerusalem in February 1997. The European response was, in one sense, predictable and not dissimilar to earlier interventions. There were numerous declarations, the most significant of which was the Luxembourg Declaration of October 1996, that were highly critical of Israel.[28] For the most part, blame for the deterioration in the peace process was laid squarely at the feet of the new Netanyahu government. Also characteristically, France, under its newly elected president Jacques Chirac, pursued an independent and overtly pro-Arab policy which managed to irritate not only Israel and the United States but also the more Israeli-supportive EU states, such as Germany and the United Kingdom.[29]

Unlike previous occasions, though, this time the European activism was not limited to bluster and rhetoric. Despite US uneasiness, France did contribute diplomatically to the resolution of the 'Grapes of Wrath' intervention through its contacts with Syria and Iran, which made possible a compromise between Israel and Hizbullah, which in turn facilitated an Israeli withdrawal.[30] In October 1996 the EU appointed a special envoy to the peace process, the Spanish diplomat Miguel Angel Moratinos, who was given the task of maintaining contacts with all the parties to the dispute and providing support to the EU presidency. Although his appointment was initially treated with traditional Israeli condemnation and US disdain, he assumed a deliberately low-level and uncontroversial profile that aimed to build up trust and to project a constructive EU role. The appointment in 1999 of the former Secretary-General of NATO, Javier Solana, to the post of High Representative of the Common Foreign and Security Policy (CFSP), provided enhanced political credibility and offered a much-needed element of continuity to EU policy which could buttress the work of Moratinos.

From Clinton to Bush

The eventual outcome of all these initiatives and institutional developments was that when the Clinton administration decided to play a much more intensive hands-on role in the peace process, the EU was finally granted the diplomatic role which it had so long sought. This was a role that the EU recognized could not and should not seek to supplant or even 'balance' the primacy of US mediation but one whereby Europe could 'complement' the efforts made by US leaders and diplomats. This promotion of a more modest European role significantly defused the transatlantic tensions that had undermined previous attempts at coordination and provided clear practical advantages for the United States administration to utilize EU good offices in the search for a settlement.[31] In particular, the United States began to recognize that the EU could play a critical third-party role in relation to the Palestinians, who were naturally sceptical of the ability of the United States to be a fully impartial mediator and who also naturally turned for diplomatic support to the Europeans, to whom they were so financially and politically indebted. When US-promoted agreements between Israel and the Palestinians were reached, such as the Hebron Protocol of 1997 or the Wye River Memorandum of 1999, both the United States and the EU signed letters of reassurance in support of the implementation of these agreements. In March 1999 the EU issued the Berlin Declaration, which proclaimed the landmark decision to support a Palestinian state, but whose diplomatic purpose, coordinated with the United States, was to dissuade Yasser Arafat from unilaterally declaring a Palestinian state.[32] It was symptomatic of the increased trust on both the Israeli and Palestinian sides that when a last-ditch effort to reach an agreement was made in Taba in January 2001, it was Moratinos who was asked by both parties to listen to their respective points of view.[33]

In retrospect, the period 1998–2000 can be seen as the historic high point of an intensive and constructive EU presence and role in the MEPP. While the EU recognized that its role was to be subordinate to the United States and that it had to match its rhetoric with practical policy initiatives, the United States accepted that the EU could play a facilitating and complementary role. Even the Israeli government under Ehud Barak began to discard some of its entrenched suspicions of European intentions.

However, with the failure of the Camp David summit in September 2000, the rise of a more vicious and bloody Palestinian uprising, including the repeated use of suicide bombings against civilian Israeli targets, and the election of a right-wing Likud-led government, the momentum of the peace process ground to a halt. The administration of President George W. Bush, which came to power in 2001, also decided to adopt a more low-key and limited engagement in the MEPP, seeking to distance itself from the intensive personalized diplomacy of the Clinton period. With the ensuing violence, Europeans tried but failed to fill the diplomatic vacuum and confronted an Israeli government which manifested an instinctive distrust of European intentions and relied almost entirely on the sympathetic reception from its traditional US ally.[34] In the process, Europe's financial investment in the Palestinian Territories and its support for the Palestinian Authority were made practically worthless as Israeli military reoccupation severely damaged the Palestinian infrastructure and greatly reduced economic activity.

The crisis of the new Intifada appeared to return Europe to its traditional role of diplomatic impotence and marginalization. The impact of the terrorist attacks of 11 September 2001 seemed, for a while, to offer the prospect of a more intensive focus on the MEPP. In November, President Bush indicated that the United States was now willing to support publicly, for the first time, the creation of a Palestinian state. However, the subsequent wave of Palestinian suicide bombings undermined the US resolve to engage more fully in the peace process and to exert pressure on Israel, which Washington judged was engaged in its own 'war against terrorism'. Moreover, as the international focus inexorably moved from Palestine to Iraq and the issue of Iraqi disarmament, European divisions over US policy and frustrations over the failure to advance the MEPP only intensified.

Yet even in this deeply inhospitable environment for European peace-making, the fruits of earlier transatlantic cooperation were not entirely lost. The Mitchell Report of April 2001 was co-sponsored by the EU, and a central diplomatic role in the formulation of the report was played by Solana. In April 2002 a new diplomatic initiative from the United States resulted in the creation of the so-called quartet – the United States, the EU, the UN and Russia – as an informal but institutionalized forum for advancing the MEPP. By the end of 2002 this new body had established a 'road map' for an Israeli–Palestinian settlement which would lead, through various stages, to 'two states, Israel and an independent, viable and democratic Palestine, living side by side in peace'.[35] Although the Israeli elections in 2003 and preparation for war against Iraq initially inhibited US efforts to push the 'road map', key US administration officials affirmed that creation of a Palestinian state would be a leading priority after any war against Iraq.[36] The visit by President Bush to the Middle East in June 2003, which included a summit with the key parties to the conflict, underlined the commitment and resolve of the US administration. However, the formation of the quartet is in itself indicative of a US realization that it cannot deliver the 'two-state solution' without the support of other key regional actors, including, most significantly, the EU.

Yet despite this potential compensation, the Middle East crises in 2000 and 2003 highlighted an EU in seeming paralysis, unable to reach a consensus between its member states, not only over Iraq but also over the MEPP. For example, the raising of the prospect of sanctions against Israel, and then the failure to reach a consensus for this, damaged EU credibility. The inability to protect the billions of euros of investment in the Palestinian Territories exposed European impotence and the EU's ultimate dependence on the United States for any effective influence on Israel. With the knock-on impact of the crisis also threatening to leave the Barcelona Process in tatters, to what extent have this Arab–Israeli crisis and the war in Iraq again exposed the essential weakness and lack of strategic capability of the EU and its member states?

Strengths and weaknesses of Europe's role

It is certainly the case that when the relations between Arabs and Israelis deteriorate and the peace process is in abeyance, Europe's structural weaknesses and problems are immediately made transparent. It is natural that unfavourable contrasts are made with the United States. First, it highlights the most salient fact that the EU, unlike the United States, is not a unitary actor and that there does not exist in reality a common European Middle East policy. For historical, cultural and geographical reasons, the EU member states have differing interests in, and diverging levels of engagement with, the countries of the region. This can be illustrated by Europe's relations with Israel. France, with its historic ties to Syria and Lebanon, its sympathy towards Iraq and its close linkages with the Maghreb, inclines towards a pro-Arab stance. Other Mediterranean EU states, such as Spain, Italy and Greece, have a similar tendency to favour the Palestinian cause. The United Kingdom, while trying to differentiate itself from the instinctively critical stance taken by France, also finds its historic relations with Jordan and the Gulf States promoting a pro-Arab orientation. In contrast, Germany and the Netherlands have strong historical and ideological reasons to be considerably more supportive of Israel.

The problem of the divergences between the European states is exacerbated by the institutional complexity of the EU itself. In terms of EU foreign policy, there is a division between its external economic relations, which operate within the partially supranational decision-making of the European Community, and the foreign and security policy, which lies within the intergovernmental framework of the CFSP.[37] Formally, there are four institutions which are involved in foreign policy: the European Council, the General Affairs Council, the European Commission and the European Parliament. The question of who runs EU policy over the

Middle East is not easy to answer, as those potentially involved include the High Representative, several commissioners, including most notably Chris Patten as commissioner for external affairs, the special envoy to the peace process, and 15 foreign ministers. In a region where personalized diplomacy is so important, this multiplicity of potential EU actors, many of whom do not necessarily have a high profile, complicates the task of diplomacy. For the countries of the Middle East, this institutional complexity projects an image of the EU as lacking transparency and predictability. When ambitious projects like the Barcelona Process appear to be undermined by a Byzantine bureaucratic structure, this can breed a more general sense of disillusionment.

These institutional constraints within the EU are reflected in its preference for an economic rather than a political engagement. This is especially evident in the EMP, in which the economic component of the partnership, the Association Agreements and the objective of a free trade area, have assumed a far greater prominence than the politico-security and socio-cultural components of the Partnership, which formally are supposed to have equal footing.[38] Whenever there is an attempt to insert a degree of political conditionality in this economic interaction – whether to impose sanction against Arab states for abuse of human rights or Israel for its treatment of the Palestinians – consensus for action is rarely obtained.[39] In contrast with other neighbouring regions, such as ECE and even the western Balkans, the economic incentives for changes in political behaviour are not supported by the political incentive of possible future EU membership. This greatly reduces Europe's power of leverage. In practice, it is difficult to dispel the impression that the EU's Mediterranean policy is a second-order priority compared to the objectives of integration of ECE and conflict resolution in the Balkan states.

Finally, in terms of structural weaknesses, there remains the historical legacy of a deeply embedded Israeli distrust of European intentions and good faith. It does not take much for the Israeli political establishment to articulate its suspicions towards the Europeans and to argue that Europe has disqualified itself from a broker role. Israel's principal ally, the United States, is not only more sympathetic to Israeli policies, having the political and military clout which the Europeans lack, but also tends to concur with the view of the essential illegitimacy of a European role. Richard Haas argues that Europe's alignment with the weaker Arab states has meant that

> Europe has forfeited much of its ability to influence Israel but has gained little in so doing: indeed, there is not a bit of evidence to suggest that Europe has been able to elicit much flexibility from the Arab states and the Palestinians.[40]

Israeli criticisms not only include Europe's perceived pro-Arab line but also the belief that Europe's policies are driven primarily by economic motives, which engender a lack of appreciation of Israel's security concerns.[41] In darker moments, Israelis detect a continuing element of anti-Semitism and Europe's failure to deal with its Muslims at home as factors informing European policies towards Israel.

These structural weaknesses in Europe's engagement in the Middle East and with the peace process are certainly significant obstacles. However, these weaknesses have to be counterbalanced by proper recognition of some of Europe's strengths, which in certain circumstances give it a comparative advantage in relation to the United States. One such strength is that the Middle East is geographically closer to and economically more dependent on Europe than the United States. Europe is the main trading partner of practically all the Middle Eastern states, including Israel. In 2000, half of the trade of the Mediterranean partner countries was with the EU, as compared to 14.1 per cent with the United States.[42] The programmes that the EU has promoted for the region, such as the EMP, will tend to enhance and strengthen these strong trading and economic links. The dominant role that the EU has played in support of the Palestinians is indicative that the future economic prosperity of the region will be closely related to the financial support and the prospects for integration with Europe. The United States itself recognizes that the lion's share of the financial support for reconstruction of the region in the event of a comprehensive settlement will come from Europe.[43] Moreover, the experience and the impetus that Europe brings to the region in terms of the importance of multilateralism, of the need to strengthen civil society and the rule of law, and the imperatives of economic and political integration are the key elements for medium- to long-term stability in the region. Over this longer-term perspective, Europe's role is only likely to increase rather than diminish.

Certainly, in the shorter term, Europe's lack of political unity and military capability, and its identification with the Arab position, inhibits its peacemaking prospects. But it is important to counterbalance this realization with an understanding of the problems that the United States faces in presenting itself as a neutral and disinterested mediator. For the Arab parties to the dispute, the US and Israeli positions often appear conflated, and there is a justified scepticism towards the ability of US administrations to apply pressure on Israel. It is now generally recognized, including in Washington, that any sustainable settlement will demand concessions from Israel which the United States alone will be incapable of imposing and which will require a concerted international effort, including not only by the Europeans but also by other external actors, such as Russia and Saudi Arabia. The establishment of the Middle East Quartet represented a de facto US recognition of this reality. Also, the fact that Europe is less associated with Israel also makes European states preferred interlocutors with a number of regional actors with which they often have historical ties and a deeper local knowledge. European states have a role to play in maintaining dialogue and seeking to integrate into the peace process countries such as Syria, Lebanon and Iran, which have non-existent or poor relations with the United States. There is also an important function that Europe can play in supporting the weaker bargaining position of the Palestinians and the Arab states. It is to ensure that this weakness is not translated into the making of concessions that would be perceived locally to be unjust and thus would not lead to a sustainable long-term political settlement. This is especially the case with the Palestinians, who should not be expected to make significant territorial concessions on the West Bank and Gaza Strip when these territories are already very densely populated and barely economically viable.

The final point to make, as this chapter has sought to demonstrate, is that Europe has become more realistic about its capabilities, has a better recognition of its weaknesses and has sought to promote policies which build upon its comparative strengths. There is less of a tendency to grandstand, or to attempt impotently to 'balance', the United States, and a greater commitment to seek to complement US efforts. The promotion of strategies such as the EMP has sought to give Europe a more long-term and structured relationship with the region. There is also evidence of a greater degree of internal coordination, with, for example, the creation of the positions of High Representative and of Special Envoy to the peace process providing a greater degree of credibility and consistency to EU policymaking. Individual European states have also appeared more willing to cede diplomatic initiative to the EU, while the United States has accommodated itself to accepting a more prominent role for the Europeans, certainly during the second Clinton administration and potentially in the post-war Bush reconstruction efforts. Even Israeli suspicions have been partially allayed, though the criticisms offered by the Sharon government have suggested that they have been far from overcome.

Conclusions

The Middle East is a region where Europe is bound to play an important role. There are close historical ties which infuse the relationship. The region is geographically close to Europe, not only in the sense that it can be considered Europe's 'near abroad' but also because the Middle East penetrates into Europe with the presence of sizeable Muslim and Middle Eastern communities. Europe's sense of vulnerability in relation to the Middle East, whether it be in terms of migration or the export of extremism, also impels an intensive engagement and involvement. The European economic penetration, and the absence of alternative opportunities for economic development in the poorer South, means that the fates of the two regions are mutually intertwined. While the states and peoples of the Middle East can fear and resent their neighbouring economic hegemon and former colonial rulers, Europe also provides a practical model for how a war-torn region can secure peace and prosperity.

In retrospect, Europe's disengagement from the Middle East during the Cold War can be considered a historical anomaly. This exclusion was driven by the imposition of the bipolar ideological struggle and by the attendant process of decolonization and imperial withdrawal. With the end of the Cold War, and the memories of European colonial rule fading or faded, Europe has regained the economic and political power to promote a legitimate presence and role in the region. To consolidate this role, Europe still has two major tasks to achieve. First, it must regain the ability to think and act with greater strategic commitment and consistency. Second, it must learn how to make its highly original new political construct, the 'less than a state but more than a regime' of the European Union, act more efficiently and in a more unified and directed manner.

Clearly, these two tasks are intimately connected. The Barcelona Process is indicative of the potential strengths of the EU's external strategy but also its weakness for rhetorical rather than strategic commitment. On the one hand, it represents a strategy which attempts to offer a holistic, economically focused and long-term vision for peace and prosperity in the region, buttressed by financial and political support from the EU and its member states. On the other, the process emerged as an untidy compromise between the EU member states, as a sort of parallel process to eastern enlargement, but without the commitment and the willingness to prioritize the desired goals and ambitions. As a consequence, the Euro-Mediterranean Partnership has tended to diffuse its energies over so many issue areas that there has not emerged, as there has with the ECE countries, a clear route map to show the Mediterranean partners how they might secure the economic and political objectives or what rewards they would obtain by fulfilling the EU's objectives. In more strictly strategic terms, the EMP has made an unnecessary linkage between the security concerns of the North African states and the Arab–Israeli conflict. At the same time, the European engagement in the peace process is harmed by the strategic failure to realize the interconnections between the Arab–Israeli conflict and the Gulf region, which is reflected structurally in the exclusion of these states from the Barcelona Process, and the more general absence of a more coordinated European policy in that region.[44]

While there is a lack of an overall strategic vision for the Middle East as a whole, a clearer and more coherent European strategy is now discernible in terms of a the Middle East peace process. In the context of a reinvigoration of the Arab–Israeli peace process, which is inevitable given that the condition of a perpetual war is ultimately unsustainable for both the local parties and the major external actors, Europe's role is not to be the major peace broker, for which it does not have the political leverage or internal consistency, but to work in close cooperation with the other parties. European unity of decision and action would need to be maintained through the European Council asserting its prerogative and exclusive responsibility over the Israel–Palestine issue so as to constrain unilateral interventions by individual EU states. In addition, an EU role would require a clear determination of its view on, and preferences for, the parameters of a peace settlement. In practice, such a determination is not so difficult to achieve since there is a clearer understanding, even among the parties in dispute, of the essential outline of a settlement. At the Taba talks in January 2001, for which Moratinos provided a full summary of the discussions, the Israelis and Palestinians came close to a mutually acceptable agreement.[45] A final settlement will inevitably have to be something close to what was almost agreed in Taba.

Notes

1 In this chapter the Middle East is taken to mean Israel, Iran, Turkey and the Arab states excluding those of North Africa/Maghreb, which is the main focus of the chapter by Tanner in this volume (Chapter 9).
2 D. Fromkin, *A Peace to End All Peace: Creating the Modern Middle East, 1914–1922*, London: Penguin, 1991; and L. C. Brown, *International Politics and the Middle East: Old Rules, Dangerous Games*, London: Tauris, 1984.
3 The EU's relationship with Turkey is both a confirmation and a potential rejection of this conception of the meaning of Europe, as highlighted in the chapter by Dorronsoro (Chapter 4).
4 Interview with Hervé de Charrette, *Les Echoes*, 8 April 1997.
5 For an assertive French view on this, see H. Védrine, *France in an Age of Globalization*, Washington, DC: Brookings Institution Press, 2000, pp. 90–100.
6 For a good overview of EU–Gulf relations, see C.-P. Hanelt, F. Neugart and M. Peitz (eds), *Future Perspectives for European–Gulf Relations*, Munich and Gütersloh: Bertelsmann Foundation, 2000. On specifically European–Saudi relations, see G. Nonneman, 'Saudi–European Relations 1902–2001: a Pragmatic Quest for Relative Autonomy', *International Affairs*, 2001, vol. 77, no. 3: 631–66.
7 For an analysis of early European initiatives, see F. d'Alancon, 'The EC Looks to a New Middle East', *Journal of Palestine Studies*, 1994, vol. 23, no. 2: 41–51; and I. Greilsammer, 'Failure of the European "Initiatives" in the Middle East', *Jerusalem Quarterly*, 1984, no. 33: 40–9.
8 Kissinger famously described the European behaviour as 'craven and contemptible'. In his memoirs, Kissinger wrote, concerning the European response to the oil embargo: 'nothing could have better illustrated the demoralization – verging on abdication – of the democracies'. See H. Kissinger, *Years of Upheaval*, London: Weidenfeld and Nicolson, 1982, p. 897.
9 'Declaration of the European Council on the Euro-Arab Dialogue and the Situation in the Middle East', European Council, Venice, 12–13 June 1980. Text found in W. Lacquer and B. Rubin (eds), *The Israel–Arab Reader: A Documentary History of the Middle East Conflict*, New York: Penguin, 1985, pp. 414–15.
10 Quoted in Rosemary Hollis, 'Israeli–European Economic Relations', *Israel Affairs*, 1994, vol. 1, no. 1: 125.
11 For a good analysis of this period, see J. Peters, 'Europe and the Middle East Peace Process: Emerging from the Sidelines', in S. Stavrides, T. Coloumbis, T. Veremis and N. Waites (eds), *The Foreign Policies of the European Union's Mediterranean States and Applicant Countries in the 1990s*, Basingstoke, UK: Macmillan, 1999, pp. 295–316.

12 J. Palmer, 'The European Community and the Middle East Peace', *Middle East International*, 16 August 1991, pp. 17–18.
13 D. Makovsky, *Making Peace with the PLO: The Rabin Government's Road to the Oslo Accord*, Boulder, Colo.: Westview Press, 1996.
14 For an in-depth analysis of the Madrid Multilaterals, see J. Peters, *Pathways to Peace: The Multilateral Arab–Israeli Peace Talks*, London: Royal Institute of International Affairs, 1996; and D. D. Kaye, 'Madrid's Forgotten Forum: The Middle East Multilaterals', *Washington Quarterly*, 1997, vol. 20, no. 1: 167–86.
15 P. Robins, 'Always the Bridesmaid: Europe and the Middle East Peace Process', *Cambridge Review of International Affairs*, 1997, vol. 10, no. 2: 78.
16 The United States has provided each year since the Camp David Treaty US$5 billion worth of primarily military aid to Israel and Egypt.
17 'Interview with European Union Special Envoy, Miguel Moratinos', *Europe Magazine*, 1998/99, no. 382: 30.
18 The Mediterranean partners are Algeria, Cyprus, Egypt, Israel, Jordan, Lebanon, Malta, Morocco, the Palestinian Authority, Syria, Tunisia and Turkey.
19 See, for example, S. C. Calleya, *Navigating Regional Dynamics in the Post-Cold War World: Patterns of Relations in the Mediterranean Area*, Aldershot, UK: Dartmouth, 1997; and O. Waever and B. Buzan, 'An Inter-regional Analysis: NATO's New Strategic Concept and the Theory of Security Complexes', in S. Behrendt and C.-P. Hanelt (eds), *Bound to Cooperate: Europe and the Middle East*, Gütersloh: Bertelsmann Foundation, 2000.
20 For analyses of the problems of this approach, see Roberto Aliboni, 'Re-setting the Euro-Mediterranean Security Agenda', *International Spectator*, 1998, vol. 33, no. 4: 11–15; and C. Spencer, 'Security Implications of the EMPI for Europe', *Journal of North African Studies*, 1998, vol. 3, no. 2: 202–11.
21 For another critical assessment, see G. Joffé, 'Europe and the Mediterranean: The Barcelona Process Five Years On', Royal Institute of International Affairs Briefing Paper 16, August 2000. For a more detailed analysis, see G. Joffé (ed.), *Perspectives on Development: The Euro-Mediterranean Partnership*, London: Frank Cass, 1999.
22 E. Keinle, 'Destabilization through Partnership? Euro-Mediterranean Relations after the Barcelona Process', *Mediterranean Politics*, 1998, vol. 3, no. 2, 1–20.
23 R. Youngs, 'The Barcelona Process after the UK Presidency: The Need for Prioritization', *Mediterranean Politics*, 1999, vol. 4, no. 1: 1–24.
24 Recognition of this from within the EU can be seen in Chris Patten, 'Common Strategies for the Mediterranean and Reinvigorating the Barcelona Process', speech to the European Parliament, 31 January 2001. Online. Available http: <http://www.europa.int/comm/external_relations/news/patten/speech_01_49.htm> (accessed 10 October 2002).
25 F. Tanner, 'The Euro-Med Partnership: Prospects for Arms Limitations and Confidence Building after Malta', *International Spectator*, 1998, vol. 3, no. 2: 202–11.
26 V. Perthes, 'The Advantages of Complimentarity: The Middle East Peace Process', in H. Gardner and R. Stefanova (eds), *The New Transatlantic Agenda: Facing the Challenges of Global Governance*, Aldershot, UK: Ashgate, 1999, p. 114; and V. Perthes (ed.), *Scenarios for Syria: Socio-economic and Political Choices*, Baden-Baden: Nomos Publishers, 1998.
27 E. Rhein, 'Peacemaking in the Middle East: Reflections on the End-Game', Brussels, 6 April 2002. Online. Available http: <http://www.euromesco.org/euromesco/publi_artigo.asp?cod_artigo=74988> (accessed 10 March 2003).
28 'EU Declaration on the Middle East Peace Process', European Union press release no. 59/96, 1 October 1996.

29 P. C. Wood, 'Chirac's "New Arab Policy" and Middle East Challenges: The Arab–Israeli Conflict, Iraq and Iran', *Middle East Journal*, 1998, vol. 52, no. 4: 563–80; and M. Bonnefous, 'Réflexions sur une politique arabe', *Défense nationale*, 1998, vol. 54: 44–67.

30 Perthes, 'The Advantages of Complementarity', p. 116.

31 For analyses of the transatlantic tensions in the Middle East during the mid-1990s, see P. H. Gordon, 'The Transatlantic Allies and the Changing Middle East', Adelphi Paper 322, Oxford: Oxford University Press, 1998; and R. D. Blackwill and M. Stürmer (eds), *Allies Divided: Transatlantic Policies for the Greater Middle East*, Cambridge: Centre for Science and International Affairs, 1997.

32 'European Union Presidential Conclusions', Berlin European Council, 24–25 March 1999. Online. Available http: <http://www.europ.int/external_relations/mepp/decl/index.htm#9 (accessed 20 November 2002).

33 For Moratinos's summary of the various positions of the negotiating parties at Taba, see 'Les Minutes des négociations de Taba, par M. Moratinos', *Le Monde Diplomatique*. Online. Available http: <http://www.monde-diplomatique.fr/cahier/proche-orient/tabaminutes> (accessed 10 November 2002).

34 For an indication of Israeli distrust, see the claims in *Financial Times*, 7 May 2002, that EU funds were diverted by Arafat to fund terrorist activities.

35 The first indications of the road map were made public in 'Communiqué issued by the Quartet', New York, 17 September 2002. Online. Available http: <http://www.un.org/news/dh/mideast/quartet_communique.htm> (accessed 10 March 2003). The unofficial text of the US draft plan for the road map was leaked to the *New York Times*. Online. Available http: <http://www.mideast-web.org/quartetrm2.htm> (accessed 10 March 2003)

36 See statement by US Assistant Secretary of Defense Paul Wolfowitz on 15 January 2003 that following the war on Iraq, 'our stake in pushing for a Palestinian state will grow', as reported in M. Brown, 'Bush Knows Best', *Middle East International*, 7 February 2003.

37 J. Monar, 'Institutional Constraints of the European Union's Mediterranean Policy', *Mediterranean Politics*, 1998, vol 3, no. 2: 39–60.

38 There are three dimensions of cooperation under the EMP: the 'political and security partnership', the 'economic and financial partnership' and the 'partnership in social, cultural and human affairs'. For a general discussion, see A. Vasconcelos and G. Joffé (eds), *The Barcelona Process: Building a Euro-Mediterranean Regional Community*, London: Frank Cass, 2000.

39 Youngs, 'The Barcelona Process after the UK Presidency'.

40 R. N. Haas, 'The United States, Europe, and the Middle East Peace Process', in Blackwill and Stürmer (eds), *Allies Divided*, pp. 61–2.

41 J. Alpher, 'The Political Role of the European Union in the Arab–Israeli Peace Process. An Israeli Perspective', *International Spectator*, 1998, vol. 33, no. 4: 77–86.

42 'EU Trade Relations with the 12 Mediterranean Partner Countries', *Eurostat/02/32*, 15 March 2002.

43 Gordon, 'The Transatlantic Allies', p. 38.

44 S. al-Mani, 'Barcelona's First Pillar: An Appropriate Concept for Security Relations', in Behrendt and Hanelt (eds), *Bound to Cooperate*, pp. 65–8; and S. Chubin, 'Europe and Iran's Role in Regional Politics', in Hanelt, Neugart and Peitz (eds), *Future Perspectives*, pp. 55–75.

45 'Les Minutes des négociations de Taba, par M. Moratinos', *Le Monde Diplomatique*.

11 EU energy security and the periphery

John Gault

Europe relies upon energy imported from regions on its periphery, especially from Russia, North Africa, the Caspian and the Middle East. The degree of this reliance will increase in coming decades. This trend of rising energy imports from countries on the European periphery has important security implications. Energy dependence will compel the European Union (EU) to pay close attention to political and economic developments in the countries of the periphery. While this import dependence is growing, the EU is seeking to liberalize internal energy markets. The liberalization process also has an impact on Europe's external energy trade relationships and on security of supply.

European energy security requires, first, that new production capacities in the periphery regions be developed in a timely manner along with adequate transportation systems to deliver the energy to European markets. European security then requires that the likelihood of interruptions to such supplies is minimized, and, in the event of an interruption, that the consequences for European consumers are moderated. Oil and gas production capacities in countries neighbouring Europe are being enlarged, and transportation systems are being planned and constructed to provide additional supplies to Europe. For the most part, private companies from both importing and exporting countries, and in some cases the national oil companies of the exporting countries, are making these investments, often as joint ventures.

The EU is trying to define a comprehensive energy security policy and to ensure that this policy is compatible with liberalized energy markets. Meanwhile, the EU already helps to provide the favourable business climate in which private energy infrastructure investments take place. To some extent, energy security can be addressed directly through energy-specific policies, but ultimately energy security is inextricable from broader economic and foreign policy challenges and solutions. A continuous flow of energy from the periphery countries to Europe will depend, ultimately, upon steady improvements in the quality of life and the comprehensiveness of political participation in the periphery countries themselves.

This chapter has three parts to it. First, there is an assessment of Europe's energy import requirements and the extent to which Europe's periphery will be the source for these supplies. Second, the role that the EU and European governments play in facilitating the necessary investment and the implementation of oil and gas projects in the periphery is analysed. Finally, the conditions necessary for ensuring European energy security are assessed, including the long-term European energy security interest in the political and economic stabilization of the oil-producing countries on the periphery.

Europe's growing reliance on energy imports

Currently, Europe is about as dependent on imported oil as is the United States, and is more dependent on imported natural gas.[1] For the purposes of my forward-looking analysis of security issues, I treat Europe as it will probably become over the next 10 to 20 years: an enlarged version of the present European Union, including not only the present EU but also candidate members and some countries not yet formal candidates (e.g. Norway, Switzerland). Thus, I treat here all the countries of Europe (excluding Russia, Belarus and Ukraine) as an entity, and the 'periphery' under consideration includes Russia, the Caspian region and the Mediterranean Basin – the 'neighbourhood' of an expanded EU.

Europe managed to reduce its dependence on imported oil during the 1990s by expanding production from the Norwegian sector of the North Sea and by delaying the inevitable decline of production in the UK sector. Substantial increases in natural gas production from both Norway and the United Kingdom restrained natural gas imports below 40 per cent throughout the decade in spite of rapid growth in European gas consumption. However, plausible assumptions about European rates of economic growth, energy prices, environmental regulations and other factors over the coming two decades lead to projections of increasing energy import dependence. All forecasts agree that natural gas consumption will grow rapidly, and oil consumption will also expand, though not as fast as that of natural gas.

Projections made by the International Energy Agency (IEA) indicate that European oil demand will rise by an average of 0.5 per cent per annum to 2030, while gas demand will expand at 2.1 per cent per annum over the same period.[2] Other projections reveal similar trends.[3] Of course, the rates of growth of oil and gas consumption will be influenced by European policies concerning market liberalization and competition, encouragement of renewable energy, excise taxes, the rate of retirement of nuclear power plants and other policies.

European oil production, primarily in the North Sea, is expected to decline from nearly 7 million barrels per day (mmbd) currently to less than 3 mmbd by 2030. Internal natural gas production, also primarily from the

North Sea, will not rise much above current levels of around 300 billion cubic metres per year (bcm/yr) in the foreseeable future. Higher energy prices and/or new production technologies could extend the life of existing fields somewhat, but substantial expansion beyond the projected levels is unlikely. Under the most plausible scenarios, Europe will import about 6 mmbd of additional oil and at least 300 bcm/yr (and quite possibly more) of additional natural gas in 2030 compared with today's import levels. This implies that import dependence for oil will increase from about 52 per cent today to about 85 per cent by 2030, and for gas from 36 per cent today to about 63 per cent in 2030.[4]

Where will the additional supplies come from?

Much of the oil currently imported into Europe (roughly 40 per cent) comes from the Middle East Gulf. But an even larger proportion originates in regions closer to Europe, especially the former Soviet Union (FSU) and North Africa, which together account for about 48 per cent of Europe's oil imports.[5] Sources of Europe's natural gas imports are even more concentrated, with the FSU and North Africa accounting for some 96 per cent of Europe's imports, including both gas imported via pipeline and gas in the form of liquefied natural gas (LNG). In any consideration of where additional oil and gas imports may originate, these peripheral regions deserve particular attention.

There are a number of reasons to expect that additional energy supplies for Europe will come first from the periphery rather than from the Middle East Gulf. Resources from the Middle East Gulf will be drawn towards faster-growing markets in Asia. During the 1990s, China changed from being a net oil exporter of 0.5 mmbd to being a net oil importer of over 1.5 mmbd. Asian markets will draw Middle East resources away from Europe and will tap hydrocarbons in eastern Siberia and in Central Asia.[6] At the margin, Europe will compete with China and other Asian markets for oil and gas supplies from these sources.[7]

The shift in direction of Middle East oil exports from western to eastern destinations has been taking place gradually for a long time. In 1980, nearly two-thirds of Middle East oil exports went to Atlantic Basin markets (North and South America, and Europe). Today, only about one-third of Middle East exports reach those markets. This trend will continue. By 2020, according to projections by the United States Department of Energy, only about 25 per cent of Middle East oil exports will flow to the Western Hemisphere and Europe. Oil has tended to move preferentially from the Gulf to Asia for many reasons, including shorter shipping times from the Gulf to Asian destinations than to Northern Europe and frequently higher netback values from Asian markets. Middle Eastern oil also has been displaced from Atlantic markets over the past two decades by increasing oil production in the Atlantic Basin.

Middle Eastern natural gas has until very recently flowed almost exclusively eastwards (in the form of LNG) to Asian markets. Natural gas, whether transported via pipeline or as LNG, costs more to transport per unit of energy than does oil. Oman, the United Arab Emirates and Qatar in 2000 together exported about 23.5 bcm, 90 per cent of which went to Japan and Korea, and less than 4 per cent went to Europe as occasional spot shipments. Recent reductions in gas liquefaction costs have begun to make Middle Eastern gas marginally competitive as new baseload supply to South European markets. For example, the following trades have been announced:

- Qatargas is selling 1.45 mmtpy[8] of LNG to Gas Natural (Spain);[9]
- Rasgas will supply Edison International (Italy) with 3.5 mmtpy LNG;[10]
- Qatargas will supply ENEL (Italy) and Repsol (Spain) with 4.8 mmtpy of LNG;[11] and
- Iran has announced its intention to sell LNG to Repsol (Spain).[12]

In addition, Qatar Petroleum and ExxonMobil have announced a project (Qatargas-2) to deliver up to 14 mmtpy of LNG to the United Kingdom, with start-up scheduled for 2006 or 2007.[13]

These new trades have been influenced by the current economic slowdown in some Asian markets, almost certainly a transient effect. The Middle East, however, will not be the primary source of incremental European gas. New gas supplies for Europe will come primarily from North Africa, from Russia and from the Caspian region (by pipeline via Russia and probably via Turkey and Greece). Gas from North Africa and from the Caspian region, delivered by pipeline to Europe, is the least expensive incremental source available to Europe, at a cost delivered to European borders of between \$2.00 and \$3.00 per million Btu.[14] Given the location of the world's gas reserves, Europe will find itself in competition with Asian markets for incremental gas. A large proportion of the world's reserves (62 per cent) lies in western Siberia, Central Asia and the Middle East, along what James T. Jensen refers to as 'the Seam' between Atlantic and Pacific Basin markets.[15] The extent to which this gas is developed to flow westwards or eastwards will depend upon many factors, and critically upon the evolution of transportation technologies and costs.

Are the periphery countries preparing to increase their hydrocarbon exports to Europe?

The outlook is good for the creation of the infrastructure necessary to supply Europe's future hydrocarbon requirements. Many of the key projects have been identified, and suppliers – mostly private firms – are mobilizing the physical and financial means for implementation. The recent track record for the development, maintenance and delivery of oil and gas from periphery countries is mostly positive. Crude oil production in the Russian Federation underwent a steep decline in the first half of the 1990s, but has begun to recover and is currently the most rapidly expanding source of non-OPEC crude oil in the world. Yukos and Sibneft have led the Russian recovery by acquiring and developing new oilfields. Caspian region production increased toward the end of the decade as new export capacity began to become available. Production in North Africa was approximately stable, as declines in Egyptian oil production in recent years were offset by increases in Algerian output. Algeria was able to increase oil production by encouraging, from the late 1980s onwards, the return of international oil companies, which re-entered in significant numbers and made major new oil discoveries (including the Hassi Berkine oil province). Production from West Africa expanded slowly during the 1990s.

Natural gas production in Russia suffered much less of a downturn than did oil production in the wake of the collapse of the Soviet Union. Caspian region gas production – especially from Turkmenistan – suffered a sharper downturn in the first half of the decade, and only in the past year or so has a recovery commenced. Turkmenistan more than doubled its production during 2001, with exports flowing northwards to the Gazprom system and southwards into Iran. Natural gas production in Algeria and, more recently, Egypt has increased considerably. During the 1990s, Algeria systematically debottlenecked and expanded the capacities of its LNG plants, doubled the capacity of the trans-Mediterranean gas pipeline to Italy, and constructed and commissioned the Maghreb gas pipeline to Spain and Portugal. Libya failed to maintain the capacity of its only LNG plant, and as a consequence its marketed gas production stagnated in the 1990s.

Overall, the track record of oil and gas production in the periphery regions during the past decade has been positive. Periphery regions also have done a good job of replacing the hydrocarbon reserves depleted by production. Since 1990, oil and gas reserves in the FSU, North Africa and West Africa have all expanded. By global standards, the efficiency of the reserve replacement process in the periphery regions has been rather high. These regions cannot compete with the Middle East Gulf, but North Africa was able in the 1990s to achieve North Sea levels of drilling efficiency (measured as gross reserves added per foot drilled; Table 11.1).[16] The FSU had a somewhat less successful experience during the decade as a whole, but a comparison of the first five years (47 barrels per foot) with the second five years (164 barrels per foot) reflects both a significant improvement in Russian drilling efficiency and the expanding role of international oil companies and oilfield service companies in the FSU region.[17]

All indications are that new oil and gas transportation systems from the periphery regions will continue to be developed. Some of the principal projects being constructed or planned are listed here.

Table 11.1 Gross oil reserves added per foot drilled (average 1991–2000)

Region	Barrels per foot
Gulf OPEC[a]	1,663
North Sea[b]	443
North Africa	434
FSU	105
World	80

Notes
a Excludes Neutral Zone.
b Includes United Kingdom and Norway only.

Russia

Crude oil exports currently are constrained by the limited capacity of an ageing pipeline network. New export routes via the Black Sea, the Baltic Sea (where a third loading port, at Primorsk, will be developed) and the Mediterranean (at Omišalj, Croatia) are being planned.[18] An additional export port, on the Kara Sea at Varandey, is being developed to handle crude oil from the Timan-Pechora region. For gas exports, the Blue Stream sub-Black Sea pipeline to Turkey entered operation in December 2002, and plans call for the expansion of the Yamal-Europe gas pipeline to a capacity of 60 bcm/yr.[19]

Caspian region

The Caspian Pipeline Consortium (CPC) oil pipeline from Kazakhstan's onshore Tengiz oilfield to the Black Sea port of Novorossiysk entered operation in 2001, and construction of the Baku–Tbilisi–Ceyhan (BTC) pipeline to carry liquids from Azerbaijan to the Mediterranean will be completed in 2005.[20] A natural gas pipeline to carry gas from the offshore Shah Deniz field to Turkey will parallel the BTC oil line. Turkey and Greece have agreed to construct a gas pipeline interconnection, suggesting that one day a route for Caspian gas via Turkey, Greece and the Balkans to Europe may be envisaged.

Egypt

Highly successful exploration in the Mediterranean Sea offshore from the Nile Delta has vastly expanded Egypt's natural gas reserves in recent years, and no fewer than four LNG projects have been announced. The two leading projects are the ELNG project at Idku, which would export gas initially to France, with additional volumes possibly destined for Italy, and the Union Fenosa project at Damietta, which would serve Spanish markets. Construction has begun on a natural gas pipeline to Jordan, with the eventual intention of reaching Lebanon, Turkey and Cyprus via Syria. Another natural gas line westwards to Libya also has been discussed.[21]

Libya

The West Libya Gas Project involves development of the Wafa oil, gas and condensate field in Block NC-169 and gas-producing formations of the (offshore) Block NC-41, and delivery of the natural gas via a trans-Mediterranean pipeline to Sicily.[22]

Algeria

Two new natural gas pipelines from Algeria to Europe are planned. One would run from Skikda via Sardinia to La Spezia. The other is the Medgaz subsea pipeline from Beni Saf to Almería, Spain. Subsea power cables will be laid in conjunction with both pipelines. In addition, Algeria and Nigeria are studying the possibility of constructing a natural gas pipeline from Nigeria across Niger to Algeria, for eventual extension to Europe.[23]

While the projects listed here will not by themselves satisfy the whole of the anticipated increase in Europe's hydrocarbon import requirements, they nevertheless illustrate how new and diversified supply sources and routes are being developed. But such projects are expensive. The investment required to achieve the anticipated increase by 2020 in Europe's natural gas imports alone amounts to US$150 billion.[24]

What EU actions are required to facilitate such projects?

It is in the interest of European consumers that these and other important energy delivery projects be planned and constructed in a timely manner. Some important lessons emerge from the projects recently completed or currently being constructed or planned. First, private-sector firms take the initiative and respond strongly to market forces. Nearly all the projects listed here are being pursued by private (including recently privatized) firms preparing to meet anticipated customer demands in Europe. Private investors are willing to take risks on extremely large energy transportation projects if they foresee sufficient demand and an opportunity to supply the required energy within the context of reasonable political stability.

Second, nearly all the projects are joint ventures involving two or more major investors. Often the joint ventures combine companies in the exporting and importing countries. By forming cross-border joint ventures, investors spread risk and ensure that both the exporter and the importer have a mutual interest in uninterrupted operation. And third, projects transiting an international boundary require some intergovernmental agreement as a precondition. Such agreements typically cover rights of way, transit fees, environmental compliance and similar matters. The government of an importing country may also pledge (through its export–import bank) to finance some portion of the investment.[25]

The European Commission's Green Paper on energy security strategy argues that 'the Union suffers from having no competence and no community cohesion in energy matters',[26] yet there are many ways in which the EU as an entity can and does support the development of new and diversified oil and gas import sources. There is the Euro-Mediterranean Partnership (EMP), whose primary aim is to draw partner countries into a free trade area by 2010, which will (if implemented) have indirect impacts on economic development, employment, income levels, investment and economic integration in the partner countries, all of which will contribute to a stable political environment in which energy supply projects can flourish.[27] The planned Euro-Mediterranean Investment Facility within the European Investment Bank (EIB) will have similar impacts, whether or not it becomes directly involved in financing energy infrastructure projects.[28]

The EU policy of liberalizing internal energy markets will encourage the private sector to expand internal EU energy transportation interconnections, complementing the expansion of external sources and enabling new import sources to reach distant EU markets.[29] Gas market liberalization will eventually help promote security in many ways, but an abrupt switch to competitive markets can also prove disruptive to the development of new gas supplies. The EU appears to have accepted the principle of long-term take-or-pay contracts, which are necessary for the financing of new gas supply projects.[30] The EU still needs to come to an agreement with some gas exporters concerning the elimination of 'destination clauses' in long-term natural gas contracts; such an elimination will contribute to supply security by increasing the number of sources serving any particular region in the EU.[31] In general, during the transition to a single internal gas market, the EU needs to remain in continuous dialogue with gas-exporting countries in the periphery, to ensure that steps towards market liberalization are compatible with the financing and development of new gas supply projects.

The EU is also encouraging countries to implement the European Energy Charter Treaty and (when completed) the Energy Charter Transit Protocol.[32] These treaties establish common rules for energy trade, investment and transit rights.[33] Although originally created to provide a stable and predictable environment for investment in the FSU, the Energy Charter and the soon-to-be-completed Transit Protocol may gain wider application. Russia has not yet ratified the Energy Charter Treaty, and Gazprom has some significant reservations about the Transit Protocol.[34] The same issues concerning third-party access to pipeline capacity as will be covered in the Transit Protocol sooner or later will be raised concerning natural gas pipelines from North Africa, although no North African country has ratified the Energy Charter Treaty. The EU has also participated since October 2000 in the 'EU–Russia Energy Partnership', which aims to improve the legal and security framework for investment in energy transportation projects linking Russia and the EU.[35] In addition, the EU's technical assistance programme INOGATE (Interstate Oil and Gas Transport to Europe) has provided funding for metering stations along gas pipelines in FSU countries and for studies contributing to the reform of transit gas arrangements in Ukraine.[36]

The EU has also intervened successfully on behalf of European energy companies ignoring unilateral sanctions imposed by the United States.[37] Beneficiaries include European companies involved in projects in Iran.[38] The EU's stance also may have reassured partners in the planned West Libya Gas Project. Continued EU defence of its corporate citizens against extra-territorial application of unilateral sanctions imposed by the United States will be important as long as the sanctions remain in place.[39] In June 2002, EU foreign ministers agreed to open negotiations on a trade and cooperation agreement with Iran.[40]

Short-term European energy security

It is one thing for the EU to facilitate the timely construction of new energy delivery systems to meet growing demand, but quite another to ensure their uninterrupted operation. Short-term interruptions have two potential consequences: prices may rise sharply, and physical rationing of limited supply may become necessary. Either will entail undesirable political and economic impacts.

Several trends in market structure already serve to reduce the danger of short-term supply interruptions. As mentioned above, joint ownership of the production and transmission system by companies from the exporting and importing countries creates a mutual interest in avoiding interruptions. Fortunately, joint ownership is becoming increasingly common. Many of the projects previously mentioned are jointly owned. More generally, downstream investments by the national oil companies of major exporting countries, pioneered by Petróleos de Venezuela, the Kuwait Petroleum Corporation and Saudi Aramco in the 1980s, have continued into the era of privatization. Both Gazprom and Lukoil, for example, have invested in downstream European gas and oil facilities.[41] This trend should be encouraged.

In some cases, pipelines can be constructed or deviations can be created around regions or countries where interruptions have been experienced or seem likely. Transneft has constructed an oil pipeline around Chechnya for this reason, and Gazprom nearly announced in January 2002 a plan to bypass Ukraine.[42] In addition, the Energy Charter Transit Protocol, when completed, will contain provisions to prevent the unlawful taking of hydrocarbons from pipelines by transit countries.[43] Fortunately, interruptions to date of energy supplies destined for European markets have been rare. Deliveries to Europe of gas from Russia and Algeria have been, overall, highly reliable.

It should also be taken into account that the periphery countries already exporting oil and gas to Europe are at present more dependent on European markets than Europe is dependent on the suppliers (Table 11.2).[44] Europe is already more diversified in terms of sources of supply than are Europe's suppliers in terms of outlets for their resources. However, the degree of dependence of the FSU on Europe may be expected to decline as Russia and the countries of Central Asia develop their links to Asian markets.

However reassuring the above considerations may be, they by no means guarantee that Europe will be free from short-term supply interruptions or sharp price swings in the future. The development of new sources of supply from the Caspian region or new gas export pipelines from North Africa in particular does not constitute a countermeasure against unexpected price movements. The reason is that these suppliers will not maintain idle production capacity which could be called upon to replace interrupted supplies or moderate upward price movements.

Today, nearly all idle oil production capacity is in the Middle East Gulf. A small amount of idle capacity – less than 500,000 bpd – was held in non-OPEC countries during the first half of 2002 as a temporary measure of cooperation with OPEC to support oil prices. Any consistent or permanent maintenance of idle production capacity in non-OPEC countries is unlikely, and would be resisted by the private companies investing in petroleum production capacity in those countries. OPEC members have used their idle capacity to moderate oil price upswings in the past – notably at the onset of the Iran–Iraq War in 1980 and the Gulf War in 1990.[45] The overhang of more than 6 mmbd of idle capacity in early April 2002 was sufficient to prevent any hike in oil prices when Iraq announced its unilateral export 'boycott'. European governments and the EU have no

Table 11.2 Mutual energy interdependence, 2000

Supplier	Europe's dependence on supplier[a]		Supplier's dependence on European markets[b]	
	Oil	*Gas*	*Oil*	*Gas*
FSU[c]	29%	66%	78%	98%
North Africa	19%	31%	77%	96%

Notes
a Share of Europe's total imports coming from supplier. 'Europe' includes all of Europe other than Belarus, Russia and Ukraine.
b Share of supplier's total exports going to Europe
c Former Soviet Union.

control over the amount of idle capacity at any time, or the use of that idle capacity to moderate oil price swings.

The EU could consider other policies to minimize the impacts of oil and energy price swings. One would be the maintenance and utilization of strategic petroleum reserves with the specific intention of intervening to influence prices. The intention of intervening explicitly to modify prices would go beyond the present strategy of emergency petroleum reserves to be used in the event of 'supply interruption'. The IEA was created, in part, to prepare for and manage severe oil supply disruptions. Members of the IEA are required to maintain emergency petroleum reserves equivalent to 90 days of net oil *imports*. The EU imposes a somewhat stronger requirement on its members, which must hold emergency reserves equivalent to 90 days of inland *consumption* of three types of petroleum products.[46] The IEA coordinates among its members, in the event of a serious supply disruption (defined as a loss of 7 per cent of supply), a programme of demand constraint, stock draws, and sharing of available supplies. The IEA thus has a primary coordinating responsibility in the event of a supply disruption. A more flexible intervention programme, called the Coordinated Emergency Response Measures (CERM), was introduced at the IEA in the early 1980s. The CERM was intended to allow the drawing upon of strategic reserves even before the 7 per cent loss of supply threshold was reached.

In September 2002 the European Commission proposed increasing the emergency oil stock requirements, more clearly separating emergency stocks from operational stocks, facilitating the coordination of EU decisions to draw on stocks, and introducing natural gas emergency stock requirements.[47] The Commission proposal included the possibility that emergency stocks could be maintained in member countries, in candidate countries, 'or equally in producer or even transit countries'.[48] A policy of using oil stocks to regulate prices is filled with potential perils, and the experience of the United States in drawing down its strategic reserve during the Gulf War and in the autumn of 2000 is not encouraging. The first drawdown was too late to have any market impact (and the offered crude was not taken up by the market), and the latter drawdown had unintended negative consequences on the New England heating oil market it was supposed to assist.[49] Strategic reserves have not yet demonstrated their potential as a subtle tool for influencing prices.

A second policy which the EU could follow to prepare for future price swings would be to encourage large energy users to hedge their future energy requirements. Many corporate energy users already engage in hedging. Such a policy would have to be accompanied by accounting regulations to ensure that consumers correctly evaluate the long-term viability of hedging counterparties. The recent collapse of Enron in the United States should encourage hedgers everywhere to re-examine carefully their contracts for future energy supplies.

European policy options are limited, however, because oil markets are global by their very nature, and a supply interruption anywhere – even of supplies not serving European markets – has a worldwide price impact, including an impact on Europe. The greatest price swings of the past 30 years, those that have contributed to significant economic slowdowns in industrialized countries, have been instigated by, or coincidental with, political turmoil in the Middle East: the October War in 1973, the Iranian Revolution of 1979, the onset of the Iran–Iraq War in 1980, the Gulf War of 1990, and the Iraq crisis of 2002–3.

This suggests that, for Europe, the avoidance of future price 'shocks' ultimately requires long-term efforts to attack conditions in periphery countries which underlie political instability: poverty and inequality, unemployment, corruption, poor governance, lack of political and economic opportunity, and perceived injustice. In general, the periphery countries from which Europe needs to draw additional volumes of oil and gas, and upon which Europe will become increasingly energy dependent over the next two decades, have significantly lower incomes per capita than do European countries (Table 11.3).[50]

Many of these countries – especially in North Africa – have high rates of population growth. Large amounts of investment will be required to raise productivity and reduce unemployment in these countries. Yet in the eight-year period 1992–9, Russia and the countries of North Africa together received only 1.5 per cent of EU-15 outward direct investment – a minuscule amount considering the important roles these countries will play in Europe's energy future. EU policies designed to make these and other energy periphery countries more attractive to investors will be an important element in ensuring energy security over the long run.

Table 11.3 Income per capita, selected European countries and periphery energy suppliers

Country	Income per capita[a]
Russia	6,990
Azerbaijan	2,450
Kazakhstan	4,790
Egypt	3,460
Algeria	4,840
France	23,020
Germany	23,510
Italy	22,000
United Kingdom	22,220

Note
a 1999 gross national product per capita, purchasing power parity (ppp) basis.

Conclusions

Europe is tied to its periphery by umbilical cords carrying energy, the lifeblood of Europe's economy. The capacities of the oil pipelines and natural gas transportation systems bringing energy to Europe from Russia, the Caspian region, the Middle East and North Africa will need to expand sharply in coming decades to meet Europe's expanding energy requirements. European policies that encourage investment will most likely be sufficient to allow private companies to build the required capacity. Indeed, some of the projects needed are already under construction. The energy reserves in the periphery countries are sufficient. However, Europe's options for protecting itself from sharp energy price swings, often associated with political instability in major oil-producing countries, are limited. In this sense, Europe's efforts to develop an energy security policy are intertwined with Europe's more general policies of economic assistance and development promotion, because ultimately Europe's energy security will rely on political stability in the periphery.

Notes

1 We focus on hydrocarbons because hydrocarbons constitute the largest energy imports by far (whether measured in terms of heating value or monetary value), and because they present substantial security issues. Other potential European energy security issues not discussed here include nuclear fuel cycle security in periphery countries and electrical grid interconnections with the periphery (especially in the Mediterranean region).

2 International Energy Agency, *World Energy Outlook 2002*, Paris: IEA, 2002. 'Europe' here refers to OECD Europe.

3 See, for example, United States Department of Energy (DOE) and Energy Information Administration (EIA), *International Energy Outlook 2002*, Washington, DC: DOE and EIA, 2002. Three scenarios are offered by J. Stern, *Traditionalists versus the New Economy: Competing Agendas for European Gas Markets to 2020*, Briefing Paper 26, London: Royal Institute of International Affairs, November 2001.

4 Similar conclusions about increasing European import dependence are expressed in Commission of the European Communities, *Green Paper: Towards a European Strategy for Security of Energy Supply*, Brussels, 29 November 2000, Document COM (2000) 769 final (hereafter referred to as 'Green Paper'), at pp. 20–1 and at p. 80. 'The Union's external energy dependence could reach 90% for oil and 70% for gas by 2020', as quoted in Commission Communication to the European Parliament and the Council, 'The Internal Market in Energy: Coordinated Measures on the Security of Energy Supply', COM (2002) 488 final, 11 September 2002, p. 6.

5 *BP Statistical Review of World Energy* (annual), and International Energy Agency, *Monthly Oil Report* (monthly). Various issues.

6 J. P. Dorian, 'Oil, Gas in FSU Central Asia, Northwestern China', *Oil and Gas Journal*, 10 September 2001, pp. 20–32. See also J. Nanay, 'Prospects for Alternative Export Routes for Caspian Oil: Turkey, Iran and China', *Middle East Economic Survey*, 17 September 2001, pp. D4–D7.

7 See K. Wu, 'Asia–Pacific Oil Dependence, Imports to Grow', *Oil and Gas*

Journal, 15 April 2002, pp. 20–3. Wu projects that Asia-Pacific crude oil imports could increase by 6 mmbd between 2000 and 2010, and that by 2010 the Middle East will supply 84 per cent of all Asian country imports, up from 74 per cent in 2000.

8 mmtpy = million tonnes per year. One million tonnes of LNG is equivalent to approximately 1.38 bcm.

9 *Middle East Economic Survey*, 14 May 2001, p. A15.

10 *Middle East Economic Survey*, 2 July 2001, p. A13, and 24 September 2001, pp. A14–A15.

11 *Middle East Economic Survey*, 8 October 2001, p. A8.

12 *Middle East Economic Survey*, 19 November 2001, p. A12.

13 *Oil and Gas Journal*, 1 July 2002, p. 9; *Middle East Economic Survey*, 1 July 2002, p. A8.

14 N. Ait-Laoussine, 'Fundamental Supply Developments within a Liberalizing European Market: A Producer's Perspective', paper presented to the Flame 2002 European Gas Conference, Amsterdam, March 2002.

15 J. T. Jensen, 'The LNG Option for Middle East Gas Trade', paper presented to the Sixth Meeting of Experts from Energy Exporting and Importing Countries, Abu Dhabi, January 2002. Jensen also points out that the 'Seam' region contains 75 per cent of the world's 'exportable surplus' gas – that is, gas which is not reserved for future domestic consumption, is required for reinjection in oil-field pressure maintenance programmes, or otherwise is unavailable for new export projects.

16 Table 11.1 is based upon the author's calculations.

17 At least one observer foresees FSU oil production peaking before 2010. See A. M. Samsam Bakhtiari, 'Expectations of Sustained Russian Oil Production Boom Unjustified', *Oil and Gas Journal*, 29 April 2002, pp. 24–6.

18 N. Mikhailov, 'Russian Oil Pipelines Set for Expansion', *Oil and Gas Journal*, 25 March 2002, pp. 62–8, and 'Tariff Accord Clears Way for Russian Oil Exports through Med', *Oil and Gas Journal*, 4 March 2002, pp. 64–5.

19 N. Mikhailov, 'Gas Pipeline Projects Needed to Boost Russian Exports', *Oil and Gas Journal*, 1 April 2002, pp. 66–8. A study by Wood Mackenzie suggests that Russian gas exports to Europe will increase from about 130 bcm/year in 2000 to 186 bcm by 2008 and to slightly more than 196 bcm by 2020, assuming that key new fields are brought into production and that, if required, some gas from Central Asia would enter the Russian pipeline system. See I. Woollen, 'Central Asian Gas Crucial to Future Russian Gas Supply', *Oil and Gas Journal*, 13 August 2001.

20 H. McCutcheon and R. Osbon, 'Discoveries Alter Caspian Region Energy Potential', *Oil and Gas Journal*, 17 December 2001, pp. 18 25, and H. McCutcheon and R. Osbon, 'Risks Temper Caspian Rewards Potential', *Oil and Gas Journal*, 24 December 2001, pp. 22–8. See also T. Adams, 'Caspian Oil Realities', Briefing Paper 23, London: Royal Institute of International Affairs, September 2001; and W.R. True, 'Construction Plans Sag', *Oil and Gas Journal*, 3 February 2003, p. 71.

21 *Middle East Economic Survey*, 31 December 2001, pp. A5–A7, and 7 January 2002, p. A17.

22 *Middle East Economic Survey*, 29 October 2001, p. A17, and 11 February 2002, p. A13.

23 *Middle East Economic Survey*, 15 October 2001, p. A13, and 28 January 2002, p. A3.

24 Ait-Laoussine, 'Fundamental Supply Developments'.

25 Concerning the intergovernmental enabling agreements for the Algeria–Sardinia–La Spezia gas pipeline/electric transmission project and the

Algeria– Spain 'Medgaz' gas pipeline/electric transmission project, see *Middle East Economic Survey*, 13 August 2001, p. A8, and 15 October 2001, p. A13.

26 'Green Paper', p. 28. The final report on the Green Paper consultation process was issued 26 June 2002, COM (2002) 321 final. In many ways, the final report confirms that there is no consensus on European energy security policy. Suggestions gathered during the Green Paper consultation process varied widely and often failed to distinguish between the role of government and the role of the private sector.

27 *Middle East Economic Survey*, 1 April 2002, p. B1. See also A. Aïssaoui, 'European Strategy for the Security of Energy Supply: Re-evaluating Relations between the EU and the Producers and Transit Countries of North Africa', *Middle East Economic Survey*, 15 April 2002.

28 *Middle East Economic Survey*, 1 April 2002, p. B7.

29 The most comprehensive proposal concerning the single internal market for natural gas is contained in European Council document 14867/02 ENER 293 CODEC 1550, 27 November 2002. An analysis of the impact of a single EU gas market upon security of supply may be found in chapter 7 of 'A Long-Term Vision of a Fully Operational Single Market for Natural Gas in Europe', a draft strategy paper prepared in January 2002 by the Joint Working Group of the European Gas Regulatory Forum. Online. Available http: <http://europa.eu.int/comm/energy/library/strategy-paper-draft-28-01-2002.pdf> (accessed 10 March 2003).

30 European Commission, 2002/0220 COD, 'Proposal for a Directive of the European Parliament and the Council concerning Measures to Safeguard the Security of Natural Gas Supply', contained in COM (2002) 488 final, Brussels, 11 September 2002. See in particular Article 6. See also Ait-Laoussine, 'Fundamental Supply Developments'; International Energy Agency, *World Energy Outlook 2000*, p. 147; and *Middle East Economic Survey*, 8 April 2002, pp. A5 and A13–A14.

31 *Middle East Economic Survey*, 22 July 2002, p. A8.

32 'Green Paper', p. 88. The European Community deposited instruments of ratification of the Energy Charter Treaty on 16 December 1997.

33 R. Kamper, 'New Charter to Govern International Energy Transit', *Oil and Gas Journal*, 4 March 2002, pp. 20–3.

34 'Rules of the Game', *Russian Petroleum Investor*, March 2002 (interview with Ria Kamper, secretary-general of the Energy Charter Secretariat, Brussels). Online. Available http: <http://www.encharter.org>.

35 Online. Available http: <http://europa.eu.int/comm/energy_transport/en/lpi_en_3.html> (accessed 10 March 2003).

36 'Security of gas supplies: Loyola de Palacio stresses the importance of the Putin/Kuchma declaration', IP/02/843, 11 June 2002. See also <http://www.inogate.org>.

37 At a United States–European Union summit meeting in London on 18 May 1998, 'the United States agreed to grant "national interest" waivers to EU companies against liability to Iran Libya Sanctions Act (ILSA) sanctions'. See *Middle East Economic Survey*, 22 November 1999, p. A2.

38 The first two beneficiaries of the US–EU accord were TotalFinaElf (operator of Sirri A and E fields, and developer of Phases 2 and 3 of the South Pars gas field) and Shell (redeveloper of the Soroush and Nowruz oil fields). *Middle East Economic Survey*, 28 February 2000, p. A16.

39 US president George W. Bush signed a five-year extension of the Iran Libya Sanctions Act (ILSA) in August 2001 and an executive order extending sanctions against Libya in January 2002. *Middle East Economic Survey*, 14 January 2002, p. A17.

40 *International Herald Tribune*, 19 June 2002, p. 3.
41 Gazprom has been for more than a decade a partner of the German company Wintershall (owned by BASF) in the joint venture Wingas, owner and operator of natural gas pipelines and storage facilities in Germany. Gazprom is also the partner of ENI in the Blue Stream natural gas pipeline project beneath the Black Sea to Turkey. Lukoil owns retail petrol stations in the Baltic States, the Czech Republic, Poland, Turkey, the United States and other countries outside Russia.
42 *Oil and Gas Journal*, 25 March 2002, p. 66, and 1 April 2002, p. 66. The plan for the detour was dropped by Gazprom prior to the Putin/Kuchma declaration of early June (see IP/02/843, 11 June 2002). Nearly all (about 90 per cent) of Russia's gas exports to Europe currently pass through Ukraine. Expansion of the Yamal-Europe pipeline system, however, will probably be via Belarus and Poland.
43 Kamper, 'New Charter'.
44 The sources of data underlying Table 11.2 are *BP Statistical Review of World Energy 2001* and *Oil and Gas Journal*, 13 August 2001, p. 64.
45 N. Ait-Laoussine and J. Gault, 'OPEC's Delicate Balancing Act', *Middle East Economic Survey*, 24 September 2001, p. D8.
46 In June 2002, EU Energy Commissioner Loyola de Palacio called for EU oil stocks to be increased from the current 90 days to 120 days. The commissioner was reported to have compared oil stocks to central bank reserves that would rarely be called upon. *Middle East Economic Survey*, 17 June 2002, p. A9. A review of EU natural gas storage capacity can be found in 'A Long-Term Vision of a Fully Operational Single Market for Natural Gas in Europe'.
47 Commission Communication to the European Parliament and the Council, 'The Internal Market in Energy: Coordinated Measures on the Security of Energy Supply', COM(2002) 488 final, 11 September 2002.
48 Ibid., p. 18.
49 S. Emerson, 'SPR Drawdowns Trigger Law of Unintended Consequences', *Oil and Gas Journal*, 10 December 2001, pp. 24–30, and S. Emerson, 'When to Use Strategic Reserves: Reforming Multilateral Drawdown Policy', *Middle East Economic Survey*, 3 February 2003, pp. D1–D6.
50 The source of data underlying Table 11.3 is World Bank, *World Development Indicators 2001*.

12 The transatlantic dimension

William C. Wohlforth

Europe's emergence as a strategic actor in its own periphery is a development with major significance for the transatlantic relationship and indeed for international politics as a whole. In concert, the European Union (EU) and the United States can do much to advance their interests and foster stability and prosperity in Europe's neighbourhood. Increased policy competition in the regions, however, could poison the transatlantic relationship and exacerbate the challenges confronted by regional actors.

To judge by elite commentary on the overall state of the Euro-American relationship, one would expect the transatlantic dimension of the EU's new regional role to be fractious. Little more than a year after the terrorist attacks of 11 September 2001 on New York and Washington, the US and European governments were at loggerheads on a raft of international issues, and policy elites on both sides increasingly seemed to be occupying different intellectual worlds. 'The emotional gap may well become deeper than it has ever been since the end of World War II', warned Jürgen Habermas.[1] If 'Americans are from Mars and Europeans are from Venus', as Robert Kagan argued in a noteworthy essay early in 2002, nowhere should the two sides' divergent perspectives be clearer than in their approaches to regional issues.[2] And in the spring of 2003, the direst predictions seemed to have been realized, with the transatlantic relationship placed under severe strain by the war in Iraq.

Still, as the other chapters in this volume attest, the realities on the ground of Europe's periphery belied any simple portrait of steadily declining cooperation sliding into resentment and rivalry. Amid the diplomatic chafing and the inevitable expressions of pique, the two sides cooperated messily but ultimately successfully from the Gulf War to Bosnia, Kosovo and Macedonia. Diplomats on both sides could put an essentially positive gloss on US–EU cooperation in promoting peace and prosperity in Europe's periphery, citing the 1995 New Transatlantic Agenda and the regularized and expanded US–EU policy coordination that has followed, as well as a complex set of working arrangements between the European Security and Defence Policy (ESDP) and NATO.

Elite anxiety over US–EU relations is thus driven more by expectations than by current events. Given the contretemps over Iraq, the question is not whether ties will fray but how badly. The worry is that over time the two sides will be ever less inclined to cooperate and more inclined to compete. To assess this anxiety it is not enough to cite the record of US–EU cooperation on regional matters or to bewail the breakdown caused by George Bush's and Tony Blair's insistence on disarming Iraq. Editorializing about current trends in US–EU policy towards Europe's neighbouring regions – no matter how well informed and scholarly – is also unlikely to add much of lasting value. Rather, it is necessary to analyse the underlying structural setting of policymaking to see whether the early harbingers of discord are likely to grow in significance. The presumption behind such an analysis is that in the absence of major change in underlying conditions, major change in patterns of behaviour is unlikely. Any historian can name instances when this presumption was unfounded. But the point is that it is usually right.

Scholars of international relations conventionally divide the underlying structure into two broad categories. First are the 'three I's' of liberal and constructivist theories: identity, interdependence and institutions. These factors are clearly very important in explaining the ability of the United States and its European partners to work together. They have changed only marginally since the end of the Cold War, however, and so cannot explain significant change in the transatlantic relationship. Europe and the United States retain their core liberal identities; they remain deeply interdependent economically; and the democratic and multilateral institutions they built domestically and internationally during the Cold War have all remained in place. The chief changes that have occurred are increases in transatlantic economic interdependence and EU integration, neither of which should lead to a deterioration in relations, according to liberal and constructivist theories.[3] Hence, while the 'three I's' may well explain continuity in the relationship and imply certain limits to the degree of competition that might come to characterize it, to explain change we must look elsewhere.

Accordingly, this chapter sets out a perspective on the future of the transatlantic dimension of the EU's new regional role based on the second broad category: power relations, which have undergone a major shift from bipolarity to unipolarity. Does the shift to a unipolar power structure explain the changing tenor of US–EU relations, and, if so, with what portents for transatlantic policy coordination in Europe's neighbourhood? According to neo-realist theory, unipolarity begets counterbalancing against the United States by other powers, including Europe. Hence, neo-realists fit the EU's new assertiveness in its region into a narrative of counterbalancing and potential geopolitical competition. Each new assertion by a European politician or EU official that Europe must provide a 'counterweight' to the United States appears to buttress this narrative.[4] Needless to say, this is precisely how neo-realists interpreted the behaviour of

France, Germany and Russia in the United Nations Security Council negotiations regarding Iraq.[5]

In this chapter I show that the standard neo-realist rendering of the distribution of power is wrong. Balance of power dynamics are not pushing the United States and the EU inexorably towards a competitive relationship. However, key features of the transatlantic relationship – including increased EU involvement in its periphery as well as endless disagreements with the United States arising from clashing visions of world order – are all rooted in the distribution of capabilities. Change in this underlying structure is likely to be slow and subtle, but the best bet is that for the next 10–20 years, changes will augur for an increase in the nettlesome aspects of the relationship rather than a fundamental alteration in its character.

Of course, no social structure is determinate. Any structure in any social realm may be overwhelmed by other causes. Europe and the United States may fall out over the EU's policies in its own region as a consequence of causes having nothing to do with the distribution of power in world politics. Scholars disagree strongly over the causal importance of mainly material structures, such as the distribution of power, as opposed to mainly non-material social relationships and factors emanating from within the domestic politics of states. One way to test the veracity and strength of structural theories is to make predictions derived from such theories and monitor the results. That is the spirit that informs this chapter.

The distribution of capabilities: US unipolarity and US–EU incommensurability

Policymakers, pundits and scholars now increasingly agree that no system of sovereign states has contained a leading state with the across-the-board material preponderance the United States enjoys today. Less often noted than this asymmetry of power is the incommensurability of power between the United States and the EU. Europe is and will remain militarily inferior to the United States, but it matches it in aggregate economic potential. It is this mix of global unipolarity and bilateral power incommensurability that provides the material setting for the transatlantic relationship.

Unipolarity

The standard view of unipolarity is that it enables US unilateralism, which corrodes the multilateral institutions that govern the Euro-Atlantic security community and stokes European resentment. This is true, but incomplete. Unipolarity also dampens geopolitical competition among Great Powers, according to two influential theories. The theory of hegemony stipulates that leading states foster international arrangements that are stable to the degree that the leader is dominant.[6] The United States today enjoys a pre-eminence in nearly all the component elements of power that is unprecedented in modern international history. As a result, its leadership of the international system is less subject to challenge than that of any past system leader, including Britain at its peak and the United States itself in the early Cold War. At the dawn of the twentieth century, a militarily powerful Germany challenged Britain's leadership. The result was World War I. In the middle of that century, US leadership seemed under challenge by a militarily strong Soviet Union. The result was the Cold War. What explains these conflicts and many others was the fact that the leader led in one kind of power but not others, and thus seemed simultaneously threatening and vulnerable. The magnitude and comprehensiveness of the United States' lead over the other major powers makes it highly unlikely that the world will be plunged into conflict by a challenge to US leadership.

More surprising is that neorealist theory – best known for its prediction of the imminent return of multipolarity – also predicts that as long as unipolarity lasts, the major powers will not be plagued by the security dilemmas that accompany balance-of-power politics. Because the United States is simply too powerful to counterbalance, there is no need to calibrate, or possibility of calibrating, alliances to produce an equilibrium among the major powers. Balance-of-power politics make great diplomatic history precisely because they are pregnant with potential disaster; a few miscalculations can produce an arms race or a war. Pundits often lament the absence of a post-Cold War Bismarck to fashion a grand strategy for Great Power peace. Luckily, as long as unipolarity lasts, we don't need one.

The new transatlantic testiness caused by Washington's unilateral temptation is but one side of unipolarity's coin. The other side is decreased geopolitical competition among major powers, which has the effect of highlighting the apparent salience of lower-level conflicts. What used to be considered low politics has become high politics because the unipolar distribution has helped clear the *old* high politics – arms races, brinkmanship crises and wars among Great Powers – off the international agenda. So unipolarity not only enables US unilateralism but also allows governments on both sides of the Atlantic more leeway to squabble over matters that in the bipolar era would have been considered secondary.

US–EU incommensurability

Europe's aggregate economic potential matches the United States', but its military capabilities are comparatively small, and declining in relative terms. The result is an unbalanced power portfolio between the two partners. This US–EU power incommensurability creates the classic preconditions for what sociologists call *status dissonance*: the inability of actors to sort out their rank in a prestige hierarchy owing to the fact that on some dimensions of status they are peers but not on others.[7] Research in biology, psychology, anthropology, sociology, medicine, economics and history shows that humans appear to be hard-wired for sensitivity to status and that status hierarchies are universal in social life.[8] Do US and European leaders crave status? While, as individuals, policymakers may be influenced by the various status drives that science and social science have identified, does this necessarily mean that these drives will be translated into their behaviour as representative of their respective groups?

The answer is a qualified yes. One of the strongest empirical findings in social psychology is that individuals who identify with a group transfer the individual's status preference to the group's relations with other groups.[9] Hence, to the extent that Europeans transfer real decision-making power to Brussels, the officials who act in Europe's name can be expected to be just as jealous of the EU's standing in the world's status hierarchy as Washington officials already are. Close observers tend to ratify this expectation. The implication is not that the quest for status will always dictate each side's preferences, but rather that periodically they will be willing to subordinate more prosaic instrumental aims to the drive for status. The question is the degree to which the underlying material structure provides incentives or disincentives for this kind of behavior.

Status is a social-psychological phenomenon, yet sociologists from Weber onwards have postulated a link between material conditions and the stability of status hierarchies. When social actors acquire resources, they seek to convert them into something that has more value to them than the mere possession of material things: social status.[10] When this conversion process is blocked, tension builds and status hierarchies become unstable.[11]

When actors' capabilities are incommensurate on some dimensions, they experience ambiguity about their relative status and have increased difficulty reaching agreements. The reason is that all actors tend to be biased in favour of higher status. Put simply, the status-inferior actor (in this case, the EU) that achieves parity on one dimension of power (aggregate economic output) is likely to expect greater deference from the status-superior (the United States). But the status-superior actor that retains dominance on at least some dimension (military capabilities) is unlikely to treat the status-inferior as a peer.

Incommensurate capability endowments are thus likely to frustrate US–EU relations as they upset the previously comparatively clear US-dominated hierarchy. Not only will they feed status dissonance, they will complicate bargaining on a range of issues. According to social exchange theory, imbalances between reward and coercive power are likely to corrode a relationship over the long run. And standard rational choice models suggest that incommensurate power portfolios are likely to increase uncertainty and thus the difficulty of striking mutually acceptable bargains. There is, in short, a great deal of social science research suggesting that clearly equal or clearly unequal actors are more likely to get along than actors who don't know exactly where they stand.

Implications for US–European partnership

In security matters, US–European partnership remains the default option under unipolarity. While it is not mechanistically necessitated by the system's structure, it does represent the path of least resistance, and, for many of the states concerned, the optimal strategy. US grand strategy is to prevent the re-emergence of competitive multipolar regions in Europe and Asia by maintaining a substantial forward presence in both regions. The idea is to preserve the stability that US policymakers perceive is in their own best interest while retaining Washington's substantial influence in the affairs of both regions. Most officials believe that US leadership and engagement are necessary conditions of order. Many note that the United States uses the leverage it obtains by its leadership role to advance its commercial and ideological interests in promoting trade, globalization and democracy. The merits of the strategy can be debated, but the set of beliefs that undergird it is hardly surprising for a state with the extraordinary power advantage the United States enjoys. Great power usually leads to expansive definitions of interest.

The best strategic response for other powers is to engage the United States unless and until it becomes possible to create a real counterpoise. In the absence of a restored balance, the other capitals face a strong incentive to avoid becoming the focused object of US power. To be sure, the other major powers sometimes will try to coordinate policies against Washington – witness the global policy coalitions on US national missile defence, the Comprehensive Test Ban, the Kyoto Protocol on Global Warming, the International Criminal Court, and, notably, Iraq. Balancing power means increasing the real capabilities of other major powers to match those of the hegemon. None of the policy bargaining by other major powers since the end of the Cold War had even a remote potential to do this. Rather, these efforts had the effect of altering the relative political costs to the United States of pursuing various objectives. Such policy rows *are* politics, to be sure, but they are *not* genuine counterbalancing, geopolitical competition, or a struggle for global primacy.

Indeed, much of the bickering over US policies is enabled by the fact that the major issues that threaten Great Power wars are off the table. Because real balance-of-power politics and struggles for primacy are not on the cards, European and other major powers face lower risks when staking out independent stances on policy matters. But all such endeavours remain vulnerable to the collective action problem. A policy coalition against the United States is a collective good all members can enjoy whether or not they pay for it, and so it is likely to be undersupplied. Defection is always probable – as the EU and its High Commissioner for

Foreign and Defence Policy, Javier Solana, discovered when Russia opted out of the global coalition against national missile defence in the wake of 11 September.

Hence, Europe's decision to continue a close partnership with the United States is consistent with the other major powers' responses to US primacy. Unless and until the EU begins to acquire the material and decision-making capabilities of a superpower, a critical mass of European governments will probably prefer to bandwagon with the United States. Given that Beijing and Moscow also essentially opt to bandwagon with Washington most of the time, it is little wonder that Europe, which shares many more basic interests and perspectives with the Americans, has retained a close transatlantic alliance. And for their part, the Americans *could* choose to 'come home' and still remain secure, but given the temptations of the US power advantage and the manifold external demands for involvement that flow inevitably from its unipolar position, they are unlikely to do so.

An underlying preference for engaging the United States does not mean that other major powers will choose to bandwagon with Washington on every issue. On some issues, European governments will choose their own course, and on some they may seek to recruit temporary partners outside Europe. Depending on the strength of the US preference on these issues, prospective opponents of US policy risk paying some political costs for their opposition. It is impossible to predict which governments will choose to risk such opposition on which issues. When one moves from the realm of the security imperative of survival – the provenance of traditional balance-of-power theory – to the more fluid realm of political bargaining, no theory can generate specific predictions about specific state strategies. The more tractable question is how far these bargaining dynamics are likely to go in undermining regional cooperation or degenerating into real competitive rivalry.

This is the essential context for contemporary status politics and regional policy coordination among the major powers. The United States' unprecedented global dominance is thus an existential threat to the status (but not the existential security) of the other traditional Great Powers. To the extent that they prize status above material rewards, policymaking elites in other states may be willing to forgo potentially beneficial regional cooperation with the United States if it comes at the expense of their collective self-esteem. The incommensurability of their power portfolios makes the United States and the EU candidates for status rivalry. Many of the issues that divide them are complicated by status considerations. And one of the impulses for further EU integration is the desire for international prestige.

Hence the elite commentary about diverging worldviews and clashing policy stances that supposedly derive from different cultures and history misses the point that were the power relations to be reversed, so would

Europe's and the United States' attitudes regarding the use of force and the efficacy of international law. Indeed, the transatlantic gap in world-views and preferred strategies is partly an artefact of unipolarity and incommensurability. Given its power and position, it is not surprising that the United States resists further development of international regimes and institutions in ways that might constrain it in the exercise of its military power – the International Criminal Court being the best example.

The United States' military prowess also inclines its elite towards placing high value on military means in addressing security threats. Most important in this respect is the US superiority in new and extraordinarily expensive high-technology warfare. These capabilities allow decision-makers to contemplate the use of force in ways that minimize casualties in their own forces as well as among civilian populations. The result is a pref-erence for new kinds of strategies – such as pre-emptive or even preven-tive war – that other decision-makers rule out on prudential as well as moral grounds.[12] The old moral rule that one should resort to force only in clear and dire cases of self-defence is easier to follow when technology permits only bloody and hard-to-control military operations. The old pru-dential rule – best represented by the now-deceased Weinberger–Powell Doctrine – that leaders should go to war only over the gravest threats to the nation's security looks different when technology promises victory with few allied casualties. New capabilities have presented US policy-makers with new temptations that their European colleagues do not yet face.

Thus, by the time the sun had set on 11 September 2001, the Bush administration had already decided to frame its response to 11 September as a 'war' on terror.[13] The evidence concerning that decision suggests that had Al Gore been president that day, the response would have been sub-stantively identical. The Bush administration's new National Security Strategy, to cite another example, makes the case for a general policy of preventive war against rogue-state proliferators of weapons of mass destruction (WMD). The argument behind the new doctrine is that the United States and its allies will be much more secure in a world where potentially trouble-making regimes are deterred from proliferating. One of the many apparent motivations behind the Bush administration's Iraq policy is to help establish such general deterrence of would-be WMD pro-liferators. Many Washington policymakers believe that preventive war against Iraq will contribute to decades of deterrence against any who might be tempted to follow Saddam Hussein's path (in addition to foster-ing a large range of other potential upside benefits). The strategy's merits are debatable, but the point is that only a state with the global, high-technology coercive power Washington has at its command would ever conceive of such a policy.

EU policymakers also, not surprisingly, tend to place greater emphasis on strategies that highlight capabilities in which they are strong. They tend to favour multilateral institution-building on a variety of fronts and are much more inclined towards preventive diplomacy than preventive war. While their solidarity with the United States on 11 September was sincere, and their cooperation in Afghanistan and elsewhere significant, their subsequent policies have reflected a rather different view from the Americans' 'war on terror': a framing of the problem as a police, intelligence and policy issue that demands close multilateral cooperation within the EU and with US agencies. Again, the merits of the approach can be debated, but the point is that the EU lacks the material wherewithal to conduct a global, high-technology war against terror and so has framed the issue in the only way it could.

On both sides, these policy preferences easily translate into normative judgements, moral assessments, and threats to, and defences of, collective self-esteem. On the US side, the capability to use force in a wide variety of circumstances reinforces the ideological baggage of traditional sovereign statehood, especially decisive presidential leadership and old-fashioned patriotism. In this context, EU policy approaches seem to many US policy-makers and commentators to be naive, feckless, self-indulgent and irresponsible, while EU criticism of US policies is passed off as free-riding on American leadership. Many Europeans, by contrast, view Washington's inclination to stress military force as immoral, and the EU's work on human rights, protection of the environment, international law and institutions and its painstaking preventive diplomacy as morally superior to the old power politics.

In sum, the neo-realist assessment of unipolarity is premature. Unipolarity fosters strategies of hedging, free-riding and bandwagoning, not balancing. Tensions in the transatlantic relationship concern policy bargaining stoked by status politics.

The severity of this competition is limited by three factors. First, unipolarity substantially ameliorates the security problem among Great Powers. In the past, considerations of status and security were inextricably intertwined. Now, status politics may assume a more independent role, including on regional policy issues. But take away the main security threat, and they are unlikely to assume the deadly form they did in the past. Second, US–EU status politics are unlike those of earlier times, and not only because the principal actors are democracies. US–EU incommensurability is the opposite of the standard pattern of the past that featured status inferiors with outsized *military* power. This is the classic Russia–Prussia–Germany–Japan–Soviet Union problem. The EU, if it continues to develop as an economic giant while remaining a military pygmy outside its immediate region, and it unifies enough really to be considered an international actor, will reverse this pattern.

Third, status competition is attenuated by the diffuse nature of decision-making authority in the EU. Status competition presumes the existence of coherent corporate actors on whose behalf decision-makers act strategically. If the EU were a state, the world would be bipolar in economic terms. But economic comparisons between the EU and the United States ignore the fact that the Union is not a state. Except in a few areas (trade, antitrust), its formidable economic potential is not at the command of a single strategic decision-making authority but rather is diffused through extremely complex institutional arrangements.[14] Owing to this institutional gap, the transatlantic incommensurability of power is smaller in reality than it appears in aggregate statistics.

Implications for US–European partnership in the EU's neighbourhood

The global setting is thus primed for a continuance of the transatlantic partnership, but with ongoing and sometimes fractious policy bargaining that is frequently stoked by status dissonance. What are the implications for policy cooperation in the EU's neighbourhood? It is important to stress that the unipolar structure paradoxically *increases* the salience of regional international politics across the globe for two reasons. First is the declining pole-to-state ratio. The nineteenth-century international system was composed of six or eight polar states out of a total of roughly 30 significant powers. In the early Cold War there were two poles, but the number of states had doubled to just over 70. Today there is one pole in a system whose population has trebled to nearly 200 states. As a simple matter of numbers, there is bound to be more going on in regional international relations in today's system. Not only are the numbers of lesser powers growing, so are their aggregate capabilities. By one measure, the conventionally defined Great Powers comprised over 80 per cent of global capabilities in the mid-nineteenth century, 65 per cent in the early Cold War, but only around 55 per cent today.[15]

Second, many regional dynamics are measurably less constrained by Great Power politics than they were in the Cold War for purely structural reasons. The current international structure is *looser* than Cold War bipolarity, even though it is more unequal. The gap between the most powerful state and the rest is much larger now than under bipolarity, but the system is less constraining on many important regions. This comparative looseness does not mean that the system is not unipolar. On the contrary, it is a result of the fact that unipolarity limits the very intense Great Power contradictions that tend to force lesser powers to choose sides.

The contemporary international system, in short, is characterized by unprecedented US hegemony within the Great Power club, and a novel proliferation of lesser states outside that club. The likelihood that regional dynamics will fall outside the limits of a polar state's national interest or capability is thus greater than in preceding systems. Because there are now far more, and more capable, states relative to poles than in prior eras, and because the abeyance of intense security rivalries among Great Powers increases the latitude for regional interstate dynamics, there is a *heightened* demand for inter-state cooperation at the regional level. Notwithstanding US primacy, today's international system puts a premium on the ability of the United States and the EU to coordinate policy in the regions.

The bottom line is that because of the growing status dissonance between the two sides, the potential complementarity between their power portfolios and associated policy preferences is extremely difficult to realize in practice. Any joint policy endeavour demands political bargaining and the allocation of status-conferring goods, both real and symbolic. Who controls the operation? Whose officials get the 'decisive' say? Who gets how much credit? Who pays how much for what? From Bosnia, Kosovo and Macedonia further afield to the Arab–Israeli dispute, Afghanistan and prospectively in Iraq, the message from Brussels is, in Javier Solana's words, 'We are no longer just financial donors, but are striving for political influence.'[16] But because the two sides place different values on their respective contributions, determining how much political influence each side should get becomes a contentious process.[17]

The track record so far suggests that the United States, the EU and European governments face serious problems in cooperating on regional conflicts. In the Balkans and the Middle East, in particular, the newly increased demand for policy coordination was on display, as was the difficulty Europe and the United States had in rising to the challenge. In Bosnia and Kosovo a clear pattern emerged of transatlantic tension over the division of labour and political influence. In both cases, the Americans eventually insisted on control over the pre-conflict diplomacy, and de facto operational control over the military operations, but then sought to deflect much of the subsequent peacekeeping and reconstruction to Europe. The result was European rancour at having to pick up the pieces after US operations over which the Europeans felt that they had no control and for which they won no glory. The fact that the Americans' 'glorious' armed victories appear to come without shedding much American blood while subsequent low-prestige European peacekeeping operations often appeared to entail greater risk to troops only fed the bitterness. As NATO Secretary-General Lord Robertson put it, the transatlantic relationship cannot long endure 'if the Americans do the cutting edge, while the Europeans are stuck at the bleeding edge, if Americans fight from the sky and the Europeans fight in the mud'.[18] This very same pattern has re-emerged in Afghanistan.

As Roland Dannreuther demonstrates in this volume (Chapter 10), a different manifestation of the same problem occurred in the Middle East, where the differing capabilities and partners of the United States and EU might be thought to be usefully complementary. The EU's effort to enhance its role in the region at first met with concerted US resistance and even outright sabotage. In the end, Dannreuther shows, the two sides could only coordinate their policies effectively once Washington forced

Brussels to accept its subordinate role in the process. Even then, as soon as the complex, incremental, multilateral process of implementing the Oslo accords – a process so amenable to the EU's strengths as an actor – gave way to renewed crisis and conflict, Brussels lost even the modest role it had won in the latter 1990s.

Naturally, these problems arise in those circumstances where the EU attempts to stake out a measurably independent role on an issue or in a region where US policymakers have strong preferences and are accustomed to the old hierarchy entailing automatic deference from Europeans. As the previous chapters have demonstrated, this list of such issues remains short. On Russia and the East-Central European former Soviet states, Central Asia, the Caucasus, the Palestinian issue and the Persian Gulf, these conditions have not been met, and Washington deals mainly either with European governments or with a relatively incoherent EU.

Will the material setting endure?

The underlying power configuration favours a prolongation of the US–European partnership, albeit with increased chafing, resentment and discord. But how stable is the underlying power configuration? It is impossible to predict the rise and fall of Great Powers with any precision, but the preponderance of evidence suggests that those who expect the re-emergence of multipolarity to occur in the next decade are underestimating the stability of unipolarity. For one thing, the United States is not making it easy to catch up. For example, each year it spends 80 per cent as much on defence research and development as all the other major powers combined. And when it comes to high-end military capabilities, there is no need to rehash the numbers that show how hard it would be for any state to begin to close the gap. But there are several larger arguments – all grounded in long-term trends and well-understood relationships – for the durability of the current essential power configuration.

First, the overall gap separating the United States for other polar contenders is very large, so closing it will take a long time. Any countervailing change will have to be strong and sustained to produce a polarity shift. Second, the United States is both big and rich, while all other states are, at most, either one or the other. It will take at least a generation for today's poor big countries (e.g. China, India, Russia) to become rich. Given declining birth rates, the other rich countries (e.g. Germany, France, the United Kingdom, Italy, Japan) cannot get big. Third, rates of economic growth tend to converge as states approach US levels of GDP per capita. Based on what we know of long-term growth patterns, it is unlikely that the more wealthy countries of Europe and Asia will be able to grow substantially faster than the United States over prolonged periods as they approach the US level of wealth per capita. Fourth, the end of the Cold

War and other recent events suggest that it has become harder now than it was in the past for relatively backward or autarkic states to compete with the wealthiest states in military technology.[19] On the basis of what we now know of the prerequisites for producing the most modern military capabilities, poor states whose elites aspire to larger international roles will have a much harder time quickly ramping up military capabilities in order to stake a claim on the international system. Today's potentially dissatisfied states, such as China and Russia, find that they must integrate into the global economy in order to compete technologically, but in so doing they reduce their autonomy. Fifth, the geography of today's unipolar structure means that any effort by one major power to ramp up its military capability would only nudge its neighbours closer to Washington and thereby reinforce unipolarity.

Thus, taken individually, European states will in all likelihood never be capable of assuming a polar position. Only by pooling strategic resources will Europe gather the strength necessary to help resurrect a multipolar world. That will require increased military spending, extraordinarily difficult military restructuring in 15 countries, and, most important and difficult, the creation of a unified defence industry and centralized staffing, command and strategic decision-making capabilities. Creating such state-like capabilities goes to the heart of state sovereignty and inevitably is, at best, a grindingly slow and contradictory process. Many European states have been very reluctant to relinquish sovereign power in the area of defence and foreign policy. It is hard to square such concerns with the occasionally stated goal of counterbalancing US power. While they do not rule out the possibility of major progress along these lines, most students of European politics do not expect state-like foreign and defence capabilities to emerge any time soon. Unless there is some major external shock, a European 'pole' is a project for a generation.

Prediction is perilous, because the material setting is itself partly the product of human agency. Actors can choose to create the capabilities that supposedly constrain them. But barring major shocks, the choices that would generate the most consequential material shifts – that the United States would dismantle its military machine or that Europe would create one – are not on the cards. The chapters in this volume, as well as many other sources, indicate that the most likely shift is a very slow increase in the EU's ability to deploy its considerable economic power coherently. That shift would mean a slow increase in US–EU power incommensurability and an attendant increase in status competition. Hence, the best bet is that the sorts of problems in regional policy cooperation that we have witnessed over the past decade are set to increase marginally.

Conclusions

True multipolarity is not on the horizon. The most likely scenario is an uneven, marginal increase in the EU's capability to act on the world scene as a single economic actor, coupled with an even slower deepening of the European Security and Defence Policy. If this projection turns out to be accurate, then the prognosis for US–EU relations in Europe's neighbourhood is status quo plus. That is, relations will resemble the post-Cold War norm, with a marginal increase in status competition that will continue to challenge policy coordination. This analysis is based on the assumption that once shorn of the security dimension, status politics take a back seat to welfare – that is, that Europeans are unlikely to sacrifice welfare and sovereignty to purchase the military power they would need in order to balance the United States. This assumption appears to be borne out by the experience of unipolarity's first decade.

In many ways, the implications of this analysis concern Washington far more than Brussels and other European capitals. For it is the United States that operates more in the realm of choice than any of its international partners. How it chooses to manage its own global hegemony is likely to be the single most important factor shaping the future of US–EU relations. During the run-up to the Iraq crisis, it seemed to many that Washington was firmly set on a deeply destabilizing unilateral course. But a United States that is capable of seeing its own longer-term interests is likely to moderate that course over time.[20]

A review of international relations scholarship yields a nearly unanimous verdict against an aggressively unilateral course for a state in the United States' unipolar position. Legitimate hegemonies are far cheaper and safer to maintain over the long run than illegitimate ones. Institutionalized hegemonies are far cheaper and safer to maintain over the long run than non-institutionalized ones. And hegemonic powers that find ways to accommodate the status drives of lesser states face fewer costs over the long run. Aggressively unilateral policies undermine legitimacy, corrode institutions and heighten status anxieties, generating higher costs and greater instability over the long run.

While non-state threats such as terrorism may appear to supersede state-level threats, the new challenges cannot be addressed in the absence of a stable interstate order. Hence, the United States faces strong incentives to moderate the frequency with which it resorts to its unilateral option. The key problem for statesmanship is that all the arguments for avoiding aggressive unilateralism concern the long term, while all the temptations of unilateralism are short-term. The ability of US political institutions to act in the country's best long-term interests may be the single most important variable affecting the transatlantic dimension of the EU's new role in its neighbourhood.

Notes

1 'Letter to America', *The Nation*, 16 December 2002, p. 16.
2 See, in particular, R. Kagan, 'Power and Weakness', *Policy Review*, 2002, no. 113.
3 See T. Risse, 'Beyond Iraq: Challenges to the Transatlantic Security Community', *American Institute for Contemporary German Studies Working Paper*, 2003.
4 In work emblematic of this thinking, political scientist Charles Kupchan goes so far as to predict that the EU will be the next great 'peer competitor' of the United States. C. Kupchan, *The End of the American Era: U.S. Foreign Policy and the Geopolitics of the Twenty-first Century*, New York: Knopf, 2002.
5 See C. Layne, 'The Power Paradox', *Los Angeles Times*, 6 October 2002, p. 1.
6 R. Gilpin, *War and Change in World Politics*, Cambridge: Cambridge University Press, 1981.
7 See B. S. Turner, *Status*, Minneapolis: University of Minnesota Press, 1988; J. Berger and M. Zelditch, Jr (eds), *Status, Power, and Legitimacy: Strategies and Theories*, New Brunswick, NJ: Transaction, 1998; and D. Lockwood, *Solidarity and Schism*, Oxford: Clarendon, 1992 for comprehensive discussions of the concept in different schools of sociology.
8 For reviews, see R. H. Frank, *Choosing the Right Pond: Human Behavior and the Quest for Status*, New York: Oxford University Press, 1985; and R. Wright, *The Moral Animal: Evolutionary Psychology and Everyday Life*, New York: Pantheon, 1994. On the law of stratification as applied to international politics, see C. Doran, *Systems in Crisis: New Imperatives of High Politics at Century's End*, New York: Cambridge University Press, 1991; M. Wight, *Systems of States*, Leicester: Leicester University Press, 1977; A. Watson, *The Evolution of International Society*, London: Routledge, 1992; and E. Luard, *Types of International Society*, London: Macmillan, 1976.
9 For reviews, see J. Mercer, 'Anarchy and Identity', *International Organization*, 1995, vol. 49, no. 2: 229–52; and R. H. Thaler, *The Winner's Curse: Paradoxes and Anomalies of Economic Life*, New York: Free Press, 1992.
10 T. Veblen, *The Theory of the Leisure Class: An Economic Theory of Institutions*, rev. ed., New York: New American Library, 1953 [1899]. Thus, we would expect states, like people, to overconsume observable (conspicuous) status-conferring goods.
11 Weber argued that those with wealth would tend in time to acquire status: 'Property as such is not always recognized as a status qualification, but in the long run it is, and with extraordinary regularity.' Economic class and social status should correlate in the long run. Building on Weber's idea, Emile Benoit-Smullyan postulated that if this tendency to conversion of resources to social status is blocked, the resulting disequilibrium will generate revolution. See the discussion in M. Zeldich, Jr, 'Social Status', in D. L. Sills (ed.), *International Encyclopedia of the Social Sciences*, vol. 15, New York: Macmillan, 1968, pp. 250–6. If industrialization redistributes wealth, class and status hierarchies will be in disequilibrium, and conflict will ensue. The analogies to hierarchical theories in international relations are obvious. For an application of Weber's ideas to world politics, see R. Collins, *Weberian Sociological Theory*, Cambridge: Cambridge University Press, 1986, chs 6–8.
12 An invaluable source on how the very existence of the United States' powerful military machine influences US strategic choices is D. Priest, *The Mission: Waging War and Keeping Peace with America's Military*, New York: W. W. Norton, 2003.
13 B. Woodward, *Bush at War*, New York: Simon and Schuster, 2002.

14 An example of the gap between aggregate indicators and actual strategic decision-making capability is the EU's external voice on international finance. See K. R. McNamara and S. Meunier, 'Between National Sovereignty and International Power: What External Voice for the Euro?', *International Affairs*, 2002, vol. 78, no. 4: 849–68.

15 W. C. Wohlforth, 'U.S. Strategy in a Unipolar World', in G. J. Ikenberry (ed.), *America Unrivaled: The Future of the Balance of Power*, Ithaca, NY: Cornell University Press, 2002.

16 'Javier Solana Discusses EU Enlargement, Middle East Role', *BBC Monitoring International Reports*, 15 October 2002.

17 For a case study amply demonstrating this proposition, see M. J. Brenner, *Europe's New Security Vocation*, Washington, DC: National Defense University, 2002.

18 Quoted in J. Lindley-French, 'Terms of Engagement: The Paradox of American Power and the Transatlantic Dilemma post-11 September', Chaillot Papers 52, European Union Institute for Security Studies, May 2002, p. 52.

19 For more, see S. G. Brooks and W. C. Wohlforth, 'Power, Globalization and the End of the Cold War: Reevaluating a Landmark Case for Ideas', *International Security*, 2000/2001, vol. 25, no. 3: 5–53.

20 See S. G. Brooks and W. C. Wohlforth, 'American Primacy in Perspective', *Foreign Affairs*, 2002, vol. 81, no. 4: 20–33.

13 Conclusion

Towards a neighbourhood strategy?

Roland Dannreuther

The central research question which this volume has posed is the extent to which Western Europe, meaning the European Union (EU) and its member states, has emerged as a strategic and coherent actor towards the countries in its immediate neighbourhood since the end of the Cold War. The various contributors to this volume have all naturally addressed this question in different ways, reflecting their own particular perspectives and those of the specific region or issue area for which they have had responsibility. This final concluding chapter does not seek to review and summarize the preceding chapters. Rather, it attempts to determine whether there emerges a broader and more cumulative picture from these contributions which identifies the EU as a strategic actor in its immediate neighbourhood and which can be viewed as something more than the sum of the EU's various regional policies or dimensions. This is primarily an issue concerning the EU's foreign and security policy, but it also has broader and significant implications for the identity and purpose of the EU, both internally in terms of its self-identity and its geographical expression (*le finalité geographique*) and also externally in terms of Europe's status and role in the international order.

This concluding chapter has two principal sections addressing the following two issues. First, there is an assessment of the extent to which the EU has emerged as a strategic actor in its immediate neighbourhood and the strengths and weaknesses of this engagement. Second, the chapter examines the broader issue of what these findings tell us about Europe's place in the world: its relationship with the United States, and in terms of international order.

The EU and its neighbourhood: a strategic actor?

Pál Dunay starts his chapter (Chapter 3) on East-Central Europe (ECE) with an affirmation of the strategic vision underlying the European integration project which pre-dates the collapse of Soviet power in Eastern Europe. This is expressed in Robert Schuman's visionary statement from 1963 articulating the resolve to create a unified Europe which would be built upon freedom and democracy and which would be open to the peoples of Eastern Europe once 'freed from the constraints under which they live' (p. 27). As Dunay argues, the likely accession in May 2004 of 10 new members predominantly from ECE, and the creation of an enlarged Union of 25 countries, represents ultimately a vindication of this strategic vision. In the longer-term perspective, the decade or more that it has taken for the countries of ECE to be transformed from oppressed socialist countries, with discredited and defunct economic systems, to democratic and economically dynamic countries that have fulfilled the conditions for membership of the EU, is a short historical interlude. It also marks an important achievement and milestone in the prospective unification of Europe.

This does not mean, though, that the EU and the EU member states deserve the greater part of the credit for this transformation. As Dunay also notes, the negotiation process has frequently been characterized by a penny-pinching and narrow technocratic approach (p. 44). The EU has often acted as an exclusive club of existing members, more interested in preserving current privileges than in welcoming new members and being sensitive to their needs and the political costs of transition. The success of this transition should, therefore, mainly be credited to the countries and peoples of ECE, who have pursued the goal of the 'return to the West' with resolve and consistency, despite the apparent coolness and lack of enthusiasm of their Western partners. International actors other than the EU have also played a vital role in this transformation. In particular, the United States has played a seminal role in the process and, at least in part, promoted a relatively fast process of North Atlantic Treaty Organization (NATO) enlargement to stimulate a more determined and focused approach by the EU. Bodies such as the Organization for Security and Cooperation in Europe (OSCE) and the Council of Europe have also played a critical role in promoting the political conditions for stability through their support for democratic institutions, the rule of law and respect of human and minority rights.

Nevertheless, the EU maintains a certain pride of place as the key strategic prize for which the countries of ECE have struggled, and the goal of membership has represented the ultimate confirmation of their 'return to the West'. For its part, the EU has demanded, as compared to other organizations such as NATO, the most rigorous political, economic and social conditions for membership, and applicant countries have had to submit to the most intensive demands and intrusions into their sovereign affairs. Indeed, perhaps the most surprising aspect of the transition process in ECE has been the absence of a major Euro-sceptic revolt against these intrusions on sovereignty. To an extent, as Dunay notes, some of the principles underlying membership of the EU, such as that of solidarity, have yet to be fully internalized by the candidate countries, and this could cause problems in the future (pp. 39–40). However, in general, these countries have implicitly understood not only the benefits but also the costs of membership. In addition, despite a widespread sense of the West's historical obligation to ECE, there has also been some understanding of the factors behind the ambivalence of many EU member states towards the enlargement process, and their reluctance to endorse it. Inevitably, the accession of a large number of countries with lower GDP per capita than the EU average imposes costs on politically important domestic social and economic interest groups among existing EU member states.

In general, however, Dunay argues that the EU has acted as a flexible and adaptive strategic actor towards ECE and has held fast to the strategic vision which underpins the European integration project. The other contributors to the volume are noticeably less sanguine and positive about the other aspects of the EU's external projection. The problems and reservations concerning the EU's strategic role beyond ECE can be broken down into three different but interconnected concerns: the ambiguities of the EU's strategic and geographical identity; the problems of policy formulation and implementation; and the potential creation of new dividing lines, whether of a new 'welfare curtain' supplanting the 'iron curtain' or the creation of a 'fortress Europe'.

Strategic ambiguities

One of the criticisms of the EU's ambition to become an international actor in the post-Cold War period has been its deeply entrenched and seemingly irresolvable ambiguity about its external identity. The failure to define the borders of Europe has been viewed as a critical weakness in its self-projection.[1] The contributors to this volume have all recognized this strategic ambiguity, and the costs that it imposes, but also show some understanding of why such an ambiguity has been preserved. There is the fact that, as Antonio Missiroli notes, the Treaty of Rome leaves open the prospect of membership to all states that can be defined as 'European', which might exclude countries from North Africa and the Middle East but certainly potentially includes the countries of South-Eastern Europe and the Newly Independent States (NIS) (p. 18).[2] To rule out indefinitely the prospect of membership for these countries is unilaterally to define a highly divisive and normatively problematic conception of European-ness. In addition, as practically all the contributors note, the prospect of membership of the Union is the 'golden carrot' which can most effectively galvanize the necessary internal political and economic transformations among the peripheral states. As a practical policy, keeping open or leaving ambiguous the future borders of the Union preserves the most powerful instrument available to the Union for promoting the desired processes of economic liberalization and democratization.

Nevertheless, the contributions to this volume indicate that the decision to enlarge the Union to 25 members in 2004 has brought a greater clarity to the geo-strategic map of Europe. In practice, there appear to be emerging three broad categories or concentric circles of neighbouring countries surrounding the enlarged EU. First, there are the countries that have a short- or medium-term perspective for membership. These include Romania and Bulgaria, which have missed out being in the first tranche of candidates for accession but are projected to join in 2007–8. They also include Turkey, the final decision over whose potential candidacy has been postponed until December 2004. It also includes the countries of the western Balkans, where the 'general consensus' of eventually incorporating the entire Balkan peninsula into the EU has been, as Ettore Greco notes, one of the most significant and unexpected acquisitions to the geopolitical vision of the EU (p. 65). The second category of countries includes those that are neighbours of an enlarged Europe, that can be considered to be part of a 'wider Europe' but that have no immediate or medium-term perspective for membership.[3] These are the countries of the southern Mediterranean rim, from Syria and Lebanon to Morocco, and the countries of the western NIS, meaning Belarus, Russia, Ukraine and Moldova. The third category designates those countries that are considered to be geographically proximate but that neither are immediate neighbours of the enlarged Union nor have any medium-term perspective for membership. These include the countries of the Caucasus and Central Asia and the non-Mediterranean countries of the Middle East, such as Iraq, Iran and the Gulf States.

With this strategic map in mind, some of the apparent anomalies in the EU's external interaction with its immediate neighbourhood, and the differentiation in the nature and intensity of its engagement, begin to make more sense. The fact that the EU has, as Neil MacFarlane argues, a 'non-strategy' towards the southern Caucasus and Central Asia reflects, in reality, the absence of clear interests and objectives in these regions rather than a 'failure' of strategy (p. 132). Likewise, the greater priority of the EU towards the Balkans – in terms of conflict resolution, provision of aid and technical assistance – as compared to the western NIS or the southern Mediterranean, is understandable once the EU's strategic objective of the region's eventual incorporation into the Union is understood.

This more clearly defined strategic map is, though, far from set in stone, and, even if established more concretely, will not resolve all the strategic ambiguities or satisfy all the aspirant neighbouring states. There is the possible, or even probable, emergence of an 'enlargement fatigue' where European public opinion balks at extending the Union to include countries that have demonstrated a poor economic and political performance, such as Romania and Bulgaria, or where there remain high levels of criminality and lawlessness, such as in the Balkans generally, or where the country's credentials for being considered European are in dispute, such as Turkey. There is also the problem that postponing the prospect for membership to an indefinite future for those countries with a clearly expressed European 'vocation', such as Ukraine or perhaps Georgia, could radically weaken the external stimuli for reform in those countries, with significant long-term consequences. Also, for the countries of North Africa and the Middle East, the unambiguous definition of the EU as an exclusively European club accentuates the sense of exclusion and of a civilizational rather than a merely developmental barrier across the Mediterranean Sea. The fear is of the creation of new dividing lines that will cut against the strategic vision of Europe's unification, as expressed by Robert Schuman and the other founding fathers of the European project.

Despite these problems, the greater clarity of the Union's external identity does potentially give a greater strategic purpose where priorities in terms of objectives can be better identified along with the means to achieve these objectives. Implicitly, it is also suggestive that an enlarged Union is likely to be a stronger and more forceful international actor. The new member states bring into the EU's orbit new neighbours and neighbouring regions, which inevitably increases the Union's strategic reach and set of geopolitical interests beyond its borders. These interests include not only ensuring the security of the new external borders of the Union, but also in dealing with the deeper causes of instability beyond those borders. Hence, the dynamic of the EU's interest is increasingly likely to move beyond just developmental aid and assistance, to seeking to resolve the underlying conflicts that plague its periphery. As Dannreuther argues in his contribution (Chapter 10), this can already be seen in the increasing EU engagement in the Arab–Israeli conflict, which is paralleled by Greco's (Chapter 5) argument that Europe should be more ambitious in setting a road map for dealing with the suppressed causes of conflict in the Balkans. Certainly, it can be argued that *internally*, an enlarged Union can imply a possible diffusion of power within the EU, or at least greater internal differentiation between the EU member states, with the potential (or perhaps existing reality) of an internal core and periphery configuration. But *externally*, the overall impact should be of an accretion rather than a diffusion of power.

Problems of policy formulation and implementation

Strategy is ultimately about the capacity for instrumental rationality, meaning the ability both to define clear and realizable objectives and then to match these objectives with the means and capabilities of achieving them. It might be plausible or even convincing to argue that an enlarged Union should, in principle, be a more powerful and strategic actor, but this can only ultimately be guaranteed if there also exists the institutional capacity to define and, more importantly, to implement the desired foreign and security policies. Without this capacity, the EU potentially remains a toothless international actor, unable to project its influence with the necessary coherence and sustainability.

However, if there is one dominant and recurring theme in all the contributions to this volume, it is the difficulty that the EU has in defining, coordinating and implementing its various policies towards the immediate neighbourhood. For example, there is a fairly consistent record – as Hiski Haukkala notes with the Northern Dimension (ND), Fred Tanner with the Euro-Mediterranean Partnership (EMP) and Ettore Greco with the Stability Pact for South-Eastern Europe (SPSEE) and the Stabilization and Association Process (SAP) – of the EU promulgating regional initiatives that are highly ambitious but whose objectives are poorly prioritized and where the resources to implement them either are lacking or have proved clearly insufficient. In a similar vein, Missiroli highlights the lack of coordination between the various regional projects, which results in a multiplicity of Community assistance programmes – PHARE, TACIS, Interreg, CARDS, MEDA – that remain rigidly separate, both bureaucratically and procedurally, and where possible synergies through co-ordination and streamlining are lost (p. 24). More generally, there is common criticism of the highly bureaucratic and opaque decision-making and policy implementation procedures of the EU, which only serves to confuse and alienate partner countries, and which is exacerbated by the institutional separation between the Commission and the Council and the three-pillar structure of the Union.

To a considerable degree, these problems of policy formulation and implementation are a consequence of the fact that the EU is not a unitary actor. In the absence of a clearly defined central authority for foreign and security policymaking, policies tend to emerge in an ad hoc and uncoordinated manner, being driven by the impact of external events and/or the complex logic of internal decision-making within the EU, such as package deals and lowest common denominator decisions. The consequence is that often the policies that emerge are rich in rhetoric, providing a shopping list of priorities, but lacking in the resources and mechanisms to implement them. The responsibility to implement these policies is then primarily taken over by the Commission officials, who interpret their mandate in a narrow bureaucratic manner that prioritizes the technical objectives of the more quantifiable socio-economic objectives. These officials naturally tend to shy away from the broader underlying political ambitions of these policies, which they have neither the authority nor the instruments to promote in any meaningful manner. Even the hint of a strong national interest or preference against, for example, pursuing political conditionality from one of the more powerful EU member states is sufficient to curtail any independence of action from within the Brussels bureaucracy.

The manner in which the various neighbourhood initiatives have emerged over the last decade or so illustrates this mix of external impact linked to international developments and complex internal politicking. The internal dimension is itself driven by the fact that any one regional initiative is never in the direct national interest of all the EU member

states but only of a certain sub-set of them, normally those in the immediate geographical proximity. Thus, the initial agreement to recognize the
membership aspirations from the ECE countries was certainly intimately
connected to their new-found freedom and liberation from Soviet rule, but
was also driven by the specific national interests of Germany to move the
borders of the EU eastwards. Moreover, this generated a resolve on the
part of the Mediterranean EU states, spearheaded by France, to counterbalance this eastwards momentum by a parallel initiative to the Mediterranean region. Coinciding as this did with a breakthrough in the Middle
East peace process in the mid-1990s, with the Madrid Accords and the
Israel–PLO Oslo agreement, it resulted in the ambitious EMP, which
sought to provide a holistic resolution of the multiple sources of insecurity
in North Africa and the Levant.

A similar logic of 'action–reaction' can be found with the emergence of
the Balkan initiatives (the SPSEE and the SAP), the Northern Dimension
and the prospective 'Eastern Dimension'. The Balkan initiatives were certainly primarily driven by the need to promote stability in the aftermath of
the bloody wars of secession in the region, but it was also more specifically
promoted by the affected neighbouring EU member states, most notably
Greece but also Germany, Austria and Italy. The ND, as clearly described
by Haukkala in Chapter 7, was a deliberate and targeted policy initiative
of the new Northern members that joined the EU in 1995 to stimulate an
engagement in the North to match the EU's commitments to the East and
South. Finally, the prospect of an 'Eastern Dimension' that would
promote a regional policy towards the western NIS – Belarus, Ukraine,
Russia and Moldova – is itself being promoted primarily by the new
prospective members of the EU that will have these countries on their
immediate borders and that will seek an EU engagement analogous to
other neighbourhood initiatives.

The complex set of circumstances that lie behind the creation of these
various neighbourhood initiatives also explains a number of their subsequent weaknesses and deficiencies, as highlighted in the contributions to
the book. External developments that were initially propitious for the
formation of these initiatives can change in a negative fashion. Thus, the
breakdown in the Arab–Israeli peace process in the late 1990s effectively
derailed the political objectives of the EMP. The enlargement of the EU
to Poland and the Baltic States is likely to make the ND redundant. More
generally, the mismatch between the initial ambitions of these programmes, which were to a certain extent deliberately magnified to legitimize their elevation on the EU agenda, have regularly fallen foul of
limited resources and bureaucratic inefficiencies, which have plagued their
subsequent implementation. In many cases the resulting concentration on
the more economic and technocratic aspects of these programmes has only
highlighted that the underlying political problems have not yet been
resolved. Similarly, the expectation of these programmes being a powerful

instrument for political conditionality, as exposed by Andrei Zagorski in relation to EU policies towards Russia, Belarus and Ukraine (Chapter 6), has often proved not to be the case in reality.

However, the neighbourhood initiatives of the EU can be characterized as being rather like ocean liners. They might be cumbersome, unwieldy, and difficult to manoeuvre and change direction, but they rarely sink or disappear altogether. The ND might be closest to disappearing, but even there it might have a new life as a model for the newly emerging 'Eastern Dimension' or to supplant the empty Russian Strategy, as proposed by Haukkala (p. 113). The EU is also ultimately a pragmatic institution. Lessons are learned, adaptations are made, closer coordination is induced, and greater strategic consistency and policymaking can result. For example, it is now generally recognized that the broader, more holistic neighbourhood initiatives should not seek to impose a rigid template on all the different countries and sub-regions in their remit, all of which have their own specificities and particular needs and demands. As a consequence, it is widely accepted that the bulk of the hard work of promoting economic and political reforms must be done by targeted country-specific or sub-region-specific programmes, such as the Stabilization and Association Agreements (SAAs), the Partnership and Cooperation Agreements (PCAs), and Association Agreements, which have, or should have, clearly defined and progressive targets, benchmarks and rigorous annual reviews. As such, the broader regional initiatives should primarily play a supplementary role in promoting inter-regional integration and, as in the Balkans or the Middle East, by being a potential forum for resolving the deeper political conflicts which are obstacles to the regional processes of economic and political reform.

In a sense, the model is that of ECE, where there were clearly identifiable targets set, along with a 'road map' of how to achieve them. However, the ECE countries had some obvious advantages: a national consensus behind the necessary reforms and a capacity to implement them; an internal consensus within the EU that these countries belong to the European family; and a clearly defined set of goals, namely the full implementation of the *acquis* and, eventually, a clear date set for accession. It is much more difficult to apply the same model where these conditions either do not, or are unlikely ever to, exist.

A 'welfare curtain' and a 'Fortress Europe'?

The essential problem is that in an enlarged Union of 25 states, the new neighbours have a double disadvantage of generally being much poorer than their EU counterparts and with questionable credentials of a genuine European 'vocation'. If you take the 19 countries which constitute the western NIS, the southern Mediterranean and the western Balkans, the average GDP per capita for these countries is generally less than 10 per cent than that of the EU average (the notable exception here is Israel). Given that they constitute a population not dissimilar from the combined population of an enlarged Union, it is clear that there is emerging a critical welfare gap in the broader western Eurasian region which some have suggested represents a new European division, a 'welfare curtain' replacing the earlier 'iron curtain'. In addition, a majority of these states either have unashamedly authoritarian governments or have weak and poorly institutionalized democratic institutions, what Fareed Zakaria aptly terms 'illiberal democracies'.[4] Thus, even if some of these countries might uncontroversially be a geographical part of Europe, their poverty and their illiberal social and political culture greatly weaken their claim for a European vocation. This is brought out well in the contributions by Andrei Zagorski and Neil MacFarlane (Chapters 6 and 8 respectively).

In these conditions, it is much more difficult for the EU and its member states to preserve, as noted above, the 'strategic ambiguities' of the identity of the Union and the image of an ever-enlarging process that draws no clearly definable borders. There appears to be little appetite in EU public opinion for such an ambitious ever-rolling enlargement, and, from a strategic perspective, the difficulty of maintaining the integrity of the EU as a cohesive entity is generally recognized to require a certain limitation of its size. Concerns have been expressed that the accession of the ECE countries is already undermining the integrative dynamics of the EU, as exposed over the Iraq crisis in 2003.[5] The implication of this is that the EU cannot, as already recognized by the Commission, realistically offer the prospect of membership, its 'golden carrot', to a set of countries whose applications would be unwelcome and whose prospects of fulfilling the necessary conditions for membership are so distant.[6] As Missiroli notes, the challenge is therefore to formulate a new set of 'silver' or 'bronze' carrots that would meet the needs of the new neighbours, most notably alleviating their poverty, political instability and sense of exclusion, but which would fall short of the prospect of membership (p. 19).

There is also some consensus concerning what these 'silver' carrots would include. First, they would require the new borders to be as open, malleable and transparent as possible, permitting the free flow of transborder minorities and third-party nationals from these countries in the EU, and facilitating the movement of trade. Second, they would offer these countries a clear prospect of gaining, through further integration and liberalization, a progressively increased stake in the benefits of the EU's internal market and of the 'four freedoms' that underpin this market: the free movement of persons, goods, services and capital.

However, these self-evidently worthy objectives and ambitions, which fit so well with the normative sense of the EU's self-identity and its international projection, run up against some harsher political realities. First, there is the fact that, as a number of the contributors confirm, the prospect of membership is ultimately the key incentive that can most effectively promote changes in political behaviour. Without this incentive, however attractive the 'silver carrots' might be, the EU loses much of its influence and attraction. Zagorski highlights this well in exposing how the EU's expectations of imposing a degree of political conditionality through its policies towards Russia, Ukraine and Belarus have simply been ignored or resisted by the governments concerned and can generally be considered to have been counter-productive (pp. 94–5). Likewise, Tanner in Chapter 9 notes how the authoritarian regimes in North Africa often see no advantage in engaging with the EU's programme of economic and political liberalization as it would only undermine their traditional sources of power and patronage and potentially increase, at least in the short term, social and popular tensions.

The problems are not, though, limited to the political illiberalism of the neighbouring states. Within the EU, the ideal of a post-modern and post-sovereign borderless Europe runs up against the popular, and often elite-driven, fears of uncontrolled migration and increased criminality and terrorism, and the consequent demands for the effective policing and strengthening of external borders of the Union. As Tanner points out, the Arab Mediterranean states are particularly conscious of the prospect of a 'Fortress Europe' and of popular European conceptions of the links between Arabs and international terrorism, criminality and illegal immigration (pp. 146–7). As a result, European offers of engagement, and ambitious initiatives such as the EMP, are often treated cynically as designed to meet European rather than Arab interests, most notably European 'soft' security concerns and agricultural protection. The increasing importance that internal security issues have gained within the EU, arguably the most dynamic area for integration, as seen in the expansion of Justice and Home Affairs, does give credibility to these concerns.

To put it more succinctly, there is a clear contradiction between the ambitions of the EU to maintain and encourage cross-border links between an enlarged Union and its neighbours, and the internal public demands for more effective policing and isolation of these borders. In more philosophical terms, this is a contradiction between the normative vision of a post-modern and inclusive EU, which seeks to overcome rather than entrench borders, and the security demands of a state-in-being that needs to keep in mind the primary obligation of any state: the protection of its citizens. This is, though, an inevitable contradiction that reflects the complex nature of the EU – somewhere in between a state and an international regime – and the concomitant demands to engage with the socio-economic and stability problems of its neighbours while ensuring that these problems are not imported into the Union. There is also an economic dimension to this contradiction, as exposed by John Gault in Chapter 11. On the one hand, there are the obligations of aid and developmental assistance, where the neighbouring states act as *demandeurs*. On the other hand, the EU has a direct stake in the energy resources from these regions, which is, in Gault's phrase, the 'umbilical cord' which ties the economic fate of the EU with its broader region (p. 182).

Finally, it should be stressed that the EU's power and its influence on the behaviour of another state is ultimately a two-way process, critically dependent on the will of that state to respond, as well as on the capacity of the EU itself. As Gilles Dorronsoro brings out in his study on Turkey, the EU's power lies in promoting, rather than imposing, an internal transformation within that country, which is dependent on the Turkish will for Europeanization (p. 59). Without such a will and determination on the other side, the EU's powers are much more limited, as Zagorski, MacFarlane and Tanner note in terms of the successive failures of the political conditionalities introduced within the regional initiatives and bilateral programmes to the western NIS, southern Mediterranean and the Caucasus and Central Asia. As Zagorski recommends, in the absence of a potential stake in membership, it would be more pragmatic and realistic to follow a 'common interests' approach, as has been increasingly defined in the EU–Russia relationship, where the EU seeks to define areas of common interest with the state concerned, and then build relations on this more equal and targeted basis (p. 94). In the process, the trick for the EU would be to find that level of mutual confidence and commonly defined interests which would then generate the internal will for transformation for which the EU's particular strength is in providing the necessary response and support through incentives, expertise, and technical aid and support.

The EU as an international actor

Antonio Missiroli argues in his contribution that the EU should primarily be considered a regional power (p. 23). This is because the EU's capacity to use the full complement of its instruments – economic, diplomatic and military – is limited to its immediate neighbourhood or 'geographical periphery', and possibly to its 'outer historical/economic periphery', which broadly coincides with the post-colonial links and preferential partnerships of its member states, most notably the African, Caribbean and Pacific (ACP) countries. This regional limitation to the EU's projection can be seen, as Missiroli argues, in the evolution of the security policy ambitions of the Union, as expressed in the European Security and Defence Policy (ESDP), which envisages a geographical radius for EU military crisis management that roughly covers the immediate neighbourhood and does not rule out intervention in the 'outer' periphery, such as in sub-Saharan Africa (p. 23). As a truly global actor, the EU can only be a partial and incomplete power since its capacities are limited to the economic and, possibly, diplomatic arenas.

This reality of the geographical limits of the EU's power projection exposes one important facet of the relative weakness of the EU as compared to the United States. William Wohlforth in Chapter 12 also brings out well, using the neo-realist theoretical lens, how the complex distribution of power between the EU and the United States confirms and sustains US primacy and hegemony, yet also breeds tensions, resentments and conflicts within the transatlantic relationship, as has been particularly evident during the crisis and war in Iraq in 2003. In economic terms, the United States and the EU are relatively equal, which provides the basis for the European claim for equality of status and treatment. But in political and military terms, the United States remains vastly superior, and there is little likelihood that any other pole, even from Europe, will emerge in the short to medium term as being able to counterbalance or challenge US dominance. In essence, the main reason behind this 'incommensurability of power' (p. 188), to use Wohlforth's phrase, between the United States and the EU lies in the differing compositions of these entities. The United States is a unitary actor which has the capacity to centralize its decision-making processes and focus its strategic power; the EU, in contrast, is a non-state actor which can convert its underlying economic power into political and strategic capacities only in a diffused and disaggregated manner, in terms of both decision-making and policy outcomes.

This is nowhere more evident than in the military sphere. The United States is able to direct its economic recourses into a well-financed and strategically focused military capability, which gives it an overwhelming global war-fighting capacity. In contrast, the EU has only a fledgling force, with military capabilities remaining predominantly and inefficiently dispersed among its member states, and with a limited capacity to use, or threaten to use, force collectively. As Wohlforth notes, this power disparity can be rectified only if there emerges a real will on the part of the EU to integrate its military capabilities and to unify its foreign and security policy, abolishing national vetoes and creating a single, rather than a common, policy in the politico-strategic sphere (p. 198). In reality, there are few who believe that this is likely to occur in the short to medium term, even among an inner core of EU member states.

This disparity in military capabilities between the United States and the EU is also exacerbated by the post-Cold War developments in military strategy, most notably the technological innovations of the revolution in military affairs (RMA). With the RMA most fully integrated within the US military, this has considerably strengthened the belief in Washington of the political instrumentality of the use, or the threat of use, of force. As a consequence, US strategic doctrine has gradually shifted towards a recognition that military force can be utilized while minimizing those costs – such as large-scale casualties to US forces and the non-combatant civilians of the target state – that had earlier constrained military-security policy. This strategic shift has in turn increased the unilateralist 'temptation', and the willingness to bypass the multilateral constraints on US power projection, which the structural condition of unipolarity had already made attractive. At its core, the transatlantic crisis and the European divisions over Iraq in 2002–3 were primarily linked to this issue. Some allies, most notably the United Kingdom, Italy and Spain, urged the other Europeans to recognize the reality of unipolarity and to support or 'bandwagon' with the United States. Other allies, most notably France and Germany, encouraged resistance to a US policy orientation that they believed was inimical to the norms and values underlying contemporary international order.

Wohlforth has a compelling theoretically driven explanation for the resulting transatlantic tensions or the consequences of the 'status dissonance' that he believes breeds European resentments towards US primacy and hegemony (p. 189). However, there are qualifications or nuances that should be incorporated into this broad neo-realist picture of a uniquely powerful United States and an economically competitive but politically and strategically impotent EU. The first is actually derivable from the logic of neo-realism, as argued by Wohlforth himself. This is that a unipolar world represents a much looser structure of the international system than a bipolar or multipolar system (p. 195). In the current unipolar structure, the United States has neither the capacity to be equally engaged in all the different parts of the world nor the domestic support and the political will for such an extensive strategic involvement. Beyond providing the basic security framework that inhibits hegemonic challenges to its primacy, the logic of unipolarity is a devolution of power and responsibilities to competent regional powers, particularly for purposes of socio-economic development and crisis management.

This logic is clearly visible in the European/EU case. Since the collapse of Soviet power in Europe, the United States has generally sought to disengage from its Cold War European commitments and has been reluctant to be drawn back. When this has appeared unavoidable, such as during the wars of secession in the former Yugoslavia, there has been more disappointment at Europe's continuing weakness than a celebration of the reassertion of US hegemony. In reality, there has been clear US support and underwriting of the EU penetration into ECE, the more intensive engagements of Brussels with strategically important neighbouring states such as Turkey and Russia, and the Union's gradual assumption of the crisis management responsibilities in the Balkans. As in the past, the United States has, in practice if not always in rhetoric, supported and been a significant catalyst for European integration, including in the security and defence fields. It is this deliberate US-sanctioned devolution of power which has, in turn, forced the EU to assume a greater strategic involvement and capability in its immediate neighbourhood. As a consequence, it has become a more formidable international actor and an increasingly important element in the maintenance of the security and stability of western Eurasia.

A second important qualification is to note that, as with all temptations, the unilateralist temptation has its costs as well as benefits. As Wohlforth again indicates, unilateralism is a costly way to manage the international system (p. 199). Even for the leading power in a unipolar system, the failure to secure the cooperation of key allies and partners diminishes the hegemon's influence and power projection. In addition, military intervention, even given the RMA, remains an expensive instrument, both financially and politically, which limits its application. Although military power has a crucial deterrent value, the power to influence and modify the behaviour of other states requires a more comprehensive range of instruments, including economic and diplomatic ones, which is greatly aided by the cooperation of other significant external powers. The idea of complementarity, which is argued for by Dannreuther in relation to US–EU coordination over the Middle East peace process (pp. 164–5), advances such synergic advantages for transatlantic cooperation. It is also seen in other cases, most notably for Turkey, with which the United States has a close strategic and military-security relationship but where that rather narrowly focused relationship is clearly complemented by the EU's engagement with the socio-economic and cultural transformation of Turkish society. The same can also be argued for other key states in the EU's immediate neighbourhood, such as Russia, Ukraine and the larger states of North Africa.

To argue for the advantages of US–European cooperation or complementarity is, in a certain sense, a generally uncontroversial and even self-evident truth. The key test, though, comes where such cooperation is not immediately obtainable and where there exists a divergence of interests across the Atlantic. In this context, Wohlforth's argument that the EU has little option but to accept its subordination to US preferences (pp. 196–7) can be contested. The problem with demanding or expecting subordination is that it inevitably breeds an attitude of insubordination. Over time, the resulting tensions can undermine and weaken the foundations of the relationship, which in the transatlantic case depends on a high degree of trust and mutual sense of common values. In addition, the assumption that the foreign policy preferences of any individual state, whether it be the United States or the EU or any individual EU member state, necessarily represents an optimal foreign policy can be questioned. The United States, like any other state, has domestic political and historically contingent factors that inhibit the promotion of a foreign and security policy which can, in every instance, deal effectively with the multiple sources of conflict in the world.

This is perhaps most evidently the case in the Middle East, where the US hegemony is widely recognized by all the major regional actors, but its legitimacy and impartiality are doubted by much of the Arab and Muslim world. The same could be said for the EU in terms of its relationship with Israel. This provides a clear logic for the United States and EU to complement their various strengths. But, additionally, the advantages of multilateralism extend to providing a mechanism for leaders of states to justify and legitimize the overriding of the domestic constraints to policymaking as the 'necessary' price for international coordination. The spirit and implementation of multilateralism thus can be a critical component towards fashioning and devising more effective foreign policy initiatives which meet more closely the needs of the targeted country or region. In the aftermath of the crisis over Iraq, the next test for the transatlantic relationship could be over Iran, where, on this logic, the sustaining of the complementary roles of the United States and Europe would be a more nearly optimal strategic approach than a unilateralist imposition.

The final qualification to the neo-realist picture involves an area where neo-realism tends towards a certain neglect and disinterest: the role of ideology. In an influential article, Robert Kagan, who admittedly is generally regarded as being in the neo-realist camp, promoted the conception of an ideological divide between a Kantian post-modern Europe and a traditional, sovereignty-promoting and *realpolitik*-focused United States.[7] As with all polemical arguments, this involved a mix of insights and questionable generalizations. As regards the latter, it would be a great discredit to the historical legacy of the US to ignore the continuing liberal internationalist impulses of United States foreign policy, which are intimately connected to the domestic liberal traditions and practices and the long-term support for the worldwide promotion of human rights, the free market and liberal democracy. Similarly, the contention that Europe has a common commitment to a liberal internationalist agenda ignores the considerable differences between EU member states, with countries such as France and the United Kingdom notably embracing, in thought as well as in practice, the perceived instrumentality of the use of force in international relations. More generally, the sense that the EU can and should remain a purely 'civilian power' has increasingly lost support to a realization that Europe's self-identity requires a military dimension.

The insights found in Kagan's thesis can thus be redefined in a way that takes in these considerations. This would involve a fuller recognition that the United States and the EU have common liberal foundations – the commitment to human rights, the rule of law, the free market and liberal democracy – which represent their shared values and act as the bedrock of the transatlantic relationship. However, owing to their contrasting historical experiences and the specific contingencies in which the liberal orders have been constructed in the United States and Europe, they do nevertheless symbolize and represent differing liberal conceptions or 'models' of a liberal political system. The achievement of the United States has been the integration of a radically multicultural immigrant society, with a highly institutionalized and legally protected regime of civil liberties within the framework of a symmetric federal system and a clear separation of powers between the executive, legislative and judicial branches of the state. As an actor in international affairs, though, the United States has tended towards a strong defence of US sovereignty and political independence, primarily because of the dual foreign policy prerogatives of the Congress and the Presidency.

The 'liberal model' that has emerged through the process of European integration is subtly but significantly different. The process of integration has been less radically inclusive than in the immigrant-incorporating United States, with, in Europe, the ethnically demarcated nation-states preserving their separate identities and sovereign rights. This has resulted in a looser and weaker EU federal structure, with a corresponding weakness in external projection as compared to the United States. However, as an external actor the EU suffers from fewer internal constraints to devolving powers to other multilateral institutions or initiatives. This is partly due to the more limited separation of powers as compared to the US political system, but also derives from the greater habituation of European elites to the practice of devolving or pooling sovereignty for collective purposes. The European integration process also has a certain dynamism in that it remains incomplete, with its historic vision and strategic mission for the unification of Europe remaining unfulfilled. As such, the European project remains a powerful and potentially attractive model for neighbouring states that can benefit from their incorporation into its economic and political structures. But even for regions far from Europe, which nevertheless remain predominantly separated into nation-states, the integrative model of the EU has arguably as great a practical applicability as the US model, and perhaps greater.

Again, this is not to promote any sense of competition between the US and European liberal political models. They are clearly complementary, with respective strengths and weaknesses, and their essential compatibility is seen in the continuing support, with admittedly some reluctance at times, that the United States has given to the European integration process. More broadly, the fact that there exist significant divergences between US and European political evolution confirms that there is no one template for a liberal political order but that liberalism adapts to the specific historical, cultural and political traditions of the country or region to which it is applied. However, this argument does suggest that the EU, as a model of political integration, has a practical and normative global resonance that must be considered alongside the question of whether the EU can translate its integrative experiment into a greater strategic engagement in international relations.

Notes

1 See, for example, J. Zielonka, *Explaining Euro-Paralysis: Why Europe Is Unable to Act in International Politics*, Basingstoke, UK: Macmillan, 1998.
2 In terms of the NIS, Russia, Belarus, Ukraine and Moldova are generally recognized as being European countries; the countries of the south Caucasus define themselves as Europeans, a claim which is also generally recognized; the countries of Central Asia are generally viewed as Asian rather than European,

but being members of the OSCE and NATO partners gives them a potential claim for European status.

3 The most comprehensive indication of the EU's thinking towards the emergent 'wider Europe' can be found in a Communication from the Commission of the European Communities to the European Parliament, 'Wider Europe – Neighbourhood: A New Framework for Relations with our Eastern and Southern Neighbours', COM (2003) 104 Final, 11 March 2003.

4 F. Zakaria, *The Future of Freedom*, New York: W. W. Norton, 2003.

5 For an interesting debate on this, see F. Heisbourg and C. Grant, 'How Should Europe Respond to the New America?', *Prospect*, April 2003, pp. 16–20.

6 See comments by Commissioner Chris Patten in 'Wider Europe – Neighbourhood: Proposed New Framework for Relations with the EU's Eastern and Southern Neighbours', Brussels, 11 March 2003. Online. Available http: <http://www.europa.eu.int/comm/external_relations/we/intro/ip03_358.htm> (accessed 28 May 2003).

7 R. Kagan, 'Power and Weakness', *Policy Review*, 2002, no. 113. Online. Available http: <http://www.policyreview.org/JUN02/kagan.html> (accessed 2 June 2003). See also the book on the same theme: R. Kagan, *Of Paradise and Power: America vs. Europe in the New World Order*, New York: Knopf, 2003.

Index

Note: Where a page number is followed by an '*n*' this indicates a reference to an end note.